MW01000055

HOME TEAM

HOME TEAM

The Turbulent History of the San Francisco Giants

ROBERT F. GARRATT

To Greg: for a baseball fan who knows Candlestick! Best, Rob Garratt

UNIVERSITY OF NEBRASKA PRESS | LINCOLN & LONDON

Library of Congress Cataloging-in-Publication Data
Names: Garratt, Robert F., author.
Title: Home team: the turbulent history of the San
Francisco Giants / Robert F. Garratt.
Description: Lincoln: University of Nebraska Press, [2017] |
Includes bibliographical references and index.
Identifiers: LCCN 2016031549 | ISBN 9780803286832
(cloth: alk. paper) | ISBN 9781496201232 (epub) | ISBN
9781496201249 (mobi) | ISBN 9781496201256 (pdf)
Subjects: LCSH: San Francisco Giants (Baseball team)—
History. | Baseball—California—San Francisco—History.
| New York Giants (Baseball team)—History. | Baseball—
New York (State)—New York—History.
Classification: LCC GV875.S34 G27 2017 | DDC
796.357/640979461—dc23
LC record available at https://lccn.loc.gov/2016031549

Set in Minion by John Klopping.

For my grandchildren:

Leighton Mae, Hudson, and Aidan;
Madeline and Sofia;
Elliott and Olivia.

Touch all the bases
and be safe at home!

CONTENTS

ILLUSTRATIONS

GRAPHS

PREFACE

The Giants' move from New York to San Francisco has been long overshadowed by an emphasis on the Dodgers and their colorful owner, Walter O'Malley, who masterminded his team's move from Brooklyn to Los Angeles the same year that the Giants came west. This book widens the focus on West Coast baseball to treat the story of the Giants' move in its own right, rather than as a footnote to the Dodgers' story. It also looks at the development of the Giants as a San Francisco team, forging its own history.

The Giants coming to San Francisco involved more than a change in location and an assumption of a new name; it also involved the cultivation of another identity, an important theme in their California story. For all the joy at the beginning of the move, this transition for the Giants was far from easy. Once they settled into their new home and the initial enthusiasm of the relocation had worn off, difficulties arose. After early successes with near misses at league pennants and a World Series championship, there were troubled times, both on the field and at the box office, when attendance slumped so badly that the team almost left town, not once but twice. These periods of ups and downs over the years were indicative of a team struggling with its connection to the city. The story concludes happily, however. The ball club's fortunes improved dramatically with a move to a new baseball park at the turn of the century; the Giants grew into a stable franchise and became an integral part of the city's cultural life.

This version of the Giants' story develops in the form of a biography, not of a human subject but of a team, following a traditional biographical pattern with emphases on the phases of a life: beginnings, with early growing pains; then adolescent-like problems; then adulthood, with certain mid-life crises; and, finally, ending with maturity, an established and comfortable identity. The focus is chiefly on owners, managing partners, team administrators and officials, city politicians, journalists, and individuals behind the scenes, in the background of the game itself, who played an important role, not only in bringing the team from New York to California but also in keeping the team in San Francisco when it appeared that certain conditions might drive the ball club away. These people were part of the business of baseball in the city, running the ball club, coordinating events related to baseball and, especially, dealing with the important and difficult issues about where the team will play and in cultivating the team's relations with the community.

Most of the contemporary writing on the Giants concentrates on their time in AT&T Park, where they won world championships in 2010, 2012, and 2014 and have drawn fans at an extraordinary rate. According to national journals such as *Forbes* and business websites such as bizjournals.com, the Giants rank in the top five Major League Baseball franchises for profitability, team worth, success on the field, and overall stability. A good example of that stability can be seen in the smooth succession of recent corporate management. When Peter Magowan retired in 2008, Bill Neukom became chief managing partner; and then in 2012, when Neukom left, Larry Baer became the chief executive of the franchise. During this period of change, the ball club has remained not just efficient and secure but also phenomenally successful.

While all of the attention given to the recent success is both relevant and appropriate to the story of the Giants in San Francisco, it is not the primary focus here. This story goes back to the beginning of the move west, to feature both the Giants' early years in a new city and their gradual development there over four or five decades, in both rough times and smooth, the years that serve as the bedrock for the ball club's recent achievements and triumphs, both on the balance sheet and the field of play.

I

HORACE

In late October of 1954, Horace Stoneham, longtime owner of the New York Giants, was on top of the baseball world and, more important to Stoneham at least, his team was finally the toast of the town, eclipsing both the Brooklyn Dodgers and the New York Yankees. The Giants had just swept the mighty Cleveland Indians to win the World Series. The Indians, winners of 111 games that year, were heavy favorites, bolstered by a formidable pitching staff with twenty-game winners Early Wynn and Bob Lemon and a great offense anchored by American League batting champion Bobby Avila and power hitters Larry Doby and Al Rosen. But the Giants felt the magic and shocked the baseball world. The Series turned on Willie Mays's famous over-the-shoulder catch in game one, and the Giants never looked back. Defense, speed, timely hitting, and an uncanny knack for substitution in manager Leo Durocher's use of pinch hitter Dusty Rhodes were all too much for Cleveland.

The future seemed bright indeed, and thoughts of returning the Giants to their pre–World War II eminence in the National League danced in Stoneham's head. He had a young superstar in Mays, a solid if not outstanding pitching staff, a brilliant and feisty manager in Durocher, and, more critical for Stoneham, an enthusiastic fan base. The Giants drew 1,155,067 for home games during the 1954 season, more than they had in five years. With such a result and so much promise, Stoneham was poised for a great run. Happy days seemed here again.

The baseball gods are fickle and cruel, however. The Giants' perch *atop the heights of New York's sporting world would be momentary, and their reign as world champions brief, lasting only one season. They would not enjoy such glory for another fifty-six years, and in a likeness and at a location that could not have been even remotely imagined by mid-1950s New Yorkers.*

ONE

Sunset in New York

By the summer of 1955, Horace Stoneham began to sense the dire circumstances of playing baseball in the Polo Grounds. A true Manhattanite with genuine affection for the city and the urban life it offered, he had been willfully blind to the growing number of empty seats in his ballpark in the hopes that the Giants might catch fire and climb back into the National League pennant race. Stoneham's connection to New York was not just as a lifelong resident but also through baseball. Born in New Jersey, he moved with his parents to Manhattan as a young boy and except for a few years in boarding schools such as Hun and Pawling and a six-month stint working out west as a twenty-year-old, he spent his entire life in the city. His father, Charles A. Stoneham, bought the Giants in 1919. Soon thereafter young Horace began lifelong employment with the ball club, beginning in 1924 with ticket sales, gradually moving to field operations, travel arrangements, and eventually working his way into the front office in the early 1930s. He learned the operations of player personnel, salaries, and trades from his father, from John McGraw, a fellow owner and manager of the ball club, and from Bill Terry, who would succeed McGraw as team manager in 1932. When Charles Stoneham died suddenly in January 1936, Horace, now almost thirty-three years of age, became the youngest baseball owner in National League history. Given his family connection, Horace always felt that his ball club was an integral part of New York history. This assumption made the present circumstances of so many empty seats in the ancient Polo Grounds particularly troubling in a deeply personal sense.

Against that foreboding, Stoneham applied a strong sentimental feeling for New York, hoping that the previous year's championship season might signal the beginning of a shift for his club, in both on-field success and increased interest among fans. His thinking was not unreasonable or far-fetched. The Giants' 1955 roster was nearly identical to that of his World Series winners. With a team led by Leo Durocher and Willie Mays, lightning might indeed strike twice; the Giants could win another pennant. Baseball is a game of streaks and rushes; the 1951 team overcame an apparently all-but-insurmountable Dodgers lead to win the pennant dramatically.

But Stoneham waited in vain; the momentum of the Giants' championship season did not carry over and 1955 remained a big disappointment both on the field and in the stands. Part of the Giants' fate was due to fortune and the shifting ways of baseball history. It turned out that 1955 was Brooklyn's year. The Dodgers ran away with the pennant. The Giants would finish a distant third in the National League, eighteen and a half games behind their archrivals, despite a winning record of 80-74. It was their plight that year to contend with what many called the greatest Dodgers club of all time, whose players finally gelled to bring down the formidable Yankees in the World Series and produce Brooklyn's only championship.

But Stoneham sensed something far more ominous that season in the Giants' third-place finish and dwindling gate receipts. He began to realize that his location, the aging Polo Grounds, was a great liability, dimming opportunities for his beloved club in New York City. Giants attendance for the 1955 season would total 824,000, down considerably from the 1,155,067 of the previous year's championship season. Although Stoneham could seek some solace in baseball's overall numbers—the mid-1950s attendance throughout baseball was down almost 40 percent from an all-time postwar high in 1948—he could not deny the blunt fact that his New York Giants suffered the greatest slide among National League clubs despite playing in its largest market. In 1955 only the small-market teams of Pittsburgh and Cincinnati drew fewer fans.[1]

Moreover, Stoneham could no longer ignore the fact that his attendance problems went beyond his team's wins and losses. He understood that where the Giants played had as much to do with the club's present circumstances as how they played. It dawned on him that despite its tradition and history, the Polo Grounds, both as a facility and a location, was past its prime. A dilapidated stadium situated in what many considered a deteriorating neighborhood, the Polo Grounds would require major renovations to bring it up to the standards of the day. One of the oldest parks in baseball, it predated even Ebbets Field and was showing its age in seating, fan facilities, façade, and pedestrian traffic, especially the egress, when after a game the crowd would pour onto the playing field to exit through the center field gates.[2] Repairs and remodeling would be costly if Stoneham wanted to improve fan comfort, and these expenses would cut into his already dwindling bottom line. The stadium's famous horseshoe design, part of its charm, posed financial difficulties for Stoneham as well, severely restricting the number of premium box seats he could offer. Many of the so-called "infield" box seats were far away from home plate and the baselines, putting fans at a distance from infield action.[3] The majority of the general admission seats were wrapped around the outfield. Those fans that sat above the bullpens in left and right fields were 450 feet away, and those in the center field bleachers were 460-plus feet from home plate.[4]

Repairs and renovation of the ballpark, however necessary, were only part of Stoneham's stadium woes. Even more troubling was the changing nature of the neighborhood surrounding the park. In the late 1940s, a number of housing projects were planned for Harlem, the first of which was Colonial Park, which opened in 1950 opposite the Polo Grounds. By the mid-1950s the perception among middle-class white fans that the area around the park was becoming dangerous made a trip to the ballpark seem like a risky affair. Stoneham believed fans might feel safer if they could drive to the ballpark. Though he spent the majority of his life in Manhattan, with its extensive and reliable transportation system, including its famous subways, Stoneham sensed that future American life would be shaped and determined by the automobile. He watched postwar automobile production and sales boom, in large part to meet the needs of young families leaving the cities for the suburbs with their promise of affordable housing, convenient shopping centers, and new schools.

The movement that came to be designated "white flight," characterized by the largely white middle classes leaving their ethnically mixed urban neighbors, was most pronounced in northeastern cities such as Cleveland, Philadelphia, Detroit, and especially New York, where there was a great shift from the city's boroughs to Long Island, New Jersey, and Connecticut.[5] Knowing that these young families would come into the city with their cars for shopping and entertainment, Stoneham fretted more over the Polo Grounds' lack of parking than he did about the ballpark's aging facilities.[6] It was becoming clear to him that regardless of the quality of the team he put on the field, attendance would continue to dwindle unless fans had a convenient way to come to the ballpark in their cars. Nowhere in the environs of the Polo Grounds was there space to develop parking.

The shift in postwar baseball attendance was also affected by a burgeoning television industry, whose meteoric growth in the 1950s would change American culture. More and more Americans were buying television sets and staying home for their entertainment, sending shock waves through giant industries such as American cinema, Broadway theater, opera companies, symphony orchestras, radio, and professional sports. Naturally, baseball owners like Stoneham, Walter O'Malley of the Brooklyn Dodgers, and Dan Topping and Del Webb of the New York Yankees were terrified by what they imagined might be the consequences of the success of this new medium, and they scrambled to adjust. Like Stoneham, O'Malley was aware of his own problems in Ebbets Field, another aging ballpark, and was hypersensitive to attendance figures. Stoneham and Topping huddled to see about limiting the televising of home games. They also approached O'Malley about the problem.[7] The three clubs had been televising a selection of home games from the early 1950s, but they were unclear about the practice's effect on home attendance. Indeed, the jury was out even in the commissioner's office on whether television increased or hindered interest in seeing live baseball.[8] Though he held a fear about the place of television in the game, Stoneham certainly profited short-term from the Giants games that were broadcast; television revenue allowed him to post a profit even with sagging home attendance.[9] But Stoneham and O'Malley knew that television deals would only buy them a little time while they sorted out their respective stadium woes.

At the end of the 1955 season, with all of these concerns troubling his daily operations of the team, Stoneham began to weigh his options on the future of Giants baseball in New York. One idea surfaced as a reversal of history and gave him some hope that he might remain in the city. Recalling that the Giants were landlords to the Yankees in the early years of his father's ownership, he pondered playing his home games at Yankee Stadium in the role of tenant. In his characteristic style of diffidence, reticence and, some would say, cunning, he approached Yankees owners Del Webb and Dan Topping indirectly, first through some offhanded remarks at an owners meeting in winter of 1955. He floated a vague idea of tenancy and told Topping that he would get back to him in the near future. Stoneham never followed up on his suggestion, however, and the two owners never met face to face to discuss the possibility. The primary contact between the Giants and the Yankees was conducted through a third party, the New York sportswriters, essentially orchestrated by Stoneham, who, through hints and intimations during interviews, set in motion the Giants' tenancy idea as a solution to his problems with the Polo Grounds. The rumors about the Giants playing in Yankee Stadium persisted for three years. Eventually the sportswriters bristled at their own role in the stadium wars. At one of the rare Giants owner's press conferences, one writer asked bluntly whether Stoneham would simply pick up the phone and call Topping or Webb directly.[10]

Stoneham also had another card up his sleeve in the form of an idea for a new ballpark to be built and shared by both the Giants and the Yankees. The idea was more of a pipe dream, doomed from the start since it required public financing that the city could not provide and cooperation from the Yankees, who were happy in their present location. In his characteristic taciturn manner, Stoneham would be vague about details, hinting about the project in nebulous remarks.[11] During the late spring and summer of 1956, he also entertained what was surely the most far-fetched and elaborate scheme for a ballpark, even one intended for the Giants.[12] The notion, put forth by Manhattan city politician Hulan Jack, was to build a one-hundred-thousand-capacity stadium to rise above the New York Central's West Side railway location that would also provide parking for about twenty thousand cars. Jack argued that he had planners and investors to advance the project and thereby keep the Giants in Manhattan. Stoneham is on record as showing interest, meeting with Jack and his committee but expressing his characteristic caution.[13] As the costs estimates for the project continued to rise, the city's enthusiasm fell and the railway company remained distant; plans for the so-called "stadium on stilts" faded away.[14]

These suggestions about Stoneham's solutions to the Giants' ballpark woes were always devoid of particulars and served as diversionary tactics, allowing him to play a waiting game and consider his alternatives and a course of action. Stoneham gave no public indication of real concern, and certainly none of panic; it was business as usual for the New York Giants. He simply behaved publicly as he always had done, generous to a fault, providing hospitality for sportswriters and standing rounds at Toots Shor's famous Manhattan saloon, which catered to New York sports celebrities, bantering hopefully about his ball club. He could be as enigmatic as the best of them, almost as inscrutable as his friendly rival and fellow owner across the river, Walter O'Malley, whose reputation for fogging a press conference was legendary. With rumors flying about the Giants moving out of the Polo Grounds, and even out of the city, Stoneham would calmly dismiss everything as speculation, saying he had a lease with the Coogan family and he planned to be in New York for "years to come."[15]

At the same time he insisted that the Giants would stay put in New York and were committed long term to the Polo Grounds, he began entertaining a radical idea, something that just two years before would have been unthinkable. He gave serious consideration to moving the team out of New York. His first thoughts were to plan simply, minimize complications, keep costs manageable, and hold his cards close to his vest. Stoneham was well aware of the astounding success at the turnstiles of the Milwaukee Braves, leading the National League in attendance every year since their move from Boston when, in their last year there (1952), they drew a miserable 281,279.[16] That the Braves' change of fortune came once they moved to a new city with an excited fan base was not lost on Stoneham. In early 1956, he knew he could not remain much longer in his present location. Minneapolis, home to his Triple-A farm team, the Millers, and a major midwestern city, seemed a very attractive option.[17]

As a Giants franchise, the Minneapolis Millers granted Stoneham rights to the city's territory. With the recently transplanted Braves nearby in Milwaukee, and with St. Louis and Chicago as Midwest neighbors, there would be no travel objections from other National League owners. Minneapolis officials were eager to please Stoneham and approved plans for a new stadium that would offer plenty of parking.[18] Stoneham and Chub Feeney, Stoneham's nephew and second in command of Giants operations, had visited Minneapolis off and on over the past few years to check on the Millers, had built good relations with the city's planning commission, and felt comfortable with the designs for the new ballpark, which could be expanded for Major League crowds. They went so far as to contact a steel company for a reconstruction of the Millers' present park to improve seating capacity, an interim arrangement until the new park would be ready.[19] The move to Minneapolis, welcomed by the locals, with minimal disruption to the league, appeared to provide a soft landing for the Giants' flight from New York.

But as he contemplated his move to the Midwest, Stoneham did so in his customary wary and discreet manner. Making up his mind to move and selecting a date to do so were two very different undertakings for Stoneham. With his lease with the Coogan family for the Polo Grounds securely in hand, he could afford to sit back and let the action come to him. Whenever he was asked about the Giants' future, he responded as the loyal son he was, suggesting that things might work out somehow and the Giants could be in New York for a long time to come. Even with his awareness of the problems with the Polo Grounds, Stoneham was not quite ready to establish a deadline, nor to go public with any decision. Admitting to O'Malley in a confidential, informal conversation in March 1957 that he had made up his mind to move to Minneapolis, he did not feel an overwhelming urge for any public pronouncement just yet.[20] His waiting game would prove momentous. In the late spring of that year, he would be lobbied by three different parties, each of them urging him to expand his horizons westward another two thousand miles to consider San Francisco and the lucrative California market.

TWO

Dawning in the West

As it was for Stoneham's New York Giants, the year 1954 was an annus mirabilis for baseball in San Francisco. The year's crowning moment came not from the exploits of the city's beloved Seals, who finished the 1954 season at an even .500, 84-84, good enough for fourth place in the Pacific Coast League, seventeen and a half games behind the champion San Diego Padres.[1] It was rather an off-field, political event that proved so extraordinary. On November 2, 1954, after a long campaign in which newspapers, sports celebrities, and civic leaders such as Mayor Elmer Robinson and members of the board of supervisors touted its benefits for sports fans and businesses alike, Proposition B was approved by the city's voters, authorizing a five-million-dollar bond to build a stadium for the sole purpose of attracting a Major League Baseball franchise for San Francisco. The measure was overwhelmingly successful, passing at more than a 2.5:1 margin, 168,997 for and 63,282 against.[2]

Proposition B

Recreational Center bonds, 1954. To incur a bonded indebtedness in the sum of $5,000,000 for the acquisition, construction and completion of buildings, lands, and other works and properties to be used for baseball, football and other sports, dramatic productions and other lawful uses as a recreational center.[3]

Although the listing of alternative activities such as "dramatic productions" appears in the legal language of the proposition, undoubtedly to ameliorate the non–sports fans among the voting public, the essential intent of the funding was to bring Major League Baseball to San Francisco. The focus on baseball was made emphatic in the local press, especially in the columns of Curley Grieve, the sports editor of the *San Francisco Examiner*, the most vociferous and fervent of the advocates of big league baseball for the city. Indeed, this particular use of the bond was underscored in an important caveat that appeared in the proposition's fine print. The authorization came with a designated shelf life. If the city found itself unable to attract a Major League Baseball franchise within five years of voters' approval—that would be December 31, 1959—then the bond issue would be null and void and the funding for the stadium would disappear.

In 1955, Mayor Robinson's final year in office, Francis McCarty, president of the board of supervisors, began some preliminary work on behalf of the city with informal queries to a small sampling of clubs, including those in Cleveland and Washington, that led to some optimism that Major League Baseball might come to San Francisco by the 1956 season. Adding to that hope was a proposal at the January 1955 baseball's owners' meetings by Phil Wrigley, owner of the Chicago Cubs and the Pacific Coast League's Los Angeles Angels, and Bill Veeck, former owner of the St. Louis Browns and a close friend of Wrigley, to expand the National League to ten clubs, adding the cities of San Francisco and Los Angeles. McCarty thought the Wrigley-Veeck initiative might lead to an early and successful outcome for the city. For their part, the owners thought the idea intriguing but premature. After lengthy discussion, the proposal was tabled for future consideration.[4]

Undeterred by the leagues' reaction to Wrigley's and Veeck's thinking, McCarty began contacting certain owners, setting off a rash of speculation in the San Francisco press about a future Major League team, a bizarre mirroring of the rumormongering about the Giants and the Dodgers playing out in the New York newspapers during the same period. Oddly, in this early phase of the search, there was almost no mention in the San Francisco papers identifying the New York Giants as a possibility. Sportswriters like Grieve, and Prescott Sullivan, also of the *Examiner*, churned out series of columns that had Cincinnati, Washington, or Cleveland coming west. By year's end, however, prospects had dimmed considerably. Cincinnati and Washington showed no real interest in the West Coast, and Cleveland, after some initial contact with McCarty's committee, expressed little enthusiasm for any change in location.[5] All of this disappointed McCarty and the board of supervisors, who both soon realized that their task would be more difficult than they had imagined—well into the second year after the bond issue had passed, the city was still dreaming, with no serious suitor in sight.

New mayor George Christopher, who took office in January 1956, replacing Elmer Robinson, was not easily discouraged; moreover, he sensed the urgency of the bond's time constraint. In one of his first acts as mayor, he appointed an official search committee, chaired by McCarty and composed of prominent businesspeople and members of the Downtown Association. Their task was to identify viable Major League clubs who might be interested in moving to San Francisco. By forming this committee, Christopher announced a priority for his term in office and formalized the more casual efforts by McCarty the previous year.

As a first generation San Franciscan, he was well motivated to lead the push to bring Major League Baseball to the city. His ascent to the city's top political office might serve as a plot summary for a rags-to-riches Horatio Alger novel. Born in Greece and brought to the United States at a young age by immigrant parents, Christopher lived out the classic American dream. Forced to leave school and take a full-time job at the age of fourteen when his father died, he supported his family, studied at night for an accounting degree, and eventually bought a small dairy that grew into a prosperous company. He was elected to the San Francisco Board of Supervisors in 1945 and became board president in his second term. An enterprising and successful proud American, he wanted the most for the city that gave him so much opportunity and fortune. Acquisition of a Major League Baseball team would be only one of the many changes—in housing, schools, and recreation facilities—that took place in San Francisco under his two terms as mayor.[6] He had not only the drive and energy to pursue his goal but also the political savvy and skill to keep others on the board of supervisors focused on the task at hand. As his first year in office came to a close, Christopher looked ahead to 1957, in the hope that his project for Major League Baseball would show some signs of fruition.

Early in the new year, his hopes brightened considerably as the result of a stunning move by Walter O'Malley. According to Los Angeles sportswriter Vincent X. Flaherty, O'Malley passed a note to Phil Wrigley during the annual dinner of the New York Baseball Writers in Manhattan at the Astor Hotel in early February 1957 offering to buy Wrigley's Los Angeles Angels Pacific Coast League franchise— Wrigley returned the note listing his terms and O'Malley signaled his consent.[7] Later that month, at the Dodgers' Vero Beach spring training site, O'Malley revealed the details of his Los Angeles purchase publicly for the first time to an astonished New York press corps.[8] His announcement stirred a flurry of speculation in the newspapers about a Dodgers move from Brooklyn to Los Angeles, something that O'Malley continually trivialized but did not controvert. O'Malley's biographer Andy McCue argues that the agreement with Wrigley gave O'Malley two advantages. It secured his rights to the promising Los Angeles market and it put pressure on the New York officials to find a way to keep the Dodgers in Brooklyn.[9] One might also contend that O'Malley's purchase of the PCL Angels effectively set in motion events that would culminate in San Francisco's bid for Stoneham and his Giants to relocate in the Bay Area.

Certainly Christopher and McCarty felt that way. In retrospect, Christopher called O'Malley's purchase of the Angels "the break we needed."[10] Emboldened by the Dodgers' move, Christopher and McCarty, each in his own way, became more aggressive. McCarty's committee made their interest in Major League Baseball known to Stoneham in an informal presentation in New York sometime in late February. Stoneham's reaction was cautious and lukewarm at best— while San Francisco's search undoubtedly intrigued him, his public statements were almost dismissive.[11] Nonetheless, McCarty had planted an idea, however embryonic, into Stoneham's head, setting the stage for future negotiations.

Meanwhile, Christopher contacted his compeer in Los Angeles, Mayor Norris Poulson, encouraging his efforts to bring the Dodgers to Southern California. Christopher had always considered Los Angeles a partner in luring Major League Baseball to California and viewed his relationship with Poulson as collaborative. On March 2, before Poulson and other Los Angeles officials traveled to Vero Beach for a spring training meeting with O'Malley to follow up the purchase of the Angels, Christopher wired his best wishes and admitted that Los Angeles was closer than San Francisco in landing a team.

> We commend your effort regardless of when San Francisco may be considered. . . . We desire to give you our fullest support and hope you will be successful in your mission—we consider this practically a joint venture and know that if you are successful San Francisco also will eventually receive Major League Baseball.[12]

While his enthusiastic rhetoric masked what must have been at least a tinge of disappointment, Christopher, a consummate politician, understood the pragmatic side to collaboration: if Los Angeles landed a Major League Baseball team, surely it would be easier for him to entice another one to relocate in San Francisco.

Apparently Poulson was of the same opinion. Given scheduling and travel issues, both mayors knew their chances of bringing Major League Baseball to their cities improved considerably with two teams on the West Coast—when Poulson returned from his Florida meeting with the Dodgers, he invited Christopher to join him and his search committee to discuss the progress made with the Dodgers. Over the next two months Christopher conferred often with Poulson, sometimes by phone and occasionally in person. These meetings with Los Angeles officials raised Christopher's hopes and rekindled activity with McCarty and the committee.[13] The clock was ticking on the bond's time limit, but the sense of urgency was coupled with prevailing optimism in city hall.

The crucial breakthrough for San Francisco came on May 3, when Poulson invited Christopher to Los Angeles to join him, Walter O'Malley, and Matthew Fox, the entrepreneurial owner of Skiatron Television, who was promoting pay-per-view baseball with the Dodgers. According to Christopher, the meeting was a secretive and urgent discussion of the final stages of bringing Major League Baseball to the West Coast. Arrangements took on a cloak-and-dagger atmosphere, with Christopher being met in a plain car at the airport and brought to the Beverly Hilton Hotel's meeting rooms through the service entrance to avoid any detection by local press. It was at this meeting that Christopher and O'Malley agreed that San Francisco's chances to land the Giants were best pursued with a face-to-face conversation among Stoneham, Christopher, and McCarty. O'Malley promised that once he got back to New York he would arrange something with Stoneham and get back to Christopher.[14]

O'Malley was true to his word and, knowing that Stoneham had made up his mind to move the Giants out of New York, suggested that Christopher fly east immediately.[15] On May 9, less than a week after the meeting in Los Angeles, Christopher and McCarty were on their way to New York to meet Stoneham. O'Malley gathered the parties at the Hotel Lexington in Manhattan, and by the time the afternoon was over, Christopher and McCarty had convinced Stoneham that San Francisco presented an attractive possibility as a new home for the Giants.[16]

After a whirlwind twenty-four hours that concluded with Christopher and McCarty attending a Giants game as Stoneham's guest in his owner's box, the San Franciscans caught a night flight home, exhausted but buoyed by the prospects of landing the Giants. On May 10, Ford Frick, the commissioner of baseball, learned of the meeting among Christopher, McCarty, Stoneham, and O'Malley and cautioned all parties against any public statements or premature announcements. Specifically he wrote to O'Malley that

> any publicity relative to future action is to be avoided by all clubs. I hope you will also point out to your conferee that headlines and publicity statements at this time will only delay and perhaps upset the program they have in mind.[17]

While essentially admonitory, the language of Frick's telegram reveals the commissioner's awareness and even tacit approval of changes to come even as it muzzles the proposers and listeners. Many obstacles lay ahead, but after this meeting all parties could sense real headway in bringing Major League Baseball to the West Coast.

The real target for the commissioner's words appears to have been Christopher and McCarty. Frick reasoned that both men, as strangers to the ways of baseball's culture, would be unaware of the difficult politics inside and outside the sport regarding teams changing locations and might be more inclined to speak openly about any progress made during their talks with the owners. Frick was blunt in his telegram to O'Malley that any publicity about "franchise transfers" during the season would be "harmful to baseball." Stoneham, given his cautious manner, certainly would not make any statement, and O'Malley, as an interested observer, would not want to jeopardize any chances for success. Moreover, as businessmen, Stoneham and O'Malley knew that there was at the moment nothing official on the table, which meant no real commitments from the interested parties. The waiting game would continue for both New York teams.

Christopher apparently sensed Frick's concern—when he and McCarty arrived back in San Francisco, they were very guarded in their remarks on the meeting with Stoneham, although they were unable to disguise their sense of accomplishment. At a hastily organized press conference for San Francisco journalists, they admitted meeting with both Stoneham and O'Malley, acknowledged that there was a discussion "with Mr. Stoneham of the possibility of transferring a major league franchise to San Francisco," and called their visit to New York "time well spent." They went on to indicate that in the near future they planned to submit a "letter of intent" to Stoneham in which they would give the details of an offer. In closing, they explained the brevity and vagueness concerning their conversations with Stoneham by acknowledging Frick's explicit request that team owners not discuss these matters "while the season is underway." Their final words, however, made it quite clear, nonetheless, that they were extremely satisfied with their efforts. "We feel certain that definite progress has been made. Meantime, we will continue to advance San Francisco's program to achieve big league baseball."[18]

A week later Christopher wrote to O'Malley, thanking him for his efforts in facilitating the discussions with Stoneham and politely nodding to the commissioner's directive.

> Upon my return to the city I was met by representatives of the press, television and radio, and upon questioning I confined my remarks, as previously agreed by us. However, representatives of the various media on occasion take the liberty of elaborating on certain remarks made, as you so well know. This, we must understand, is beyond our control. In this connection, and in deference to Baseball Commissioner Ford Frick's wishes, we will confine our remarks pending the finalization of plans for Major League Baseball in San Francisco.[19]

Christopher concludes his letter to O'Malley by informing him that the city of San Francisco would be writing Stoneham "a letter of intent" in the near future, inviting the Giants to relocate in San Francisco. Meanwhile, thickening the plot, at a late May meeting National League owners gave both Stoneham and O'Malley permission to move their ball clubs to the West Coast.[20]

For the next two months, Christopher settled into a persistent mode, engaged in what he called "bird-dogging," in constant communication with Stoneham, O'Malley, and Fox.[21] His first task was to extol the virtues of a city that Stoneham had once identified in conversation with O'Malley as unimpressive for baseball.[22] That Christopher and McCarty had made great headway in this regard was evident in the guarded remarks Stoneham made immediately after their May 10 visit to New York, when he told the press that he was pleasantly surprised by his meeting with the San Franciscans and liked what he heard.[23] At the same time, Stoneham played a cautious, business-as-usual approach, announcing the day after the San Franciscans left that he had renewed his lease for the Polo Grounds with the Coogan family.[24]

In the next few weeks, as Christopher began unfolding the details of what the city could offer, Stoneham warmed even more, especially when he learned of the potential for parking. Throughout the late spring and early summer, Christopher continually applied the pressure, mainly through phone calls, sometimes two or three a day. He traveled to New York only once after his initial meeting with Stoneham in May, en route to the American Municipal Association convention at White Sulphur Springs, West Virginia, in mid-July. He called Stoneham from a pay phone for the sake of privacy. This covert activity was deemed necessary by all parties, primarily to keep the press in the dark about the delicacies of negotiations. For his part, Stoneham was fixated on parking and consistently drifted back to that topic in the conversations. Christopher, as seller, pressed hard about the attraction of San Francisco as a major city, the city's legal commitment to building a stadium, and the history of the area as a sports venue.[25]

By mid-July, Christopher's efforts came to fruition; Stoneham decided to settle on San Francisco as his new home, once he had a firm offer in hand. He testified to that effect on July 17, 1957, before Congress at baseball's antitrust hearings, presided over by Rep. Emanuel Celler of Brooklyn. In sharp contrast to Walter O'Malley's evasive and equivocal testimony before the same congressional committee almost a month earlier, Stoneham was remarkably forthcoming, especially on two essential points.[26] When asked about his plans to move the Giants to San Francisco, he was direct and clear. A member of the committee asked, "Am I correct in understanding that if a suitable proposition is made, you would move the Giants to San Francisco next year?" to which Stoneham responded unambiguously, "I would recommend it to our board, yes, sir." The second question revealed Stoneham's resoluteness. The same member asked, "Would you recommend this move to San Francisco even if the Dodgers remained in Brooklyn?" Stoneham: "I think I would, yes sir." Congressman: "In other words, your decision would not be predicated on any decision that the Dodgers would make?" Stoneham: "No, sir."[27]

While sports pages across the country exploded with the news, Stoneham fell back upon his characteristic reticent manner. Explaining to members of the local press that he could not play another year at the Polo Grounds, he nonetheless refrained from any official announcement, stating that he had no authorized proposal from San Francisco and therefore nothing definitive to announce. Once an offer arrived, he claimed, he would schedule a board meeting to vote.[28]

By early August, the pace of negotiation between San Francisco and the Giants hit light speed. On August 6, at the annual meeting of the stockholders of the National Exhibition Company, the corporate organization that owned and controlled the Giants, Stoneham laid out the advantages of moving to San Francisco and why he decided against Minneapolis. Everything had to do with issues of the bottom line—costs and profit—things that shareholders would be interested in hearing. Minneapolis wanted too much rent, and in San Francisco, Stoneham said, the company would exceed last year's profit in New York ten times over.[29] He also mentioned that the potential for pay-per-view television in San Francisco would add to the company's profits. After weeks of discussion with city lawyers and the board of supervisors, Christopher was able to present Stoneham an offer he could not refuse, something that New York officials found impossible to do: a guarantee for a new stadium with a seating capacity over forty thousand and parking for ten to twelve thousand cars.

San Francisco's official letter of intent arrived the very day that Stoneham held the annual stockholders' meeting, signed by both Christopher and Supervisor McCarty, laying out the terms of the city's offer. Stoneham now had before him the sanctioned offer, stating what the City of San Francisco was prepared to do for the Giants if they would agree to come west. The essential conditions of the proposal were the construction of a stadium with a seating capacity between forty and forty-five thousand; parking for ten to twelve thousand cars; that all revenue from concession would go to the baseball club; that the cost to the Giants would be 5 percent of the gross receipts, or an annual guarantee of $125,000 rent to the city, whichever was greater; and that the final plans for the stadium would be subject to the approval of the baseball club. In an addendum to the letter of intent, Christopher added a short memorandum explaining that the contents of the letter had not been made public. He asked whether there could be a joint statement made by the city and the ball club once Stoneham had his board's approval.[30]

As his testimony before Congress and his remarks to the shareholders indicated, Stoneham had made up his mind. On August 19, 1957, the board of the National Exhibition Company met in special session. Eight of the nine-member board voted for the transfer: Charles H. (Pete) Stoneham, Horace's son and club president; Charles S. Feeney, Horace's nephew and club vice president; Edgar P. Feeley, club treasurer; Joseph J. Haggarty; Max Schneider; Charles Aufdehar, husband of Horace's sister, Mary; and Dr. Anthony M. Palermo. Voting against the move was M. Donald Grant, a Wall Street broker (and future president of the board of the New York Mets).[31] Once the vote was taken, at this stage in the negotiations largely a symbolic gesture, Stoneham announced that the Giants, after seventy-four years of baseball in New York, would be moving to San Francisco, effective for the 1958 season.[32]

A good deal of shock accompanied Stoneham's announcement, but nothing like what would come two months later when O'Malley followed suit with his declaration that the Dodgers would move west as well. The exodus of these two established institutions unleashed an outpouring of criticism and regret that coalesced among New York writers into a tale of villainy. In a reversal of Winston Churchill's oft quoted line "history is written by the victors," journalists of the day like Red Smith, Dick Young, Arthur Daley, and later, in book form, Roger Kahn, Doris Kearns Goodwin, and Robert E. Murphy, among others, perpetuated a view of baseball history in which the departure of both the Giants and the Dodgers was described as "loss," "betrayal," "rupture," "abandonment," and "tragedy."[33] What emerged was a nostalgic tale of old New York and Brooklyn, the end of a golden era of baseball, and a shattering of community. At the center of the story stands Walter O'Malley, cast in the role of arch villain, publicly insisting he wants to stay in Brooklyn but privately planning to relocate in Los Angeles. "Only the elastic O'Malley can ride two horses in opposite directions at the same time," wrote *New York Times* columnist Arthur

Daley.[34] Knowing that his move out of Brooklyn would be made easier if another ball club moved with him, it was said, O'Malley turned to his shy, gullible, bibulous, and friendly rival Horace Stoneham and quietly convinced him of the riches the two of them would make in the wild west—and when the 1957 season ended, O'Malley skipped town, taking the ingenuous Stoneham along with him.[35]

Versions of O'Malley as mendacious conniver, a Svengali to Stoneham's Trilby, have had a powerful effect on the history of baseball coming to California. It dominated the New York news in 1957 and has persisted ever since, even as we have come to know a great deal more about the Giants' and the Dodgers' moves—especially that Stoneham had decided as early as 1956 to move out of New York, independent from any Brooklyn Dodgers plans. Of course, O'Malley preferred that the Giants move to San Francisco, and his role as facilitator between Stoneham and the San Francisco principals is an indication of that preference. No doubt his interest in Los Angeles had some effect on Stoneham's decision to consider San Francisco. But what O'Malley did not do was to dupe Stoneham into leaving New York City to follow the Dodgers west.[36]

The most extreme variant of the O'Malley-as-Great-Manipulator story comes in the form of an urban myth that still circulates about the Giants' move to San Francisco. The story grows out of two essential views of O'Malley, first as a determined manipulator of Stoneham and second as a master of human psychology and business negotiations. His duping of Stoneham has its origins in the New York presses' views of both men. O'Malley's understanding of the predispositions of his fellow owners and baseball officials derives from baseball's inner circles. Phil Wrigley was reported to have remarked at the beginning of an owners' meeting that O'Malley should tell the assembly what everyone is thinking in order to save time. Baseball commissioner Bowie Kuhn observed that O'Malley was a master of human relations, able to dominate others better than anyone Kuhn had ever seen.[37]

Planning for the exodus from New York, the Dodgers boss applied his penchant for psychology when trying to convince Stoneham to join the Dodgers in California; such a location, O'Malley intimated to Stoneham, would keep their storied rivalry intact and make them both rich. O'Malley knew Stoneham to be an urban type, deeply attached to city living. To get Stoneham to commit to the move, O'Malley merely played to Stoneham's interests. Convinced that, if given a choice, Stoneham would opt for the city life that San Francisco offered, O'Malley proposed that the Giants' boss take his choice of cities, either Los Angeles or San Francisco: O'Malley would take the other. The important thing, O'Malley stressed, is that they seize the rich opportunity awaiting them in California and commit to move. Playing true to form, Stoneham gladly took San Francisco. This left O'Malley not only with a partner in the move but also with his preferred choice of location and the greater business potential of the huge area of Southern California.

The veracity of this story is dubious—Walter's son, Peter O'Malley, denies it.[38] Former Giants owner Bob Lurie doubts that it happened.[39] Andy McCue, Walter O'Malley's biographer, thinks it unlikely.[40] They all say that O'Malley was too focused on Los Angeles to risk losing the territory. But others claim its authenticity. Ron Fairly, one of the early Los Angeles Dodgers players and a close friend of Walter O'Malley, repeated it, as did Jaime Rupert, Stoneham's granddaughter.[41] It has even made it into print, although in a slightly different version and under the heading of baseball mythology.[42] Myth, as the scholars tell us, often wanders into the fabulous and the marvelous, but it conveys nonetheless a truth of its own, revealing and explaining type and character. The story of O'Malley's offer and Stoneham's response, however uncertain and suspicious, goes a long way in portraying the predilections of each man that many of the writers, players, and storytellers who knew them would identify as distinctive and defining characteristics.

The O'Malley trickster myth has also been served by the cult of personality, as the writers judged O'Malley to be loquacious and gregarious, and Stoneham retiring and taciturn. All of these facets contributed to the invention by the press of O'Malley as a manipulator who convinced Stoneham to move. But even a cursory view of Stoneham's planning and thinking challenges this singular and, one has to say, stubborn view of baseball history. As attractive, and perhaps cathartic, as such a narrative might be for certain New York writers who incredulously watched the Giants and Dodgers leave what they regarded as America's greatest city, it must be seen as a willful exaggeration, nonetheless, when measured against the factual evidence of the thinking and action of both men in the spring and summer of 1957.

The emphasis on O'Malley as chief catalyst also slights the role George Christopher played in Stoneham's decision to settle on San Francisco. His tenacity, persistence, and tact had much to do with convincing Stoneham that San Francisco would be an attractive choice. Christopher's ability to keep the board of supervisors focused on acquiring Major League Baseball allowed him to present a united front in dealing with the Giants. Also, it must be remembered that when Stoneham cautioned Christopher that the initial five-million-dollar bond passed by San Francisco taxpayers would not properly fund the construction of a Major League stadium, Christopher did not panic but rather drew on his political savvy to find the additional money so as not to jeopardize the negotiations with the Giants.

But if one must have a single individual whose role in the Giant's move was crucial in persuading Stoneham to settle on San Francisco, one might look past both O'Malley and Christopher and settle on Matthew M. Fox, the colorful, fast-talking, hard-driving entrepreneur, whose future-sounding company Skiatron Electronics and Television Corporation was developing and promoting pay-per-view television. Fox's name is largely confined to marginalia and asides in the story of baseball's great western migration in 1957; yet his role in the move of the Giants and Dodgers to California is significant, even crucial.[43] He was in constant touch with O'Malley during the early months of 1957 and attended the critical meeting in Los Angeles in early May when Poulson, O'Malley, and Christopher discussed plans to approach Stoneham about relocating in San Francisco. Fox had previously convinced O'Malley of the promise of pay television in

Los Angeles.[44] He then turned to Stoneham and suggested that once the Giants moved out of New York they would be free to negotiate new contracts with Skiatron.[45]

Matty Fox was always in the moment to seize an opportunity to turn a profit. Serving as a theater usher at the age of nine in his hometown of Racine, Wisconsin, Fox rose in the entertainment industry to become the youngest executive for Universal Pictures at the age of twenty-five. When the war broke out, Fox joined the army in 1942 in the War Productions Board and took charge of salvaging scrap metal, tires, and other materials for defense industries. Always the operator, he went into the army as a private and three years later left the service as a major without ever having shipped out. A stout man of 5'8" who weighed over 200 pounds—Fox often joked that he could not pass a delicatessen window without putting on weight—he nonetheless had the charm and wooing power to court and marry Yolande Betbeze, Miss America of 1951. Always alert to business deals, he befriended the ambassador from Indonesia and secured an exclusive contract for all imports and exports between that country and the United States, earning him the title of the economic godfather of Indonesia. The U.S. State Department soon looked unfavorably upon the arrangement, and Fox's contract with Indonesia was not renewed. Undeterred, Fox saw opportunity back in the entertainment industry, especially in the field of television, which was just beginning to take hold in American households in the early 1950s. He was always alert to new developments in entertainment and made considerable money in the early stages of 3-D movies, especially in the production and distribution of 3-D glasses. With his keen business sense and imagination, Fox saw in television a growth industry of boundless opportunity for profit.[46]

O'Malley was certainly intrigued by Fox, and Stoneham felt so strongly about Fox and his ideas about promoting West Coast baseball that the Giants' owner bought shares in Fox's company.[47] Fox's name was mentioned in the New York, San Francisco, and Los Angeles sport pages in the late fifties, as well as appearing occasionally in the *Sporting News*. His potential business connections with the Dodgers and the Giants in 1957 were deemed significant enough that he was asked to appear as a witness before Rep. Emanuel Celler's House Justice Subcommittee hearings on baseball in the summer of 1957.[48] Fox was also known to the city councils in San Francisco and Los Angeles. His general business plan was to put baseball on a pay-per-view basis in both cities on the West Coast.

Sometime in early May 1957, after Christopher and McCarty had come to New York, Fox met with Stoneham to discuss a business plan for wiring San Francisco and offering pay-per-view programming for baseball. But Fox did more than simply lay out a business plan. He offered Stoneham an escrow payment—one million dollars to be paid in October 1957 with a remaining one million on January 1, 1958.[49] Stoneham appeared even more enthusiastic than O'Malley about the promise of Skiatron pay-per-view. During the Celler hearings, Fox was asked by the congressional committee members whether he had any contractual dealings with Stoneham and the Giants. His answer, while guarded, indicated that the prospects of closed-circuit television broadcasts of Giants games had developed to advanced planning stages.

> Our costs for the greater bay area including San Francisco would be less than $6 million to lay the so-called grid, which is the wire network from which individual homes would be connected—we have an agreement (with the Giants) which is in escrow . . .—we told Mr. Stoneham that we would be prepared to go forward (in San Francisco) . . .—whenever he was free to contract with us.[50]

Further questions at the hearing revealed Fox's abilities as a smooth communicator and shrewd businessman. When asked about his dealings with the Dodgers, a question that insinuated O'Malley's lack of candor when speaking publically, Fox jumped to the Dodgers owner's defense.

CONGRESSMAN: What is your status with Mr. O'Malley?

FOX: There is no status at this point.

CHAIRMAN CELLER: Is there never a status with Mr. O'Malley?

FOX: Yes there is. As a matter of fact, he is a fine gentleman and I would rather have his word than contracts with many people I have known.

CHAIRMAN: I don't doubt that and I am just speaking facetiously. . . . He is a fine gentleman, a very astute and able one too, with accent on the astute.

FOX: I agree.

CHAIRMAN: It strikes me, Mr. Fox, he has met his match with you.

FOX: Thank you.[51]

With his San Francisco plans Fox spoke to others beside Stoneham. In the summer of 1957 he was in touch with Christopher and the board of supervisors. Christopher spoke publicly about the importance of Skiatron's plan for the pay-per-view deal, saying it was crucial in landing the Giants.[52] Back in New York, Stoneham, reluctant to reveal financial specifics publicly, was singing another tune, denying that Skiatron was the essential factor in his decision to move. It was all about the new fans waiting for big league baseball, Stoneham insisted. At the same time, privately, he thought it was essential that he own a piece of the action and bought one thousand shares of Skiatron stock, which gained in value amidst the speculation of San Francisco and Los Angeles business.

Matthew Fox's dream to wire San Francisco and Los Angeles and make Skiatron the first company to offer pay-per-view sports in the United States ended unhappily. Political road blocks, including hesitancy from a Federal Communications Commission that was unclear how to deal with subscription television in a growing industry, opposition from entertainment groups including Hollywood filmmakers, complications in both cities to begin wiring, and insufficient capital investment cost Fox his contracts with both the Giants and the Dodgers. O'Malley, who never had a legal contract with Skiatron, arranged with a local station to televise the Dodgers' away games with the Giants.[53] Stoneham continued to be interested, but by 1961, getting no real commitment from Fox on a date for broadcast, he had agreed to televise the Giants' away games with the Dodgers on a local

San Francisco television station. Meanwhile Fox had transitioned Ski-atron into Subscription TV and was continuing his negotiations with both the Giants and the Dodgers. The company had attracted outside investors, who joined with Fox to continue serving the San Francisco and Los Angeles markets with a limited wiring of certain target neighborhoods in both cities.[54] He also went ahead on the planning for the technical infrastructure for wiring private homes. But in the late spring of 1964, Fox died of a heart attack at the age of fifty-three. Later that year in California, backed by the entertainment and television industries, Proposition 15 passed at the ballot box, outlawing pay television. Fox's scheme of pay-per-view television would have to wait twenty years before becoming a reality, but his importance to the western expansion of baseball was certainly significant. The promise of his ideas for baseball broadcasting had a powerful influence on O'Malley's and Stoneham's plans to move to California.

THREE

Reinvention

As soon as he arrived in San Francisco, Stoneham began to reap the benefits of his historic move. The city officially welcomed the Giants in early April with a ticker tape parade on Montgomery Street in the heart of downtown San Francisco, lined with over 200,000 euphoric fans. The celebration made the cover of the April 28, 1958, issue of *Life* magazine. The Giants were instant Bay Area favorites and Stoneham was the toast of the town, a celebrity among the press and an honored guest at a number of preseason luncheons and banquets. Settled into the tidy confines of Seals Stadium, which had been expanded to seat 22,900, the newly transplanted Giants opened on April 15, 1958, against, appropriately enough, the Los Angeles Dodgers. The Giants' Rubin Gomez threw the first pitch, to Dodgers centerfielder Gino Cimoli, a San Francisco native, inaugurating Major League Baseball on the West Coast. The home team won before a delirious sellout crowd, 8–0. Fan interest would remain enthusiastic throughout the year and the Giants responded with a competitive and successful run. By the season's end, Stoneham was thrilled with both the reception he received and the team's performance. He had not even the slightest tinge of regret over his monumental decision to move his team. He knew that he had made the right choice in choosing San Francisco.

Seals Stadium was a jewel in the Pacific Coast League and many thought it perhaps the most beautiful Minor League park in the country. After Paul Fagan bought the Seals in 1946, he began to refurbish the ballpark, repainting the interior, working on the infield, and removing all advertisements from the outfield walls. In the winter of 1957, Stoneham was able to convince Fagan to add about twenty-five hundred more outfield seats, but with a seating capacity of just under twenty-three thousand it remained a cozy, fan-friendly place. Fans appreciated the close-up atmosphere and the proximity of the players; the players, in turn, fed off the intimacy. Rookie Orlando Cepeda noted "the warmth and sense of community" in the place; Willie Mays said it was similar in atmosphere to the "friendly confines" of Wrigley Field; and Willie McCovey remembered that players were close enough to fans to have conversations.[1] It was in so many ways the perfect ballpark in which to play for a transplanted baseball team that was growing a new fan base.

After all the welcoming and civic ceremonies, the Giants settled into West Coast life playing to near sell-out crowds. Given the seating limitations of Seals Stadium, most Bay Area fans got to know the Giants by listening to KSFO radio broadcasts with Russ Hodges and Lon Simmons, the voices of the Giants. As fans adjusted to the pace and schedule of Major League clubs coming and going and the ball club began its daily routine of home and away baseball, the local press settled into their work, a strategic campaign of reinvention, converting a New York team into something distinctly San Franciscan. The plan to "make it new" grew from a local pride that rejected New York claims of grandeur and sophistication, as well as the implied reproach of California coming from East Coast journalists still smarting from the loss of its fabled National League teams. The loss had a personal edge to it—and therefore was more deeply felt—as many of the New York beat writers for the Giants and the Dodgers would lose their assignments with only one baseball team (the Yankees) left to cover.[2]

Some New York commentary, *New York Herald Tribune* Red Smith's for example, mixed lamentation and criticism, touching on the genuine feelings of loss that many New York fans felt. "The departure of the Giants and the Dodgers from New York is an unrelieved calamity, a grievous loss to the city and to baseball, a shattering blow to the prestige of the National League, and indictment of the men operating the clubs and the men governing the city."[3] Other reactions shifted the focus to the Giants' new home, citing the shortcomings of San Francisco as a Major League city, especially the unsuitable weather and the ignorant and unsophisticated West Coast baseball fan.[4] Noted *New York Times* columnist Arthur Daley expressed his distraught frustration with a touch of the zany, speculating that, with the new burden of coast-to-coast travel, "careers of big leaguers, already shortened by unrestricted night ball, will be further abridged by the expansion to California. Ball players will have to develop the digestive systems of ostriches or goats in order to absorb these violent fluctuations in their eating habits. They will have to learn to sleep like sloths, who can catch their shut-eye while hanging upside down from trees."[5] Reports from New York about Mayor Christopher attempting to "steal" the Giants implied that San Francisco was attempting to raise its profile as an American city by pirating big league baseball.

The notion that San Francisco would need something from New York to establish its greatness, or to render it a "big league" city, grated on the sensitivities of natives convinced of the city's importance and its status as a center of business and culture. Sportswriters like Curley Grieve would write enthusiastically about a "new age in the city's history" but would be careful to declare the appropriateness of Major League Baseball in the Bay Area.[6] Natives understood San Francisco's place as an uniquely cultivated and sophisticated American city, clearly "major" before the addition of the Giants. Some were disapproving of the enthusiasm and the euphoria expressed in welcoming the Giants to town. "Good grief, they will think we are from Kansas," one reserved citizen observed of the parade to welcome the Giants.[7] Despite the great efforts of politicians and officials to land big league baseball, and the genuinely enthusiastic reception toward the team that prevailed citywide, an attitude of cool and self-assured nonchalance toward all things New York prevailed among many of the local writers, energizing the project of reinventing the Giants.

Of course these writers had to tread warily not to be hoisted by their own petards. The umbrage and fits of pique motivating them were bred of the same provinciality attributed to New Yorkers. They also had to be careful not to appear being out of touch, too elite even, given the warm excitement expressed by civil authorities and the public in welcoming the Giants to town. Charles McCabe, a columnist for the *San Francisco Chronicle*, described the delicate balance. Commenting on the excitement the Giants had brought to town, McCabe suggested a tension that found a resolution. "San Francisco has been saying for decades that it is big league. In its secret heart, it has never been sure. These days it is."[8] While the writers acknowledged the fervor throughout the city and paid tribute to the history of the transplanted ball club, they nonetheless remained true to their project of reinvention: how to transform a New York team into their own.

Nowhere was this more apparent than in the local reception of the one genuine box-office attraction the Giants had: Willie Mays. Mays arrived in San Francisco as an established superstar whose very presence symbolized the New York Giants. Charles Einstein, of all Mays biographers the one who probably knew him best, summed up Mays's reception by San Francisco writers and fans as "restrained" in comparison to the enthusiasm accorded the team in general. "To chauvinistic residents of the Bay Area, Mays was the hated embodiment of New York. Also he had the temerity to play center field at Seals Stadium where the native-born DiMaggio had played it in his minor-league days."[9] Years later, Mays admitted he felt some of this prejudice in the fans' reactions during his first year in San Francisco, when they booed him at times.[10] Eventually Mays, whose greatness was undeniable even to the most "restrained" eye, would win over the most xenophobic among his new audience. But initially, as Einstein suggests, he was perceived as a New Yorker, whose legendary play and stardom evoked memories of the Polo Grounds: the catch in the '54 World Series, league-leading home runs in 1955, stolen bases in 1956 and 1957, and a Gold Glove in 1957.

The history of Mays's reception among San Francisco's revisionist sportswriters illustrates clearly the process taking place in the remaking of the Giants, especially in the early years between 1958 and 1962. Some local scribes went so far as to adopt an "I'm from Missouri" stance, not wanting to be too effusive in their recognition of Mays's status as one of baseball's greats. James F. McGee, applying a reversal of logic, reminded his readers that the Giants would be the beneficiaries of a storied tradition of Pacific Coast League baseball and listed all the great Seals who played in San Francisco before they went on to Major League careers. In an article entitled "Rich Inheritance for Majors Here," McGee cautioned against being too swept up by "the Major League mystique," especially the play of a certain center fielder. "Willie Mays, the Giants' wizard, will be playing in the shadows of two Italians from North Beach this season."[11]

McGee's approach represented a distinct kind of revisionism, one rooted in a rejection of New York influence. Others adapted a different approach to reinvention, widening their focus and perspective. Writers like Bob Stevens of the *San Francisco Chronicle* and Roger Williams of the *San Francisco News* did not deny Mays's ability or stature; nor did they compare him to the DiMaggios. Rather, they simply treated him with something akin to benign neglect, noting his achievements but limiting any praise or admiration. They turned their attention instead to new Giants who had no history in New York, especially Orlando Cepeda, a sensational power hitting rookie from Puerto Rico, who was voted the fans' favorite in a 1958 poll conducted by the *San Francisco Examiner*. Cepeda finished the 1958 season with a .312 batting average, 25 home runs, and 96 runs-batted-in and was voted unanimously the National League Rookie of the Year.[12]

The reinvention project was aided unwittingly by the Giants' front office in a dramatic overhaul of the roster that began in 1956. Young players were signed, especially from the Caribbean and the southern states, and developed in the Giants' Minor League clubs. The 1958 opening-day lineup included three rookies: Cepeda, Willie Kirkland, and Jim Davenport. By June, they had added catcher Bob Schmidt and outfielder Felipe Alou. None of these men played in New York. Indeed, manager Bill Rigney remarked that the first two years in San Francisco the Giants adhered to a revolving-door policy: the roster was fluid with a steady flow of players coming and going almost weekly.[13] Fan favorites and future Hall of Famers Willie McCovey (1959) and Juan Marichal (1960) joined a number of veterans who arrived via trades, like Sam Jones, Billy Pierce, and Harvey Kuenn. By 1962, the year the Giants won the National League pennant, the only player on the opening-day lineup with any connection to the New York team was Mays, who by now, after four brilliant seasons in a San Francisco uniform, had become a local hero, even among the most provincial of the city's sportswriters.[14] It would have been difficult for any of the restrained among the revisionists to ignore Mays's 1962 season: he led the league in home runs with 49, finished second in the league in runs scored with 130, and finished second in runs batted in with 141. Without him, many argued, there would be no National League pennant and no World Series appearance for the Giants. Moreover, as Einstein points out, 1962 meant that the Giants had been in San Francisco five years, giving fans and sportswriters a good stretch of time to experience Mays's greatness. It also meant that the memories of Lefty O'Doul and the Seals were receding into the past, while the Giants were engaged in a furious pennant race and nail-biting playoff with the Dodgers. Mays began to gather the testimonials that would rank his play equal, if not superior, to that of the preeminent San Francisco center fielder, the great Joe DiMaggio.[15]

One remarkable aspect of reinventing the Giants into a San Francisco club had nothing to do with the local sportswriters. Rather, it grew out of Horace Stoneham's pioneering commitment to bring Latino players into Major League Baseball. With the Negro Leagues nearing collapse in the late 1940s and early 1950s, Stoneham hired Alex Pompez, former owner of the New York Cubans, and placed him in charge of player acquisition in Latin America and the Caribbean.[16] Pompez, who was acquainted with legendary Hispanic baseball men such as Pedro Zorilla and Horacio Martinez, brought a number of players into the Giants' fold, many of whom would become standouts in San Francisco. Orlando Cepeda, Felipe Alou, and Andre Rodgers played in 1958; Juan Marichal arrived in 1960; Matty and Jesus Alou began in 1962; Jose Pagan and Tito Fuentes had started by 1964. As Mays's biographer James S. Hirsch observed, the Giants arrived in San Francisco "unlike any other team that had played in the league. [They] fielded four blacks and six Latins. . . . It was the Giants, not the Dodgers, who now set the standard for integration. They were Major League Baseball's melting pot, and their outreach brought in some of the finest players of the era."[17] Stoneham broke another barrier in

1964, signing the first Japanese player in the Major Leagues, Masanori Murikami, who pitched for the Giants in 1964 and 1965.[18] Ironically, Stoneham's commitment to integration played no small part in ridding the San Francisco club of one of its last New York vestiges. Alvin Dark, long associated with the New York Giants as a player in the 1950s, was fired in 1964 after four years as manager, principally because he could not connect with his Latino players.[19]

All this roster activity was not only effective in a redefinition of the ball club as unique, giving Bay Area fans a sense of the Giants as their own, it also produced results on the field that bore no resemblance to the last few years of the team in New York, especially 1956 and 1957, when they finished in the National League's second division. In a complete reversal of the pathetic 1957 season, the Giants played winning baseball in their first season in San Francisco, challenging for the pennant. Making it easy for those writers in the reinvention business, this team had become transformed, not just geographically but athletically. In late August they eventually faltered, finishing third. What was a mild disappointment to local fans proved a great surprise to baseball's pundits who had picked the Giants to finish once again in the second division. Success at the box office showed an even greater disparity to that of the 1957 New York team. Despite playing in Seals Stadium, where seating was limited, they drew 1,272,625 fans, easily doubling attendance for the previous year in the cavernous Polo Grounds. They also established the highest Giants' attendance figures since 1948.[20]

Their second year in San Francisco proved an even greater success at the gate and on the field. Still playing at Seals Stadium, the Giants nonetheless increased attendance from the year before, drawing 1,422,130. Bay Area fans were treated to a great Major League pennant race with a heartbreaking ending. In late September, the Giants were leading the Braves and the Dodgers by two games with eight left to play. The city, flush with pennant fever, dreamt of hosting a World Series as the Dodgers came to town for three dramatic games at Seals Stadium. That Series, and the Giants' season, turned on a single play in game two. Having lost the Series' opening game 4–1, the Giants were ahead in the second game 1–0 in the seventh inning when the Dodgers loaded the bases with one out. Manager Bill Rigney decided to go for an inning-ending double play when slow-footed Chuck Essegian pinch hit for pitcher Don Drysdale. When Essegian obligingly grounded a two-hopper to third baseman Jim Davenport, it looked like Rigney might be prescient. Davenport fielded it cleanly and threw to shortstop Daryl Spencer, covering second, who dropped the ball. A run scored, everyone was safe, and the Giants never recovered. The Dodgers went on to score four more runs and won the game. Dazed and shocked, the Giants lost the next day and dropped four out of their last five games, finishing third behind the Dodgers and the Braves.

Deflated for the second straight year, fans nevertheless felt the excitement of the chase. Moreover, they had cause for celebration in their hopes for the future. In addition to a competitive pennant race, they knew the Giants were loaded with young talent, a great harbinger of future success. Also, the year 1959 marked the inaugural season for Willie McCovey, named the National League Rookie of the Year, who would go on to become one of baseball's premier power hitters and one of San Francisco's favorite players.

A full reinvention of the New York baseball team required more than focusing on the players. It entailed a makeover of the face of the franchise as well, that of owner Horace Stoneham, a true-blue Manhattanite, whose family had been in control of the Giants since 1919. Long before the first pitch in Seals Stadium on April 15, 1958, the leading forces of reinvention, especially sportswriters Curley Grieve and Prescott Sullivan, introduced Stoneham to Bay Area readers and began the conversion of a New Yorker into a San Franciscan. The emphasis was on the urban as a location and the urbane as an individual. Stoneham was presented as a man committed to city life, one who loved refinement and sophistication, and who was attracted to good restaurants and the theater. A favorite denizen of the legendary Manhattan watering hole Toots Shor's (Shor preferred "saloon" as the description of his place even though it was well known for dining), Stoneham was quick to adapt to San Francisco's rich array of great eating establishments. Eventually he settled on Bardelli's restaurant on O'Farrell Street, whose owner, Stu Adams, a bon vivant and raconteur every bit as outgoing as Toots Shor, welcomed Stoneham and his entourage regularly.[21] Bardelli's epitomized vintage San Francisco with its high vaulted ceilings, beautiful stained-glass windows, and its waiters in tuxes who treated patrons as though they were guests rather than customers.[22]

Stoneham's choice of a place like Bardelli's was made much of by Grieve, Sullivan, and especially Herb Caen, whose daily columns in the *San Francisco Chronicle* were read by locals as a "who's who" guide to the city's society. To be mentioned in Caen's columns was a kind of acceptance or recognition as part of the fabric of the city. William Hogan, Caen's editor at the *Chronicle*, described the writer's significance and importance. "Caen is the best known man in town. You must read Caen to be in the know. You find out what's doing, who's who, how it is, and where it happened. . . . Caen's column is a love letter between you and him and the city."[23]

Stoneham moved to San Francisco at the beginning of October 1957. By the year's end—only three months' time—he was mentioned in Caen's column five times.[24] Throughout 1958 Stoneham was regularly cited in Caen's columns, always as one of the city's great personalities, hobnobbing with important locals.[25] Caen's item in his January 21, 1958, column is characteristic. "Giants boss Horace Stoneham, dining at the Owl n' Turtle, hosted six pals. When the check arrived Horace displayed an autographed baseball and grinned to owner Bill Varni, 'Have we got a deal?' Varni was quick to respond, 'Well if the autograph is Bill Rigney, you pay half the check. If it is Willie Mays, dinner is on the house.' It was. Now do you think Willie Mays is overpaid?"[26]

Prescott Sullivan emphasized Stoneham's baseball background and love of the game but was quick to tout the Giants boss's love of San Francisco. Sullivan recalls a conversation with Brick Laws, owner of the PCL Oakland Oaks and one of Stoneham's oldest friends in the Bay Area. "Ten years ago," Laws says, "when he had no thought of moving, he told me how much he loved this city. 'Brick,' he said, 'I don't ever want to leave New York. But if ever I have to get out, you can be sure that San Francisco will be where I light.'"[27] Ward Morehouse, writing in the *Sporting News*, testified to the great results of the reinvention of Stoneham as a native San Franciscan. In an article entitled "It's 'Goodbye Broadway'—Horace Now a Native Son," Morehouse remarks on how ebullient Stoneham was about his newly adopted home. "People out here have been wonderful to us. . . . The city has more than lived up to everything it promised. Personally, I'm not really missing Broadway and New York so much. . . . San Francisco is the same kind of city as New York. You have great variety here, fine restaurants, good theater. . . . Everybody here is for the home team, and that's a change for us."[28]

In these stories of Stoneham the San Franciscan, great emphasis was placed on his generous character, his love of good food and drink, his deep affection for his newly adopted town, his familiarity with the neighborhoods and restaurants, and his genuine lack of remorse over leaving New York. Introducing Stoneham to San Francisco readers, Curley Grieve highlighted the Giants' owner's loyalty as a personal quality: loyalty to his players, to his colleagues, and to his staff. Moreover, Grieve added, Stoneham's loyalty also applies to his commitments, including his choice of San Francisco as a home for his team. Grieve's portrait of Stoneham allows the owner his own voice, quoting him liberally especially on his decision to move the Giants from New York with Walter O'Malley's Dodgers: "If Brooklyn had picked San Francisco first, I would not have gone to Los Angeles. . . . This was the one place I preferred. Believe me when I say— San Francisco first, Los Angeles never."[29]

It should be noted that the efforts of Grieve, Sullivan, and other local sportswriters to reinvent the Giants, while driven by a particular agenda, fit aptly into a larger, more pervasive pattern of change running throughout San Francisco during the twentieth century. It might be said that "reinvention" was an essential part of the city's nature. After the famous 1906 earthquake and fire that destroyed almost 80 percent of the city, the process of rebuilding began almost immediately. Only a few years later, in the fall of 1911, President William Howard Taft visited the city, whose progress in rebuilding and penchant for change greatly impressed him. In a speech before local officials he remarked that San Francisco is "the city that knows how," a phrase that became a watchword.[30]

Post–World War II San Francisco saw a new push for reinvention that manifested itself in two distinct phases. The first, largely cultural and ideological, grew out of the columns of Herb Caen, who designated the city "Baghdad by the Bay" and portrayed San Francisco as a romantic and enchanted place like no other. California historian Kevin Starr credits Caen with creating a locale that appears as a magical land of promise, a beacon to the great influx of population coming to the Bay Area in the decades after the war. "San Francisco was a city so beautiful, so favored by nature and history, that it was not quite real and hence offered new comers a setting in which to remake themselves anew."[31] Caen's description of San Francisco falls within the genre of literature of place, similar to Yeats's Ireland, Faulkner's American South, Joyce's Dublin, Steinbeck's Monterey, or, the example Starr prefers, Durrell's Alexandria. "Caen attempts to do for San Francisco what on a more ambitious level the English writer Lawrence Durrell would be seen doing for Alexandria: fuse the city, that is—people, places, sunlight, fog, seabirds, and bridges—into an alembic of magic memory: make of San Francisco a unified symbol, an image in the mind, a work of art."[32]

The second phase of reinvention owes little to Caen, however powerful his Baghdad mythmaking was to the city's changing ethos. This phase involved blueprints, traffic studies, building codes, skyscrapers, demographics, road construction, health, and sanitation, carried out by practical men in engineering, architecture, and social planning. Politicians also took their turn in this enterprise of change, and credit should be given to Mayor Christopher and others on the board of supervisors in the mid-1950s. They activated the discussions and thinking of the late 1940s when planning agencies and citizen advisory committees proposed transformation of certain districts in the city, some of which were deteriorating. Under Mayor Christopher the push toward modernization began to take flight with the appointment of a redevelopment czar named Justin Herman, who resembled New York's Robert Moses in responsibilities and personality. Herman came to his role in the city's redevelopment project after heading the United States Housing and Home Finance Agency in the western states. He was organized, driven, and autocratic, with a strong work ethic. For the next fifteen years, he pushed through much of the work on neighborhoods, such as the Western Addition, Diamond Heights, and the Golden Gateway that, according to Starr, "significantly remade the city."[33]

The changes afoot in San Francisco, including the addition of Major League Baseball, were happening at a state level as well. In postwar America, more than baseball teams were on the move to California. Attracted by weather, housing, scenery, the California lifestyle, and the prospects of growing numbers of businesses, such as Lockheed, International Business Machines, Fairchild Semiconductor, and Hewlett-Packard, young Americans moved west for employment and a new life. Many in this workforce had experienced California in the armed services and were eager to get back. Like the Bay Area, Los Angeles and greater Southern California were being changed by newly arrived transplants seeking jobs amidst the legendary natural beauty of sunshine, beaches, palm trees, and orange groves. Disneyland opened in 1955, calling itself a magical kingdom. It served as a kind of barometer for life in Southern California and was a great attraction for families from all over the country. The Dodgers were part of the change as well. Playing in the spacious Los Angeles Coliseum from 1958 through 1961, they energized the sports public of Southern California, attracting huge crowds. Although they began remaking their ball club a bit later than the Giants did, by the time the team moved into their new stadium in Chavez Ravine in 1962, they would field a lineup with little resemblance to Brooklyn's "boys of summer."[34]

The activity in California reflected a change taking place across the country at large. The expansion of baseball, finally living up geographically to its claim as the national pastime, mirrored the general population movement, not only to California but from eastern and midwestern cities to suburbs, close by, where young families could find more affordable and spacious housing. Those moving were accommodated and expedited by national transportation and infrastructure rebuilding. Construction of President Dwight Eisenhower's national freeway system was underway in the late 1950s, redesigning the nation's traffic grids and constructing superhighways, thereby making interstate driving much easier and more convenient. Towns were being expanded or created with subdivisions and new housing developments. Commercial jet travel would begin in the late 1950s, not only facilitating the two West Coast ball clubs' travel but also changing the idea of distance in the country. Businesses and tourism would soon adapt. Airfreight would transform commerce throughout the United States and would eventually alter the diets of Americans by making fresh food available all over the country regardless of the seasons or origins. The advent of television in the 1950s created a national popular culture. As more and more Americans bought television sets, exposure to national shows, stars, and personalities gave them a sense of a common culture, regardless of where they lived. Monday mornings at the office, people from New York, California, the Midwest, and the South could discuss what happened on the Ed Sullivan Show, or savor the antics of Milton Berle, Dean Martin and Jerry Lewis, or Jackie Gleason from their weekly comedy shows.

However profound all these changes were, they seem more powerful, even overwhelming, in retrospect and from the distance of time. Those living through them took them in stride, as part of the experience of life in a certain era and moment. For people in and around San Francisco, a transformation occurred in 1958 that enriched their lives and broadened their horizons. A long time coming, Major League Baseball had arrived. San Francisco now had its home team, one that would be shaped and given its own identity, as part of the ongoing process of the city's change and reinvention.

FOUR

Scandalstick

In the spring of 1960, his stadium woes at long last behind him, Horace Stoneham had little doubt of the soundness of his move to San Francisco. What was there not to like? For the first two years on the West Coast the Giants drew well in Seals Stadium, despite its modest seating capacity of 22,900. Astonishingly, in 1959 they set a ten-year attendance mark, higher than every year in New York since 1948, including the pennant-winning 1951 season and the World Series championship of 1954. Now that the Giants were ready to move into their brand new home at Candlestick Park, Stoneham could reasonably plan for even greater numbers at the turnstiles. The new stadium could seat in excess of 42,000.[1] The reality of a new stadium was certainly appealing for Stoneham, but he appeared more excited by his coveted parking, which would afford fans the convenience of driving to the ballpark. The adjacent lots surrounding Candlestick would hold over 10,000 cars, an impossibility at the Polo Grounds, making travel to the ballpark convenient and accessible. All in all, it was for Stoneham a dream come true. The Giants would be playing in a state-of-the-art facility, with ample parking, which was what Stoneham was promised by both Mayor Christopher and Supervisor McCarty in the late spring of 1957. His problems in New York City seemed like ancient history.

Stoneham was only one of many who were giddy over the Giants' new home. The greater San Francisco Bay Area community, by now connected with the Giants as the home team, awaited the opening of the ballpark with excitement and enthusiasm. Having delivered on the stadium pledge to Stoneham and the Giants, Mayor Christopher,

Francis McCarty and others on the board of supervisors were not shy about celebrating their achievement. They took every opportunity to remind folks that San Francisco was the "city that knows how."[2] City officials and bureaucrats were particularly proud of their efforts in pushing through the process of the stadium's construction, staying on schedule, and meeting deadlines. Groundbreaking and preliminary excavation began in June of 1958, followed by the start of construction in September by Charles Harney, a native San Franciscan and well-known contractor whose firm had built roads, bridges, freeway projects, and dams.[3] Overall, the project to completion took less than two years. Christopher and McCarty took special pleasure and satisfaction because San Francisco would have its new stadium two years before the Dodgers would open theirs in Los Angeles.[4]

Candlestick's inaugural festivities on April 11 and 12, 1960, attracted politicians and celebrities from far and wide, including Vice President Richard Nixon; California governor Edmund "Pat" Brown; Commissioner of Baseball Ford Frick; Mrs. John McGraw, widow of the legendary New York Giants skipper; Joe Cronin, native San Franciscan and president of the American League; Warren Giles, president of the National League; and actor Jeff Chandler, who served as master of ceremonies for the festivities. Some of the guests were conspicuous in their attendance and unctuous in their remarks. At the dinner on April 11 at the Garden Room of the Sheraton-Palace Hotel, Vice President Nixon, a native Californian, sang the praises of Candlestick—"the finest park in America"—and predicted a pennant that year for the Giants.[5] Not to be outdone, Governor Brown had glowing remarks for the stadium and, with an eye on his statewide constituency if not the alignment of National and American League teams, announced he was looking forward to a Giants-Dodgers World Series in Candlestick.[6] The next day, April 12, Nixon threw out the ceremonial first pitch, when the Giants hosted the St. Louis Cardinals.

Local writers joined the celebratory chorus with rave reviews in their approval of the Giants' new home. Curley Grieve, whose tenacious lobbying in the early 1950s proved influential in bringing Major League Baseball to San Francisco, saw a new day for Bay Area fans.

"Mourners of Seals Stadium for sentimental or proximity reasons," he wrote, "will dry their tears quickly once they see this modern, beautiful baseball plant, surrounded by acres of parking and catering to the comfort of viewers."[7] Bob Stevens, echoing Vice President Nixon, predicted a pennant in large part because of the great new facility in which the Giants would play.[8] Bill Leiser dubbed Candlestick Park "one of the finest plants ever constructed."[9] Charles McCabe folded praise of the ballpark into his tribute to legendary New York Giants skipper John McGraw.[10] Charles Einstein followed a similar strategy in his "Ball Park Ballad," a lighthearted treatment of Giants history in a parody of "Casey at the Bat."[11] Even out-of-town writers chimed in. J. G. Taylor Spink, editor of the nationally circulated *Sporting News*, pronounced Candlestick Park a sensation. "It's simply wonderful, marvelous, unbelievable. Baseball has never known anything to compare with it."[12] Spink's observation about Candlestick's incomparability would prove exact and prescient, but for reasons much different than Spink intended.

Initial reactions among players, however, were not so sanguine. Willie Mays didn't have to wait for a game to be played to recognize that Candlestick posed a big problem for right-handed power hitters. "During our first batting practice I noticed how the wind would knock down anything hit to left. I couldn't hit anything out. Neither could Cepeda. I told them then that they needed to bring in the left field fences."[13] After the first game, St. Louis Cardinal left fielder Leon Wagner (who, coincidentally, hit the first home run in Candlestick—on opening day, to right field) commented on the wind coming in behind him. "I like it out there in left as a fielder. The wind holds the ball up and gives you time to go three or four steps backward." St. Louis pitcher Larry Jackson, the first to lose a game in Candlestick, remarked that the wind was going to make it rough on everybody, fielders and hitters alike. Solly Hemus, the St. Louis manager, said the Giants hitters would suffer. "The wind blowing out toward right will stop their right-handed hitters, like Mays and Cepeda, from hitting it out of the park. It's a pitcher's stadium."[14]

Given the hindsight of forty years of baseball history, the players turned out to be harbingers of a bitter truth. Candlestick was a terrible place to play baseball, so much so that it would have a profound effect on the Giants' fortunes as long as they called the place home. To be fair to the writers, it didn't take them long to rethink and then rewrite their views on the ballpark. After only two months of baseball in Candlestick, the bloom was off the rose and articles began to appear about the downside of the park and especially of *watching* baseball there.[15] There were the elements of course. Night games, often played in bone-chilling cold and occasional fog, were, as Roger Angell observed, akin to an Aleut rite of passage, especially for the fans who sat immobile for nine innings.[16] Willie McCovey felt sorry for the fans. "We saw them sitting in the stands, freezing at night games, and wondered how they did it. At least we were moving around on the field."[17] Afternoon games were breezy, a consequence of the park's location directly east of the Alemany Gap, the most notorious of several wind tunnels caused by the city's many hills and valleys. The Alemany Gap regularly funneled cold air eastward off the Pacific, especially in the summer time.[18] Jim Murray, the *Los Angeles Times* sportswriter who visited Candlestick often when covering the Dodgers, lamented the plight of the Giants' power hitters "trying to hit homers through a wall of wind that could turn back bullets."[19]

But wind was only the most conspicuous problem. The stadium itself also came under scrutiny: its layout, design, and facilities were austere, both in appearance and in utility. Constructed entirely from reinforced concrete, the place was utilitarian and soulless, devoid of any amenity or charm. Dodgers broadcaster Vin Scully called it a "mean" park.[20] Many of the planned embellishments needed to be eliminated due to budgetary restraints. Even its ingress and egress for automobiles and pedestrians alike proved problematic. Getting from the parking lot to the seats became a deadly affair due to the design of a steep incline dubbed "Cardiac Hill"; during the first season seven fans suffered fatal heart attacks in their ascents.[21] Postgame traffic was also an annoying experience as people were delayed in their cars exiting the ballpark due to the bottleneck from the parking lot to the freeways. Candlestick's location may have given Stoneham his sought-after parking, one of the few places in the city were that kind of space was available, but it also brought with it the conditions that would inspire some of the harshest criticism ever leveled at an American sports facility.

"Candlestink"; "The Temple of Winds"; "Field of Screams"; "Harney's Horror"; "Foggy Field"; "Valley Forge": these were just a few of the names from a list making Candlestick Park the most vilified baseball venue of the twentieth century. Even those who referred affectionately to the place as "The Stick" saw their term of endearment denigrated as "The Stink," a reference not precisely aimed at the wind but rather at the wafting strains of garbage smells coming from the county landfill across nearby Bayshore Freeway. As writers began to rack up their hours at Candlestick, they were more forthcoming, not only about the weather but also about the park's deficiencies in general. Close to the sportswriter's heart, the press box proved woefully inadequate, as the seating was too low for viewing the game, one of the many design failures due to last-minute budget cuts.[22] Even Stoneham's treasured parking lot left much to be desired. As Candlestick was situated ten miles from downtown, getting to and from the ballpark on game days with even normal attendance was a chore with its freeway entrances and exits and small side-roads.[23]

Even after the enclosure of the stadium to accommodate the 49ers in 1971 (and, it was hoped, to obstruct the wind), weather was still a problem, more unpredictable in fact, with the wind dipping into the bowl and randomly swirling in all directions.[24] Hank Greenwald, who suffered the harsh conditions of Candlestick for seventeen years as the radio voice of the Giants, identified the stadium's location as the essential feature of the Giants' story in San Francisco between 1960 into the 1990s, both for what happened and especially for what didn't happen.

If you were to write the definitive history of the San Francisco Giants, long before the mention of Willie Mays, Willie McCovey, Juan Marichal or anyone else, there would be Candlestick. There's no way of calculating exactly how damaging Candlestick Park was to the Giants franchise, and to the city, but some things are obvious.[25]

Stories about the elements at Candlestick—the wind, made apparent by dancing hot dog wrappers and swirling dust clouds; the fog, giving the stadium an eerie perspective; the teeth-rattling temperature at night games—and their effects on both players and fans are the stuff of modern baseball legend and lore. Felipe Alou said the wind blew so hard toward right field that as an outfielder he could lean into it to rest.[26] Casey Stengel brought his Mets to Candlestick in 1963 and saw something he had never seen in his fifty-plus years in baseball: during batting practice a rogue gust swooped up the batting cage and spun it seventy feet away beyond the pitcher's mound. Lon Simmons, longtime voice of the Giants in the early years in San Francisco, recalls a 1960 night game with the Dodgers when Willie McCovey hit a towering pop fly that soared above a fog bank that had settled over the outfield. None of the Dodgers fielders could find the ball until it landed with a thud in left-center; McCovey ended up on third base.[27] Al Michaels, broadcasting Giant games in the mid-1970s, remembers a time when Dodgers infielder Bill Russell's cap was blown off his head and wound up pinned against the left-field wall without hitting the ground.[28] Robby Thompson remarked that when he and Will Clark were rookies in 1986, Bob Brenly, the veteran catcher, told them not to be in any hurry with infield pop flies in Candlestick. Brenly cautioned not to call for the ball right away. Instead, he suggested, wait and surround it; then decide in the last few seconds who will take it.[29] When right fielder Jack Clark was asked what would improve the conditions at Candlestick, he immediately answered, "Dynamite."[30] The quintessential Candlestick story, about Stu Miller, all 160 pounds of him, knocked off the mound by a quick burst of wind in the 1961 All-Star Game, has been told so often and, befitting Candlestick fashion, blown so far out of proportion that it is held that Miller might still be caught up in the jet stream, soaring somewhere over San Francisco Bay. (The truth is that he rocked a bit in his stretch and was called for a balk.) When the best thing that can be said about a ballpark is that it didn't fall down during an earthquake—as was the case in the 1989 World Series—one senses the limitation of praise. Even this commendatory observation has its detractors. Hank Greenwald lamented Candlestick's earthquake-proof qualities. "Distressingly, this may have been the best chance we had of getting rid of this ballpark."[31]

All ballparks affect the fortunes of their occupants in important ways and influence a style of play, some as pitcher-friendly, some as hitters' parks. There have been arguments and speculation about the effects of ballparks on the achievements of individual players—how would Ted Williams have fared playing regularly in Yankee Stadium?—and on various franchises. Many have commented on the dimensions at Fenway and how they have played into the Red Sox's history. Others point out the benefit of the so-called short porch in right field for Yankee sluggers. Some claim the ivy walls at Wrigley and the intimacy of the park have played a role in the Cubs' fate over the years.[32] But no post-1960 park in the Majors has been deemed negatively influential by so many as has Candlestick. The notoriety of Candlestick in this regard has become commonplace, so much so that it masks a crucial part of the baseball park's story that has nothing to do with ballplayers, games, spectators, or weather. Candlestick's notoriety began long before the first pitch was thrown on April 12, 1960. The story of the stadium's planning, financing, and building was something of a scandal in its own right—and part of the colorful history not only of Major League Baseball in San Francisco but also of the city's political past.

It is crucial to remember that the chief reason for baseball's great western migration in 1958 had everything to do with ballparks, first in the extreme dissatisfaction with the Polo Grounds for the Giants and Ebbets Field for the Dodgers and, second, in the attractive promises of new facilities by officials in San Francisco and Los Angeles. Once the Giants and Dodgers moved, they both had temporary homes, negotiated in part by local officials and businessmen, until such time as their respective new ballparks could be built. The temporary venues—

HORACE

Seals Stadium and the Los Angeles Coliseum, each a quick fix as the teams put down roots in California—form an important albeit brief chapter to the history of West Coast baseball. Both Stoneham and his Dodgers counterpart, Walter O'Malley, were willing to make do with these temporary locations, each of them insufficient for Major League Baseball in different ways, knowing that permanent and new Major League facilities were on the planning boards, soon to be completed.[33] The exciting 1959 National League pennant race was played out in Seals Stadium and the Los Angeles Coliseum, although neither place was really suitable for Major League Baseball.

So too did the events surrounding the planning and construction of the new ballparks become part of the history of West Coast baseball. The Dodgers story of the building of the new stadium in Chavez Ravine has been widely reported.[34] After a tough two-year struggle that included political wrangling between Los Angeles City Council members, public hearings, ballot measures, lawsuits, Supreme Court action, and evictions of the last residents of Chavez Ravine, O'Malley felt optimistic enough in late 1959 to begin construction. After all the legal and political issues, he must have viewed the actual construction and building of the ballpark and its surroundings as relatively routine. Dodger Stadium opened on April 10, 1962, to celebration and fanfare. It was a great success and a huge emotional relief for O'Malley. Los Angeles sportswriter Jim Murray summed up the feelings of many when he declared Dodger Stadium the Taj Mahal of baseball.[35]

With the beginning of the 1962 season, the Giants and Dodgers were settled in their permanent homes, fixed within their respective communities and secure in their West Coast identity. At least this was the initial perception, and it would certainly apply to the Dodgers' history in Los Angeles. The Giants' story in San Francisco would be more troubled. The prevailing version of the histories of Candlestick Park and Dodger Stadium would have it that O'Malley faced all of the difficulties in the creation of his new park early in his time in Los Angeles and prior to actual construction, whereas Stoneham's route went in a different direction. The planning and permitting of the ballpark in San Francisco were seemingly smooth and without political and public resistance. While there were the usual minor glitches during construction, the story goes, it was only after the Giants settled into Candlestick for a few seasons that the park's deficiencies became apparent to the players and, more important, to the fans, whose attendance began to dwindle.

But a closer look at the events leading to the planning and building of Candlestick will show a different picture, one that suggests tension, confusion, shenanigans (if not duplicity), underhandedness, and backroom deals between city hall and the builder. Candlestick was trouble from its conception, long before any dirt was moved, plans sketched, or pilings sunk. The city's rush, first to secure a stadium proposal as part of the hurried efforts to woo the Giants, and then to complete the construction of the new stadium as soon as possible, was misguided. Pressure to open for the 1960 season, exerted by the city and the Giants, produced cost-overrides and corner-cutting that would greatly affect both the pace and the workmanship in the stadium's construction. The park's notoriety would also become apparent in veiled backroom deals within city hall, and then in public political squabbling between the San Francisco Board of Supervisors and the contractor, both of which would lead eventually to a grand jury investigation and a myriad of lawsuits. In important ways, the early dealings and complications with the construction stage would play out over the next three decades in continual attempts to improve the less-than-satisfactory conditions at the ballpark, involving inconclusive weather studies, plans to dome the stadium, a number of citizen initiatives, and four public votes to move the team to a new venue.

When George Christopher met with Stoneham in New York in 1957, the mayor was in a curious negotiating position. He came with the security of public financing for a new stadium and a site that provided ample parking, but he had nothing tangible to offer the Giants' boss. Everything was in the planning stages; no actual stadium existed for Stoneham to consider as the Giants' home.[36] But Christopher pressed this condition as an advantage, stressing the publicly approved financing in hand and an opportunity for the Giants to be in on the design and planning of the new stadium. He explained the 1954 vote to Stoneham, by which San Francisco voters had passed a five-million-dollar bond issue for the single purpose of building a stadium to attract a Major League Baseball team. Not surprisingly Stoneham was extremely interested, even enthusiastic, when he learned about the parking, but he cautioned Christopher that the amount the voters had approved would not be enough. Stoneham emphasized that to build the kind of facility that a Major League club would be interested in moving into would take around fourteen million dollars.[37] Somewhat subdued by Stoneham's estimate but nonetheless determined to land the Giants, Christopher assured the Giants' owner of San Francisco's seriousness and returned home to secure the additional funding. Added to his concerns about Stoneham's suggested price tag was a sense of urgency about the city's bond: the 1954 measure passed by the voters had a shelf life of five years. If the city could not attract a Major League Baseball club during that time frame (by the end of 1959), the bond would become null and void.

One thing Christopher did not have to worry about, however, was the location of a ballpark. He had formed a search committee in early 1957 and charged it with finding a suitable site for a baseball stadium. By mid-summer, having vetted a number of prospective sites in the city, the committee had settled on Bayview Park, an area near Candlestick Point about ten miles south of downtown but still within the jurisdiction of the City and County of San Francisco. Christopher himself favored this site.[38] The committee had reviewed various neighborhood sites, including South Basin near Hunters Point, all of them with costs well in excess of projected financing. They also considered a renovation of Seals Stadium that included adding an upper deck, but that location offered no potential for parking.[39] The Bayview parcel came to the attention of the committee through a rather casual and fortuitous early spring meeting between Tom Gray, head of the Downtown Association and a member of the mayor's search committee, and Charles Harney, a local multimillionaire contractor. In a conversation at a University of San Francisco basketball game, Harney made it known to Gray that he thought Bayview would be perfect for a stadium. Moreover, he happened to own over fifty acres of the property and would consider selling it to the city if his construction firm were given the contract to build the ballpark.[40]

Harney's offer seemed too good to be true. The city owned almost thirty acres in Bayview; with the addition of Harney's parcel it would have the necessary space to build with adjoining parking and service roads. Moreover, acquiring the land from a single owner would greatly simplify any negotiation or possible litigation the city might face. The mayor and his committee knew their options on city land were limited by both location and costs, so they listened carefully to Harney's proposition. He had a reputation as an enterprising, hard-driving businessman and was a well-known figure around town: successful construction mogul, pillar of the Catholic church, benefactor to the University of San Francisco, local sports fan, and astute real estate wheeler-dealer. For years he had been buying small parcels of the Bayview Park property when they became available, and in 1953 he purchased forty-one acres of seemingly worthless Bayview tide flats from the city for twenty-one hundred dollars per acre. To help with the stadium project, he agreed to sell his Bayview holdings back to the city for sixty-five thousand dollars per acre, reflecting, in his judgment, its improved value in 1957.[41] The mayor and the board of supervisors were happy to meet Harney's condition of sale, especially because it solved two problems in a single stroke: sufficient land to build the ballpark and a locally known contractor who had a reputation for getting things done in a timely manner.[42] He was known throughout the construction trade as "Hurry-up Harney."[43] Once the sale to Harney was complete—his condition that he build the stadium was agreed upon—Christopher informed Stoneham in New York about developments on the ballpark, hoping to assuage any concerns the Giants boss might have about the move.[44] Stoneham, however, had made up his mind to move to San Francisco at the end of the current season, convinced that progress in San Francisco was genuine.

Meanwhile activity heated up in the Bay Area. As a shrewd politician, Christopher sensed it would be improbable that voters would approve the additional funds Stoneham felt necessary to build what he termed a "Major League" ballpark. So in late summer of 1957, the mayor and those involved with the building and planning for the stadium oversaw the founding of "San Francisco Stadium Incorporated," a nonprofit corporation—and a shadow organization of city hall— whose initial board of directors were none other than Mr. Harney, his brother-in-law C. J. Carroll, and Harney's executive vice president, Joseph Silvestri.[45] The solitary purpose of this organization was to advance the planning and construction of the stadium: specifically to issue a bond for an additional six million dollars and to assign contracts for planning, grading, fill, and construction, matters that under the city charter would require voter approval and open bidding. With the shadow company, however, there were no such constraints. Thus, although design, matters of funding, and construction of the stadium were technically subject to the city's oversight and control, and therefore transparent to the public, business was actually channeled through San Francisco Stadium Inc. This organizational ploy was necessary, reasoned Christopher and his cohorts, not only to facilitate the funding and begin the early stages of construction with grading and road work but also to assure Stoneham of the city's commitment.

Meanwhile, the Giants' boss flew from New York to San Francisco in mid-August and inspected the Bayview site, which he found to his liking. In what has become an oft-told tale, Christopher, McCarty and Harney took Stoneham to Candlestick Point on a sunny morning before the notorious afternoon winds blew through. As they were explaining their ideas for the stadium, Stoneham's gaze remained fixated on the vast acreage that would serve as the stadium's parking lot. After listening politely to the commentary and posing for a few customary photos, Stoneham said everything looked fine and suggested that they all should return downtown for lunch. His visit to the site lasted less than one hour. Later that afternoon he signed a letter of agreement with the City of San Francisco for the 1958 season.[46]

As the news of the Giants' decision to move settled in, the mayor and city hall officials in early fall turned their attention to advancing the stadium project. The formal plans and contracts were making their way through Parks and Recreation Committee and other subcommittees at city hall, but pocket resistance to the Bayview location surfaced among some in the business community who reintroduced the idea of a downtown location. But before this proposal could gain any headway, objections rose, primarily from the mayor's office. First the price tag of downtown real estate effectively added millions to the cost of the project.[47] Then a group of merchants raised their opposition to a downtown location because they thought it would have a negative effect on shopping. The downtown proposal went nowhere.[48] Lefty O'Doul, former Major Leaguer and manager of the Seals, reopened the push for an enlargement of Seals Stadium, but an annoyed mayor reminded everyone about the limitation of parking. Moreover, cost again for the Seals Stadium renovation was significantly higher than that of the Bayview project. As a final gambit in securing the Bayview site, Harney agreed to provide some of the start-up capital that would be repaid by San Francisco Stadium Inc. bonds.[49]

By the end of the year the matter of the stadium's location was settled. The mayor and the search committee convinced the board of supervisors and the city treasurer of the viability of the Bayview property, both on the merits of the site itself and on the dearth of realistic and practical alternative settings. Harney's cooperation as the owner of the property and as the potential builder of the stadium loomed large in the mayor's argument. With the Parks and Recreation Committee and the board of supervisors in agreement on Bayview, the city and San Francisco Stadium Inc. began moving forward with the planning for financing and contracts. Eventually, however, Christopher began to see the indelicacies, including a possible conflict of interest, with Harney's role as director of San Francisco Stadium Inc. In February 1958, the mayor replaced Harney and his brother-in-law with local banker Alan K. Browne, Western Pacific Railroad executive Fredrick Whitman, and Fuller Brawner, head of Fuller Paints.[50]

Even with this shadow venture, the construction of the ballpark continued to run into difficulties. Almost immediately after the ceremonial groundbreaking, Harney and architect John Bolles started feuding, each blaming the other for slow progress. In the winter the feud became particularly nasty and Harney threatened to stop work altogether if any changes were made to the plans.[51] Essential items that were somehow omitted from the initial planning stage never made it into the contractor's budget. Installation of fire equipment and safety features, landscaping, lighting, waterproofing, and irrigation had all been left out, as was the cost for additional engineering, legal fees, and design. A heating system, planned to warm reserved seating, suffered in cost-cutting and never worked properly. Bolles and the city treasurer insisted that these basic items were understood under general categories; Harney said they had to be specified and itemized.[52] Stoneham's coveted parking lot needed special ingress and egress construction that had been overlooked.

Perhaps the most egregious oversight, and one that typified the breach between contractor and architect, involved the irrigation system of the playing field. Groundskeeper Matty Schwab complained to Harney that there was no sprinkling system for the field. Harney replied that it was not specified in the budget. After a short delay in which the city attorneys overruled him, Harney authorized the installation but it was carried out carelessly, leaving the sprinkler heads protruding four inches above the ground throughout the outfield. Schwab had to point out the obvious, that playing the outfield was difficult enough for Major Leaguers without having to dodge scores of sprinkler heads. An enraged Harney had to replace the system, insisting that he would have to be compensated.[53] Eventually, Candlestick's overall construction costs soared to above fourteen million dollars. Stoneham, in characteristic reticent fashion, was decidedly hands-off on construction issues and said little publicly about any of the difficulties in the construction, concentrating instead on the ball club's daily operations in Seals Stadium.

Some city observers claimed that Harney became involved in the project to build San Francisco a ballpark not to make a huge profit but rather to be memorialized with his name attached to the finished product. During the early stages of construction, he demanded that all the plans coming to him from the architect's office be labeled "Har-

ney Stadium." All his trucks and vans coming to and from the construction site had "Harney Stadium" painted on their doors.[54] He also
lobbied the mayor's office for official designation. This practice went
on through the first six months of construction. But when the Parks
and Recreation Committee decided on a public contest to name the
stadium in early 1959, resulting in "Candlestick Park" after its historic location, a piqued Harney took the committee's decision as a
personal slight and suddenly lost his enthusiasm for the project. He
ordered a work slowdown on the site, which delayed the park opening by a year. Harney also became punctilious with the details of his
contract and demanded extra money for anything not listed in the
original. Many of these features, what Bolles called essential and Harney labeled as additional, had to be subcontracted with other construction firms or scrapped altogether. The final cost to the city for
the stadium was $15,122,700.[55]

As the snafus and delays in construction became the subject of
newspaper columns and sports radio shows, and Harney's recalci-
trance a matter of public record, some citizens called for the city's
grand jury to look into the problems with Candlestick.[56] The eighteen-
member jury, under the direction of its foreman, Henry E. North, a
prominent member of the San Francisco business community, began
an investigation in summer 1958. Six months later, in December 1958,
it released a report that found a number of irregularities in planning procedure and questionable land dealings. A majority of the
jurors concluded that the city did not get a good deal on the acquisition, design, construction, and financing of the stadium. The find-
ings were especially critical of the funding of the park and the cost
to the taxpayers.[57]

The reception of the report was surprisingly cool. The local press,
led by Curley Grieve, sports editor of the *San Francisco Examiner*,
buried the story, or characterized it as an example of North's grand-
standing and public posturing.[58] Other city journalists followed suit.
Editorials in the *Chronicle* and the *Examiner* dismissed the report
and blamed North for exceeding his authority.[59] Christopher labeled
the grand jury report a private vendetta against his office and a vote

against progress. The mayor called North a civic nuisance and, for good measure, threw in a few personal barbs, that North was unreliable, a drinker, and "fixable." An outraged North filed a libel suit against the mayor that began a legal struggle between the two that played out in city newspapers for the next few months. North's suit was eventually dropped and he and the mayor reconciled.[60] Gadfly journalist Burton Wolfe, whose magazine the *Californian* published a series of articles in 1960 critical of the tepid response to North's grand jury report, claimed that the ordeal with the mayor left North a broken man. Once a well-known and prominent businessman in the city, he was shunned by former friends and died in 1961 as an isolated figure.[61]

As the construction of Candlestick Park neared its final stages late in 1959, relations between Harney and architect Bolles grew worse. In October, Harney submitted a bill to San Francisco Stadium Inc. for $438,501; Bolles, reviewing the bill for the corporation, authorized a payment of $111,566.76, claiming that Harney had not completed contracted work.[62] Disputes between Harney, Bolles, and San Francisco Stadium Inc. continued into the new year, resulting in a standoff between the builder and the city. Early in 1960, with the baseball season opener only a few months away, Alan K. Browne, president of San Francisco Stadium Inc., informed Harney that his group proposed to hire someone else to finish the Candlestick project. Moreover, San Francisco Stadium Inc. announced that Harney had been paid 90 percent of the $7 million contract price but that $700,000 was being withheld to pay for the subcontracting for unfinished items.[63] Harney filed suit against the corporation's claims, and the city promptly filed a countersuit against Harney. As the proceedings went forward, a third party completed the last items required to get the stadium ready for the opener on April 12. When Harney died of a heart attack in 1962 at the age of sixty, the legal wranglings were still unsettled. In 1963, the city settled with Harney's estate for $430,000. There is no evidence that Harney ever attended a Giants game at Candlestick Park.[64]

The real power of the Candlestick story lies in its latency. At the time of the park's land acquisition, planning, design, and construction and the disputes between builder, architect, and the city, no alarm bells went off. There was no public outcry, no real concern among the press, nor at city hall. Local newspapers at the time, decidedly behind Major League Baseball, viewed any negative publicity on the ballpark as critical of the Giants' presence in the city; therefore they ignored the report or dismissed it as a trivial reaction. The mayor's office took exception to the grand jury report as obstructionist, labeling it a political stunt perpetrated by the mayor's enemies. It was only later, after years of reflection, and extreme disappointment with the facility, that the location, the planning, and especially the funding seemed problematic, making Hank Greenwald's negative observations about Candlestick all the more definitive.

The park's history supports Greenwald. The Giants opened in Candlestick in April 1960 and for the next forty seasons called it home. Their initial success in the early years gradually faded to decades of frustration and what-ifs. The storied franchise in New York won fifteen National League pennants and five world championships. During their forty-year tenure at Candlestick, the Giants won only two pennants; there were no world championships. Whenever teams go through these long periods of drought, baseball has a simple explanation: a curse. The man who wanted his name connected to a baseball park got his wish: the curse of Charles Harney.

FIVE

Perennial Bridesmaids

While Candlestick Park fell considerably short of the stately plea-sure dome that Stoneham had hoped for, his Giants prospered there during the 1960s. In their first ten years in San Francisco the team drew well at the gate, averaging 1.3 million fans a year.[1] It was for good reason: the Giants were phenomenally successful on the field, winning more games in the decade than any other National League team. While they had only one pennant to show for their efforts, they were competitive in every pennant race during that period, finish-ing second five times. In consecutive years, 1965 and 1966, they lost out in the last days of the season—both times to their bitter rivals, the Dodgers—stoking fan interest but also frustration. During their first ten years in San Francisco, the Giants might have been termed the greatest team never to win a world championship.

Despite the lack of pennants, Giants fans in the 1960s were treated to some of the greatest players of the era: future Hall of Famers Willie Mays, Willie McCovey, Orlando Cepeda, Juan Marichal, and Gaylord Perry, along with occasional All-Stars like Felipe Alou, Jim Daven-port, Mike McCormick, Stu Miller, Dick Dietz, Ed Bailey, and Tom Haller. With this kind of talent, the Giants were consistently play-ing winning baseball, year after year. Not surprisingly, the city, and the Bay Area in general, developed a deep affection for the ball club. All of this helped Stoneham's bottom line. Prior to the move to San Francisco in 1957, one investment unit (one share of common stock and one share of preferred stock) of the National Exhibition Com-pany, the holding organization that owned the Giants, sold on the open market for $125. In mid-summer of 1964, that same unit cost

$725. The risk Stoneham took in leaving New York was paying handsome dividends.[2]

By the time Candlestick opened in 1960 no one doubted the connection between the city and its baseball team. The two years at Seals Stadium indicated that the Giants were popular, were competitive, had great players, and would draw well. Moving to a new venue merely underscored their popularity. Initially the novelty of a new ballpark drew fans to Candlestick. Even after reality set in, that watching games in the new venue would involve braving the elements, especially the chilling winds during night games, fans continued to turn out, consistently pushing attendance past the million mark, year after year.

The Giants' NL pennant in 1962 gave fans great satisfaction, but the loss in seven games to the Yankees in the World Series increased their frustration. The world championship eluded the Giants in dramatic fashion that year when, in game seven, in the bottom of the ninth, with runners on second and third, McCovey slashed a wicked line drive that a perfectly positioned Yankees second baseman Bobby Richardson speared for the final out, clinching a 1–0 World Series win for New York. Bay Area Giants fans were crushed. The McCovey liner became a frozen moment of baseball lore for years to come, a narrative structured by a series of "what ifs"—what if McCovey's line drive were two feet either side of Richardson? What if Richardson had been playing McCovey to pull, as he should have? What if Matty Alou had tried to score on Mays's double in the previous at bat instead of being held at third? It was the closest the Giants would come to a World Series championship for almost fifty years.

The 1962 season also vindicated both Stoneham's and O'Malley's great gamble in moving out of New York and into new territory. After four years in California, each team had its own stadium, which accentuated identity and location. No longer playing in borrowed or temporary facilities, both teams could cultivate a sense of place in their respective ballparks. Each location reflected its hometown character and accentuated its strengths, and players and fans recognized a home-field advantage. Dodger Stadium, located in Chavez Ravine, catered to Los Angeles's team speed; the groundskeepers rolled the base paths rock hard for greater traction. Temperatures were balmy and games were played to shirtsleeve crowds and, during day games, to sunbathers. The Giants, on the other hand, were built on power; their groundskeeper let the grass grow and simply raked the base paths. After adjusting to the winds in the first season, designers realigned the fences to create power alleys that would accommodate home run hitters like Mays, Cepeda, and McCovey.[3] Their home crowds braced for the elements, especially the chilly nights.

The respective grooming of the new ballparks produced one of the legendary incidents in the intense and time-honored Giants-Dodgers rivalry. In the heat of the 1962 pennant race, with the Dodgers coming to town for a three-game series in mid-August, Giants skipper Alvin Dark approached head groundskeeper Matty Schwab to see whether conditions at Candlestick could minimize the Dodgers' team speed, with the likes of base-stealing champion Maury Wills and burners Willie Davis and Tommy Davis. Schwab dumped wet sand all around first base, raking it in to slow any initial steps in base stealing attempts. The conditions were so wet and sloppy that the Dodgers lodged a complaint with the umpires, who ordered Schwab to correct the situation. He responded by ordering his crew to dump damp peat moss around the base, which only made the footing worse. In the crucial three-game series—the Giants were five and a half back— the Dodgers stole one base and were swept, putting the Giants back in the race. When San Francisco traveled to Los Angeles three weeks later, they were greeted with duck calls from the fifty thousand fans in attendance. Vin Scully, the voice of the Dodgers, joined in on behalf of the home team by dubbing Alvin Dark "the Swamp Fox," after the legendary Francis Marion, war hero of the American Revolution who befuddled the British in the lowland backwaters of his native South Carolina.

The general success of the Giants and Dodgers in league play after they moved west and their subsequent competitive fervor when playing each other made apparent to baseball fans across the country what most Californians knew instinctively—that San Francisco and

63

Los Angeles had a deep antipathy for one another. It was perhaps not quite as severe as a *Time* magazine writer put it in 1965:

> Most so-called U.S. sports rivalries are frauds, preserved only by tradition. The feud between the Giants and the Dodgers is real. It was bad enough when it involved Manhattan and Brooklyn, two boroughs of the same city. Now the principals are San Francisco and Los Angeles, two cities 325 miles apart whose partisans hate each other's guts.[4]

Fans in each city, nonetheless, reveled in the joy of victory when their team trounced the other. These feelings between the cities and the regions transcended sports, originating in a historical framework and defined by cultural perceptions generated by each community. San Franciscans cultivated the reputation of their city as a place of historical significance in California, a financial and business center that had its roots in the mid-nineteenth century, a concentrated cosmopolitan urban space with great natural beauty, superb restaurants, and great artistic organizations. They looked upon Los Angeles as an upstart, a sprawling collection of suburbs unified after World War II by a series of freeways. By contrast, residents of greater Los Angeles saw their locale as more dynamic and cutting-edge, engendering a more mobile, fast paced, informal lifestyle, unencumbered by tradition, reflecting the year-round sunny climate, the proximity to beaches, and the predominance of the automobile. As the center of the country's film industry, "Hollywood," a district in Los Angeles, came to be known less as a place and more as a glamorous lifestyle. Angelenos saw San Franciscans as stuffy and pretentious, living on past glory, and smugly provincial.

The deep feeling of divide between the regions—Southern California versus Northern California (although San Francisco is really central in California geography); differences in lifestyle and culture, even in food, music, and housing—gives the lie to the notion that the spirited and heated Giants-Dodgers rivalry ended when the teams left New York. Easterners were convinced that the intensity wouldn't survive the lack of the kind of proximity the teams had experienced in New York, with both teams in the same city and fans of both teams mixing at school, at work, in the shops, and in the bars and restaurants. After all, their argument went, everything is spacious in California; without proximity feelings will dissipate. Even Vin Scully, who grew up in New York as a Giants fan, who worked for the Dodgers in the 1950s calling games at Ebbets Field, and who witnessed firsthand the tensions between the two New York clubs and their fan base, embraced these assumptions when he came west with the Dodgers in 1958.

> In NY fans rubbed against each other in daily life, literally, and they might be Yankee fans, Giant fans or Dodger fans. They would work together, eat together, play together and there would be partisan feelings and there would be arguments. There was day-to-day friction.[5]

Quickly, though, he admitted underestimating the adversarial feeling between the two West Coast cities. He recognized that the tensions between the two California cities were real, and while they might ebb and flow, they were always bubbling close to the surface.[6]

California had its own sense of proximity despite the 375 miles between the two cities, and the rivalry between the ball clubs was set to take root in spite of the geographical separation. Before the Giants and Dodgers moved west, the regional rivalry flourished on many levels of athletic competition and throughout the year: college athletics (UCLA and USC vs. Cal and Stanford); professional football (Rams vs. 49ers); and even the old Pacific Coast League (Angels and Stars vs. Oaks and Seals).[7] There was also a commercial rivalry of old money in San Francisco banking pitted against the new wealth of Los Angeles oil and entertainment business, each of which defined a cultural split. Once the Giants and Dodgers arrived, their historical rivalry was seamlessly subsumed into an existing dichotomy reflecting north-south intra-state competitiveness.

Settling into their new California cities, veteran players on both ball clubs were cognizant of the uniqueness of this rivalry. Dodgers players like Duke Snider, Jim Gilliam, Gil Hodges, and Carl Furillo all played in Brooklyn and knew firsthand the animosity between the Giants and the Dodgers. Likewise, Giants players like Willie Mays, Johnny Antonelli, and Whitey Lockman played in New York and knew the history of the rivalry. Others learned it as it was developing its own West Coast character. Ron Fairly, a Dodgers player throughout the 1960s, speaks of a Dodgers culture that valued wins over the Giants as especially meaningful.[8] Tommy Lasorda, longtime manager of the Los Angeles Dodgers, instilled a hatred for the men in orange and black and had great success against them. Whenever the Dodgers would play at Candlestick, Lasorda would provoke Giants fans by slowly striding from the visitors' clubhouse to the dugout, blowing kisses to those in the stands who would lustily jeer him.[9] Giants fans had their own response, a chant that would become an established feature of all Dodgers games: "LA Sucks!" One righteous fan appeared at a Giants home game with a scripted banner on which was written "Even God Knows LA Sucks."[10]

Felipe Alou remarked that games against the Dodgers felt different than the others, more contested and with more at stake than just wins and losses.[11] Willie Mays learned the bitter side of the rivalry from his manager in New York, Leo Durocher, who was one of the great agitators in the feuding between the clubs. But Mays was a quick study; and while he had many friends on the Dodgers teams, first in New York with Jackie Robinson and Roy Campanella and then in Los Angeles, especially with Jim Gilliam and John Roseboro, he never spoke to anyone in a Dodgers uniform once the game was underway.[12] The competitive intensity was also helped in those early years on the West Coast by the great baseball played by both clubs, who fought each other down to the wire for the pennant in 1959, 1962, 1965, and 1966.

The rivalry took its ugliest and most brutal turn in the late summer of 1965 with the infamous confrontation between Dodgers catcher John Roseboro and Giants pitcher Juan Marichal during which Marichal clubbed Roseboro with a bat. Its ferocity exceeds even the bitter hatred of the late 1940s and early 1950s in New York between the ball clubs, and the animosity between the Giants' Durocher and the Dodgers' Robinson and Furillo that was fueled by cat-calling, bean balls, and fistfights.[13] Much of the commentary on this extraordinary Marichal and Roseburo moment—the game was played at Candlestick Park, on August 22 before a sellout crowd of over forty-two thousand—suggests that the violence between the players combusted not spontaneously but rather from a slow burn in the steadily increasing heat of events that summer, both on and off the field. Mays's biographers, Charles Einstein and James S. Hirsch, stress the competitive stakes of the torrid pennant race between the two teams—Los Angeles was in first place, one and a half games ahead of San Francisco—and the significance of the four-game series between the clubs in late August that put the players on edge.[14] Other writers widened their focus, suggesting that certain players felt the tensions of the outside world, especially the social and civil unrest in Watts, a neighborhood in Los Angeles where in early August rioting caused six days of violence and civil disorder resulting in a number of deaths, injuries, and property damage.[15] Some Dodgers, including John Roseboro, lived near the troubled area, causing them to be touchy and nervous.[16] Lew Freedman, coauthor of Marichal's autobiography, explains that political turmoil that year in the Dominican Republic was troubling Latino players on the Giants' club, especially Marichal, whose family had connections with the government.[17]

The incident is part of baseball lore, first and foremost in its notoriety, described by one writer as "the worst act of player-on-player violence in major league history."[18] But it also manifests the competitive enmity between these two clubs and the intense emotions it conjures, both in the immediate aftermath of the moment, when Willie Mays as peacemaker cradled a bleeding Roseboro and led him to safety inside the Dodgers' dugout, and the more distant one, in the unlikely friendship between the principal combatants. In his last year as an active player Marichal signed with the Dodgers, much to the chagrin and even disbelief of many Dodgers fans.[19] Roseboro was on record in his support of the signing and hoped Marichal would succeed.[20] Marichal's decision to play for the Dodgers was motivated at least in part to bring closure to a painful incident in an otherwise brilliant career, although it did not sit well with diehard Giants fans. Marichal, who must have known his playing days were over, lasted only two weeks in Dodger blue, retiring on April 17, 1975. A few years later, in

1983, on hearing that he was voted into baseball's Hall of Fame, one of the first persons he called was John Roseboro.[21]

Both Willie Mays and Vin Scully agree on one thing: that the rivalry, while extant in the early days of the two teams' moves west, was energized and invigorated in the 1962 pennant race and play-off.[22] Baseball fans with a sense of history were treated that year to an uncanny repetition of the game's most famous playoff. Just as in 1951, the Giants caught the Dodgers in the last week of the '62 season and forced a three-game playoff. The series followed the '51 script with the Giants taking the first game in a rout, the Dodgers winning game two, setting up a winner-take-all third game. Played on October 3, eleven years to the day of the third and deciding game in 1951, the Dodgers took a lead into the ninth inning, as they had in 1951, only to give it up in another come-from-behind Giants win. There was no dramatic "shot heard round the world" Bobby Thomson home run this time. Three of the four runs the Giants would score in the ninth came not with a bang but a whimper: a sacrifice fly, a bases-loaded walk, and an error.

There was also a memorable difference in a key moment in the Giants' ninth. The only one in a Giants uniform to have played in both playoff games, Willie Mays, was no longer the nervous rookie in 1951 waiting in the on-deck circle should Thomson falter.[23] Now an established superstar, he eagerly came to bat with the bases loaded and one out and lined a screamer up the middle that tore the glove off of pitcher Ed Roebuck's hand as he attempted to field it, the only base hit of the inning to score a run. The Giants then managed the three other runs to take the game and the pennant, 6–4. Differences aside, for both Giants and Dodgers fans on either coast, the game struck an extraordinary chord: history repeats itself!

San Francisco's improbable win set off an incredible series of celebrations, first on the field at Chavez Ravine while the Dodgers watched in both agony and amazement and then back in the Bay Area, as thousands took to downtown streets and another twenty-five thousand stormed the airport, spilling out on the runway to welcome the victors home, causing the team plane to be diverted to an adjacent runway and airport traffic to be snarled for hours. The city quite simply went mad in its joy, confirming its attachments to this team. With streets jammed there were few cabs, and some players had to hitch-hike home from the airport.[24] The *Chronicle* acknowledged the home team's triumph by printing in bold headlines the definitive communal phrase "WE WIN."[25]

Another echo of the '51 season came in the Giants' World Series loss to the same team, the Yankees, although this time the travel between ballparks would be transcontinental rather than across the Harlem River. As it was for the 1951 Giants fans, the 1962 loss for San Franciscans, while deeply disappointing, felt strangely anticlimactic, coming on the heels of the intense playoff with the Dodgers, with one small difference. Unlike the '51 Series, the 1962 Series was close, going seven games and ending in dramatic fashion, a 1–0 game with the home team threatening in the bottom of the ninth. Bay Area fans felt enough excitement to help swallow the bitter pill of loss. They were hooked on their Giants, and with superstars like Mays, McCovey, Cepeda, and Marichal they knew great days were ahead.

The 1962 World Series would turn out to be the pinnacle of Stoneham's time in San Francisco. For the next seven years, his Giants would win more games than any National League team but would never capture another pennant and make it back to the World Series. They would finish in second place five seasons in a row, 1965–1969, four of them under manager Herman Franks, who replaced Alvin Dark in 1965.[26] Stoneham fired Dark after a disheartening finish to the 1964 season when the Giants finished fourth with a 90-72 record but only three games behind the pennant-winning St. Louis Cardinals, who totaled 93-69. Dark had a great run as San Francisco's manager, going 366-277 in four years and winning the '62 pennant; he also had impeccable Giants bona fides, as a player for Durocher during the New York years on the 1951 pennant-winner and the 1954 world championship. But his leadership faltered in late summer of 1964, and the Giants, lacking focus, stumbled down the stretch of a torrid pennant race. Stoneham felt that Dark had lost more than the pennant, however; he had lost control of the clubhouse as well. His inability to connect with minority players, especially Latinos, finally broke the morale of the likes of Orlando Cepeda, Juan Marichal, and the Alou brothers, Felipe, Matty, and Jesus.[27]

In naming Herman Franks as his manager, Stoneham followed tradition and demonstrated, again, his loyalty to the Giants family. Franks learned his management style from Leo Durocher, with whom he had a long association, first playing under him at Brooklyn (122 of Franks's 188 games as a big league player were with Durocher's Dodgers in 1941–42) and then as one of Durocher's coaches with the Giants starting in 1949. A former catcher whose Major League career consisted mostly of back-up roles and pinch-hitting, he was tough, played hard, and was always ready. He took to Durocher quickly, as Durocher did to him. His loyalty to his skipper was apparent in his involvement with Durocher's controversial sign-stealing at the Polo Grounds during the 1951 pennant race.[28] Franks had been in the Giants organization off and on from 1949, serving as a coach in San Francisco under Bill Rigney (1958) and then under Dark (1964).

As a manager, Franks could not have been more opposite from Dark. He smoked, chewed tobacco, cussed, and was willing to drink now and then with Stoneham, something that Dark, an abstinent Southern Baptist, would never do. He was stocky, had a more relaxed casual appearance, and wore loose clothes, nothing like the elegant and modish Dark. His personality was brusque and he did not tolerate what he regarded as foolish questions from the press. The sportswriters took notice. As one put it, "Herman Franks is not the most unpleasant man I have ever met. But he is close."[29]

Franks's tenure as manager must be termed a great success, despite the lack of a World Series appearance. He was less intense personally than his predecessor, and he delegated authority to his coaching staff and senior players. To restore camaraderie in the clubhouse after Dark's departure, he invited a select group of those he regarded as team leaders to go boar hunting at the Buckhorn sulfur springs in Arizona before his first spring training as manager.[30] He made great headway with Mays, who had stopped speaking to Dark in the last two months of the '64 season.[31] Mays responded to Franks's more relaxed managerial style by having one of his most productive years, hitting .317 with 52 home runs and 112 RBIs, gaining his second Most Valuable Player award. The team responded as well. They were neck and neck with the Dodgers throughout September, sometimes first, sometimes second, and lost out on the next-to-last day of the 1965 season, despite a 95-67 record.

Franks's first season as Giants skipper would be memorable for more than the torrid pennant race with the archrival Dodgers. Early in the season he would find himself embroiled in an international incident more suited to the diplomatic corps than to running a baseball team. In 1964, Stoneham and the Giants signed Masanori Murakami, a promising young pitcher from Japan, developed him in their Minor League system, and promoted him to the big leagues in September. With Murakami's debut on September 1, 1964, against the Mets in New York, the Giants became the first team in Major League history to play a Japanese national.[32] His performance in the month of September impressed the Giants so much that Chub Feeney, Stoneham's nephew and the club vice president who handled players' contracts, signed Murakami to a 1965 contract. Both Murakami and the Giants were looking forward to a future together.

During the off-season, pressures from home, both from his Japanese team, the Nankai Hawks, and from his family, weighed heavily on the young Murakami. Japanese Baseball officials wanted Murakami to return to the Hawks and through the Japanese commissioner, Yushi Uchimura, wrote to Feeney, Stoneham, and Ford Frick, the commissioner of Major League Baseball, insisting that Murakami was only on temporary loan to the Giants as a result of an informal arrangement between Stoneham and the Hawks and should play the 1965 season in Japan. The wrangling among the Giants, the Hawks, Frick, and Uchimura continued well into the spring before a compromise was reached: Murakami would return to the Giants for the 1965 season, after which the young man could decide for himself where he would play in 1966. In his response, Frick was clear to the Japanese that if Murakami decided to play in Japan in 1966, he would not be free to return to the Major Leagues with any club other than the Giants.[33]

While the sparring and negotiating took place on the administrative levels between Feeney, the Giants, and Frick on the one side and the Japanese officials on the other, Herman Franks, who had a ball club to run, made his opinions known quietly, out of the spotlight, to Stoneham. His message was simple: the Giants desperately needed help in relief pitching and Murakami could contribute. As the Giants were slow to get out of the gate—7-9 in the month of April—Franks, not a patient man, made his concerns known. After months of inactive talk and posturing by Major League Baseball and Japanese Baseball, Stoneham and Feeney, after urging from Franks, found a way to agree to certain Japanese conditions. They in turn convinced Frick, and Murakami was back in a Giants uniform. He was instrumental in the team's success that season, appearing in forty-five games, with a 4-1 record, 8 saves, and 85 strikeouts in 74⅓ innings pitched.[34]

In Franks's four years as their skipper, the Giants had the best winning record of any National League club but could not quite grasp the pennant, finishing second each season.[35] For many managers, this run might be looked on as positive, even successful; Franks, however, considered his record unsatisfactory. Despite his more relaxed approach, he was intensely competitive and disappointed at his club's perennial second-place finish. He left the Giants for personal reasons at the end of the 1968 season to concentrate on his business ventures but also out of some frustration of being "always a bridesmaid, never a bride." On the other hand, perhaps Franks was prescient, sensing a change coming for the Giants and not necessarily a good one. If he did think that way, hindsight suggests that he got it right. Forces were at work, within and without the organization, that in a few short years would bring about the unimaginable: the Giants no longer a competitive team and without a Stoneham as owner.

SIX

A Perfect Storm

The year 1968 marked the beginning of the end for Horace Stoneham in San Francisco. After a decade of great winning baseball and robust attendance, the Giants' fortunes were about to undergo a sea change. Ominous circumstances were converging, any one of which, taken on its own, might have been manageable; together they were overwhelming, especially for an old-fashioned owner like Stoneham, whose business proclivities and personal bearing were not best matched with crises. Pressure that began with one event in the winter of 1967 would continue to build with others over the next few years and lead to Stoneham's undoing, forcing an unthinkable decision: to sever a lifelong connection with his beloved baseball club.

The most significant of these events, one that would have disastrous results for Stoneham's Giants, came in the guise of baseball's progress: the relocation of the Kansas City Athletics to Oakland for the 1968 season.[1] For the two previous years maverick Athletics owner Charles O. Finley had been itching to get out of the Midwest, where he had had mediocre attendance and a terrible television contract.[2] He coveted Northern California and the Bay Area as a prime location after watching the Giants' success there. The American League felt the same way, having been caught off guard by the National League's appropriation of the California market in 1958 when the Giants and the Dodgers moved west. The junior circuit moved into Southern California in 1961 with the expansion franchise the Los Angeles Angels and saw Northern California as a good location for another team. The league had West Coast expansion in mind. Finley was granted permission to move to Oakland at the American League owners' fall meeting on October 18, 1967, when they also authorized expansion to Seattle and Kansas City no later than 1971. The latter approval by the owners was in part to mollify angry Kansas City folks who might be harboring litigation plans in response to Finley's exodus.[3] The A's arrived in California with great fanfare in the winter of 1967 when Finley greeted a welcoming group of four hundred reporters and dignitaries at the airport, promising a long and successful stay in the Bay Area. Oakland, whose residents have always felt overshadowed by neighboring San Francisco, celebrated its new membership among the ranks of big league cities with speeches and proclamations from local and state officials.[4]

Sportswriters in San Francisco appeared impervious to any downside for their home team in Finley's move and, adopting a "the more, the merrier" attitude, extended a warm welcome to the A's.[5] Not so Horace Stoneham, who felt immediately threatened. His remarks stood in sharp contrast to those of everyone who was excited about a new baseball team in the Bay Area and would prove remarkably prescient for decades to come. "Certainly the move will hurt us. It is simply a question of how much and if both of us can survive. I don't think the area at the present time will take care of us both as much as they (the Athletics) think it will."[6] Taking a more politic and diplomatic stand, Chub Feeney, Giants vice president and Stoneham's nephew, said he welcomed the A's' move and hoped it would work out for everyone, including the Giants.[7] Like many in the city, Feeney thought it was too early to pass judgment.

It didn't take long for the Giants to feel the pinch of the A's' presence across the bay. In 1968, the A's' first year in Oakland, the Giants drew 837,220, down over 405,000 from the previous year. This pattern would persist over the next seven years, Stoneham's remaining time with the club. Only once after the A's moved to Oakland—in the playoff year 1971, when the Giants won the National League West title—would Stoneham's team draw over 1 million fans to Candlestick. In 1974, attendance fell to an abysmal 519,987, almost the lowest

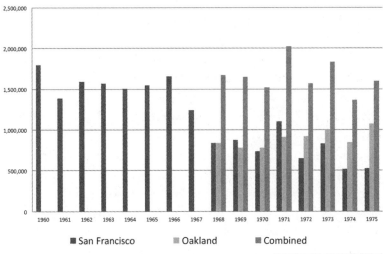

Graph 1. Bay Area Baseball Attendance, 1960–1975

Source: Thorn et al., *Total Baseball*, 6th ed.

yearly attendance ever for a Stoneham-owned Giants team in either San Francisco or New York; only twice before—in 1932 and in the war year 1943, both at the Polo Grounds—did the Giants draw fewer home fans.[8] Faced with this new reality, Stoneham was uncharacteristically blunt in his response: "Finley, the A's and the whole American League are partners in villainy."[9] Sharing the Bay Area market with another Major League ball club was proving disastrous to the Giants' ability to maintain financial health.

In stating his reasons for moving to the Bay Area, Charles O. Finley sounded much the same as Stoneham in 1957, when he announced he was leaving New York. "The population growth is the fastest of any major league city in either league, and enthusiasm for sports in the Bay Area is overwhelming," Finley told reporters upon making his bid to the American League owners. He also was happy with the ballpark arrangements, playing in a soon-to-be refurbished coliseum that was home to the National Football League Raiders, and with a television deal that exceeded anything he had in Kansas City. Like Stoneham, he claimed to be losing money where he was, and the prospects of coming west would be good for the bottom line. Plus he cited Northern California as one of the great regions of the country for climate, culture, natural beauty, and the economy.[10]

Reasons for moving a baseball team aside, it would be difficult to imagine a baseball owner more unlike Horace Stoneham in temperament, personality, behavior, and attitude toward the game than Charles O. Finley. Where Stoneham was retiring and shy, Finley was outspoken and extroverted. Stoneham relied on the advice of three or four inner-circle associates and delegated authority in almost all aspects of running his organization; Finley tightly controlled all activity in his front office and even micromanaged his team's play, occasionally ordering his managers to bench a player, change a batting order, or sit a pitcher.[11] Stoneham's relationship with other owners was cordial and convivial; his National League peers found him generous, affable, and good company. Finley's reputation among fellow owners was poor; he was regarded as petulant, boorish, and single-minded, especially with regard to ideas on how to improve the business of baseball. Finley was keen on promotions, stunts, giveaways, and entertainment exhibitions. He made much of his team mascot, a mule named Charlie O, often parading him around the park before games. One year he promoted "Hot Pants Night" for ladies. Those who wore short shorts were admitted free to the game; those who paraded around the bases in their shorts got two free passes for a future game. He advocated zany uniforms with white shoes and bright green laces and argued for colored baseballs for night games. He was a firm believer in the designated-hitter rule and pushed his fellow American League owners, without success, for a designated pinch runner to be used with free substitution.[12] With all of these schemes, he stood in sharp contrast to Stoneham, an old-school baseball purist and idealist who found continual promotions appalling and vulgar. Stoneham insisted that the game was a thing unto itself: baseball is the greatest game, played by the best who could play it, and in no need of gimmickry to attract the fans. Aside from the occasional cap-day or bat-day, and the annual season-end fan appreciation day, Stoneham disdained Finley's practices.[13]

For all the promotions and publicity stunts that Finley employed, attendance at A's home games remained among the lowest in the American League during Finley's tenure as owner. The A's' meager gate is even more surprising in the light of the great baseball played in Oakland during the early 1970s when the A's won three consecutive world championships, from 1972 through 1974, and won the American League West title in 1975. For many of Finley's years in Oakland, he drew about the same as the struggling Giants, giving some credence to those, like Stoneham and baseball commissioner Bowie Kuhn, who believed that the Bay Area could support only one Major League team.[14] From 1968 to 1975, both teams' combined attendance totaled more or less what the Giants drew prior to the A's' arrival in Oakland.

The dramatic shift in the Giants' fortunes came about primarily because of American League expansion, cutting the Bay Area fan base in half. The A's siphoned off Giants home attendance chiefly by their proximity, but also in their play: they were gelling as a ball club with a collection of great young players at the same time as the Giants were heading in the opposite direction. The A's' three straight championship seasons in the early 1970s certainly provided a sharp contrast to the poor finishes by the Giants in the same years.[15] There were some games at Candlestick Park in the dreadful years of 1974 and 1975 when attendance did not reach one thousand, prompting *Chronicle* columnist Herb Caen to write, "The Giants' annual 'Fan Appreciation Day' is coming up soon and I can't wait to see what Horace Stoneham gives him."[16] But dire as the A's' presence proved, it was not the only thing that hurt Stoneham and threatened the financial health of his National Exhibition Company.[17] Other problems were surfacing from within the Giants' organization that would add to the club's growing troubles and instability.

During his first ten years in San Francisco, Stoneham relied on a small cadre of associates who provided conversation, friendship, company, and advice on matters concerning the planning and running of the ball club. Stoneham had the final word but he listened carefully to the views of those in his inner circle: Herman Franks, coach and manager; Eddie Brannick, club secretary for over fifty years; Garry Schumacher, public relations director since 1946; and Charles "Chub" Feeney, Stoneham's nephew who became club vice president after finishing law school in 1948. These four men had long histories with the Giants; they had been with the club in New York and had come west with Stoneham in the big move in 1958. Starting in late fall of 1968, over a period of a little more than three years, all four of them would leave the Giants, greatly weakening the stability and the culture of the organization and, more importantly, isolating Stoneham precisely at a time when he faced his greatest challenges in San Francisco.

Herman Franks was the first to go. After a long tenure with the Giants that began as a coach during Leo Durocher's years in New York and continued under Bill Rigney and Alvin Dark in San Francisco, Franks was hired by Stoneham to manage the ball club in the fall of 1964, replacing Alvin Dark. In late fall of 1968, after four consecutive second-place National League finishes, no doubt frustrated that he never won a pennant and a trip to the World Series, Franks left the Giants to concentrate on his real estate development business.[18] With Franks's departure Stoneham lost more than someone who managed the ball club at a high level; he also lost a longtime club employee and, most of all, a "pal," a word Stoneham used to denote someone with whom he could have a drink and a friendly conversation. Franks was happy to oblige Stoneham as a pal, and, over his four years as manager, he gave his boss frequent opportunity to do something he loved: discuss the game of baseball and the players, especially during those exciting seasons that led to so many close chances for a pennant.

Eddie Brannick and Garry Schumacher retired in 1972, within a few months of one another. At the age of seventy-eight, Brannick decided to call his life in baseball a finished career and move back to New York and the East Coast, where he felt more at home. He began his association with the Giants in 1906 when he was hired by John McGraw to work as a club house boy: he was thirteen years old. In 1911 he became traveling secretary, a position he kept until

1936 when young owner Horace Stoneham promoted him to general secretary of the club. He remained in that position for thirty-six years. A loyal denizen of Toots Shor's saloon and a great fan of Broadway, Brannick was a well-known character around the city. New York journalist Arthur Daley once wrote that Brannick knew politicians, actors, musicians, athletes, "anyone who was worth knowing."[19] So closely and thoroughly identified as an old New Yorker, he surprised many when he agreed to follow Stoneham west in 1958 and continue as club secretary in San Francisco. In the end, his connection to the Giants and his loyalty to Stoneham proved stronger than his attraction to New York. Nonetheless he brought a New York mode with him. When he arrived in San Francisco he was conspicuous in his speech and appearance—he dressed as if he stepped off the pages of a Damon Runyon story: a floppy panama hat, two-toned black and white shoes, high collars, and bright foulards.[20] As a longtime associate of Stoneham, Brannick provided his boss not only with a sense of history, the last link to the days of McGraw and Christy Mathewson, but also with a great sense of tradition and of loyalty to the organization, traits that Stoneham particularly admired.[21]

Schumacher came to the Giants in 1946 after a twenty-year career with the *Brooklyn Standard-Union* and the *New York Journal America* as a baseball beat writer who reported primarily on the Brooklyn Dodgers. He was hired as director of public relations for the Giants and served as Stoneham's New York contact with the sportswriters with whom he had familiarity and even some deep friendships. Stoneham often relied on Schumacher to release statements concerning club business and to take questions from the press.[22] He moved west with the club in 1958 and, like Brannick, was a colorful reminder of the Giants' New York past, cultivating a Brooklyn accent that seemed to grow heavier in San Francisco. A great raconteur and a regular in Stoneham's lunch groups, Schumacher was a master of the turn of phrase. He once credited Giants junk-ball pitcher Stu Miller with the development of the "Wells Fargo pitch," one that comes to the plate in stages.[23] In a famous debate at Reno's on Battery Street in downtown San Francisco, when, according to one account, Schumacher went toe to toe, or rather glass to glass, with barkeeper/owner Reno Barsochini over the game's best center fielder, Schumacher countered Barsochini's steady insistence on DiMaggio's supremacy with a case for Mays's greatness, each of his responses thickening his Brooklyn accent.[24] Schumacher announced his retirement a few months after Brannick did, sensing that after almost fifty years in baseball he wanted a less demanding schedule. He left the Giants officially on June 1, 1972. Unlike Brannick, Schumacher did not move back east after his retirement, feeling very much at home in the Bay Area.[25] Schumacher's affection for San Francisco—what he called "the glory city"—was so great that he asked four of his closest friends to scatter his ashes at sea just past the Golden Gate Bridge.[26]

The resignations of Franks, Brannick, and Schumacher unsettled Stoneham, as the loss of daily contact with colleagues and good friends was likely to do. Their leaving also meant a passing of Giants history, something that meant the world to Stoneham. But the departure of Chub Feeney proved to have far more significance for the Giants' owner, depriving him of his closest and most reliable confidant. In December 1969, Feeney was selected by the National League owners to succeed Warren Giles as president of the National League, effective January 1970. It was a career move for Feeney, a competent and well-respected baseball executive who narrowly missed becoming the commissioner of baseball the year before, when Major League owners fired William Eckert and then voted to choose his replacement.[27] For Stoneham, however, Feeney's advancement would have personal ramifications affecting the daily routine of the Giants' front office and the running of the ball club. In announcing the move, Stoneham tried to shine a positive light on what was a great personal loss.

> It was a difficult decision for Chub. It was tough for me to let him go. We will certainly miss him a great deal. But we need leadership in the National League and the owners felt that Chub was the right man for the job.[28]

Feeney was more than a club executive; he was family, Stoneham's sister's son, with a long connection to the National Exhibition Company.[29] While he was studying law at Fordham, he worked part-time with the Giants, helping with ballpark operations. Once he finished law school in 1948, he gave up any ideas about a legal career, knowing that his future lay with the Giants. He moved immediately into the front office and gradually familiarized himself with the business of baseball. Soon Feeney was handling player trades, assuming most of the ball club's public relations duties, meeting with officials and dignitaries and accompanying Uncle Horace to owners meetings. During the difficult and crucial years after the 1954 World Series when the Giants were weighing their options about location, Stoneham sought Feeney's advice on much of club planning, especially in the discussions with Minneapolis on a possible move there, and then in the negotiations with San Francisco. Once the club came west in 1958, Feeney managed all of the player contract negotiations, payroll issues, and trades. At ease with the public and the press in a way that his shy and private uncle was not, Feeney often functioned as the club's spokesperson, even hosting his own radio show, "Call Chub Feeney," broadcasted after Sunday home games, when he answered questions from fans.[30] He was the one person in the front office who could speak candidly to Stoneham and even disagree with him on a matter of club business. Feeney understood that his uncle had the final word as owner, but on matters of salary, personnel, and dealings with the City of San Francisco, he gave Stoneham his best and most informed advice, even if it occasionally offered a contrary view. Feeney's title was vice president, but, in truth, he functioned more like an advanced general manager. He was Stoneham's sounding board and lodestar. Feeney's departure deprived Stoneham of a crucial point of view that he had come to depend upon at precisely the time in his ownership when he faced his most difficult and trying circumstances.

Without the company of these trusted colleagues, Stoneham had to look to those less familiar with the Giants' culture, like Jerry Donovan, a former Seals executive who joined the club in 1958, and Chuck Rupert, a son-in-law, who began dealing with the club's financial matters in the mid-sixties. Although Donovan knew San Francisco as a baseball man and Rupert was a family member with a good business mind, Stoneham missed those with whom he had deep and long-standing relationships, especially Feeney. As a result, he felt individually more responsible for the fate of the organization than he had ever felt before, despite the presence of his newly created front office staff.[31] Amidst this isolation and as concerns mounted over attendance, club revenue, and expenses, Stoneham sensed yet another looming problem that would cause him further anxiety: his team was aging, especially his best players.

In 1971, Willie Mays turned forty. All those around him, including Stoneham, knew that Mays's best years were behind him. But he still was an icon, the most prominent player in the game, and the heart of the Giants' team. Stoneham had a fatherly affection for him and knew he would have to do something soon to fix Mays's future in the game. Now that Mays's playing career was winding down, Stoneham wanted him to retire as a Giant—the only organization he had known for his twenty-year Major League career—and move to a lifelong association with the club like other former stars, such as Bill Terry and Carl Hubbell, who transitioned into coaching, scouting, and front-office jobs after their playing days. Maybe with Mays there would be the possibility of a managerial position someday. Moreover, Stoneham's generosity and loyalty to his players was a matter of record. After Orlando Cepeda was dealt to the St. Louis Cardinals in 1966, Stoneham would call Cepeda at Christmas time, and when the Giants' boss traveled to Puerto Rico in the winter, he would take Cepeda and his mother out to dinner.[32] In the winter of 1968, Willie McCovey signed a two-year contract with the Giants taking him through the 1970 season, an unusual practice in an era when almost every player had a one-year contract. After his 1969 National League MVP year, McCovey received a call from Stoneham requesting a meeting. During their conversation Stoneham tore up the existing contract and issued a new one with a substantial raise, saying that he wanted to reward McCovey for his great '69 season.[33]

The Giants' finances, however, no longer resembled those of the profitable early years in San Francisco before the arrival of the A's.

Simply put, Stoneham was running out of money. Major League Baseball's days of television contracts, merchandising, and playoff revenue-sharing lay in the future; in the late 1960s and early 1970s, the gate was still the primary source of income for ball clubs, and since 1968 the Giants were drawing poorly. As he looked to a new decade of shrinking revenue, Stoneham had to cut his costs, which made stripping the team of big-name and high-salaried players a practical, however painful, necessity. Cepeda left in 1966 before the club's fiscal woes were apparent, easing payroll pressure. Cy Young–winner Mike McCormick was traded in 1970.[34] Gaylord Perry was dealt to Cleveland after the 1971 season (where he was a Cy Young Award–winner the next year), and shortstop Hal Lanier sold to the Yankees for cash.[35] All-Star catcher Dick Dietz was traded to the Dodgers in 1971.[36] McCovey was sent to San Diego in the fall of 1973 and Juan Marichal was sold to the Boston Red Sox that December. Dave Kingman, who arrived in September of 1971 to be a new Giants power hitter, was sold to the Mets after the 1974 season.[37]

Shedding the high-price players posed difficult decisions for Stoneham, but no one trade or player sale brought with it the agony Stoneham felt when he realized he would have to part with Willie Mays. The blunt reality came off the bottom line: the Giants could not afford to keep Mays, at least in the manner that Stoneham intended. Once the two-year salary for Mays was cobbled together—$165,000 for the 1972 and 1973 seasons—Stoneham knew he would have to find Willie a new home, a place where he would be happy, where he could be guaranteed this two-year salary obligation, and where his future would be secure. With the Giants revenue fading fast, Stoneham put all of his effort into getting Willie settled, and quickly.

During the spring of 1972, Stoneham entered into secret negotiations with Joan Whitney Payson, New York Mets club owner, and M. Donald Grant, the chairman of the board, to trade Mays to the Mets. The Mets were the only club Stoneham contacted because he felt that Willie should be back in New York where he began his great career, had many wonderful years, and was a legend in the city. A crucial part of the trade for Stoneham involved assurances from Payson and Grant that Willie would be given some kind of extended contract with the ball club once his playing days were over. As befitting a sentimental and old-fashioned owner, Stoneham felt the need for secrecy in the event that the deal with the Mets might fall through and Willie's pride would be hurt, the result of feeling discarded by a cash-poor owner.[38] The attempts at secrecy failed, however, and newspapers on both coasts caught wind of the story. A surprised and angry Mays learned third-hand about the trade when the Giants were visiting Montreal, wondering why the organization for whom he played his entire career would not inform him about such a possibility and involve him in the talks. Briefly, he thought about retiring from the game.[39]

On May 11, 1972, the finalized negotiations became official news. Mays was traded to the Mets for a Minor League pitcher named Charlie Williams; there was also mention of an additional unspecified amount of cash from the Mets, rumored to be between fifty thousand and two hundred thousand dollars.[40] In a gesture that conveyed the highest form of respect, Stoneham brought Mays in on the final hours of deliberation with Payson and Grant and then ushered him to the press conference at the Mayfair House announcing the trade.[41] In his remarks the Giants owner tried to put on a brave face but could hardly hide his disappointment. "I never thought I would trade Willie, but with two teams in the Bay Area, our financial situation is such that we cannot afford to keep Willie and his big salary as well as the Mets can."[42] Grant followed by saying that the Mets planned to keep Mays around for a long time, securing his future in baseball. The player himself spoke briefly, that he was happy to be back in New York and looking forward to playing for the Mets, and that he was grateful to the Giants and to Stoneham for all they had given him.[43]

The press conference ended and with it one of the most fabled chapters in Giants history was over. In a bizarre twist, Mays's start in a Mets uniform would be against his former team, who traveled to New York after their series with Montreal; Mays homered to break a 4–4 tie and the Mets won 5–4. During the Mets series in New York, an emotional Stoneham asked to see Mays after one of the games. The two of them stayed up most of the night in the owner's hotel suite, Stoneham drinking and talking regretfully about the trade and Mays listening. Looking back on that night more than forty years later, Mays reflected on Stoneham's genuine concern "for my welfare, not only my salary but that I would be taken care of in the future. I realized how much he cared for me and how hard the trade was for him to make."[44]

The press's reaction to Mays's return to New York reflected the changing tides of two cities' connections to their baseball teams. In New York, Mays was treated as an Odyssean hero, home at last after years of wandering exile. "WILLIE COMES HOME" read one East Coast headline of the Alabama-born ballplayer's trade to the Mets.[45] Some of the welcome was for the player himself, his prominence and his reputation as the greatest player of his generation. Nor did his age bother some writers. Dick Young of the *New York Daily News* wrote that even a forty-year-old Mays was better than most players in the game.[46] Others saw in Mays's return a chance to rewind the clock and bask in nostalgia. *New York Times* columnist Red Smith reminded his readers of a young Willie Mays roaming the outfield at the Polo Grounds, in the golden age of New York center fielders, Mays, Mantle, DiMaggio, and Snider.[47] In another *Times* column entitled "Moments to Remember," Arthur Daley interpreted Mays's return as cathartic, healing the old painful memories of the Giants leaving New York after the 1957 season, taking with them the young superstar Mays who dazzled Polo Ground fans with his amazing exploits. Daley reverently recited the famous New York moments in Mays's career, including the "impossible" throw to nail the Dodgers' Billy Cox at home during the 1951 pennant race and the astounding catch of Vic Wertz's fly ball in the 1954 World Series.[48]

On the other coast, the reporting of the Mays trade also revealed an emotional edge, but unlike New York's in every aspect. The tone was negative, and pointedly critical toward the Giants and Stoneham. For Bucky Walters of the *Examiner* it was too little, too late. With a rebuke for Stoneham and the front office, Walters complained that instead of a no-name rookie pitcher named Charlie Williams "it would have been possible for the Giants to have gotten several established players for Mays a couple of years back when his market value was still high."[49] Other San Francisco journalists were less concerned about losing Mays and more about the sagging state of affairs with the Giants. Most took note of Mays's reduced productivity and looked upon his departure as another symptom of a ball club in decline. A few hundred miles south of San Francisco, Jim Murray of the *Los Angeles Times* used the Mays trade to fling a few barbs north. Decrying Stoneham for selling one of baseball's gods for "30 pieces of silver," Murray shifted his target to the city he loved to hate.

> San Francisco has an abhorrence of strangers and Willie was a 14-year stranger—in San Francisco but not OF it—and the townspeople kept looking at each other with a "Who invited him?" look. San Francisco frowns on enthusiasm, anyway, preferring a bored acceptance. It is not a town, it's a cocktail party. Willie must have felt like a guy who showed up wearing brown shoes with his tux.[50]

Murray's snide allusion to Stoneham's betrayal of Mays for a handful of cash set off others in the press, who castigated the Giants' owner for his plantation boss's attitude toward players, especially great ones like Mays. Initially, an emotional Stoneham didn't respond to the criticism, preferring instead a difficult and what must have been an especially painful silence. Years later, however, he corrected the record in an interview with Mays's biographer Charles Einstein. When Einstein asked Stoneham how much money he actually got in the Mays trade, the answer was surprising.

> He [Stoneham] said, "There was no money."
> "None?"
> "None. Do you think I was going to give him up for money?"
> The only element involving money, he said, was what the Mets could pay Mays over the next ten years that Stoneham couldn't.[51]

After the Mays trade things hardly improved for Stoneham. In 1973 he parted with the last of his superstars—McCovey and Marichal—and spent most of his time denying rumors that the team was for sale.[52] He was losing the public relations battle with the A's, who were enjoying unparalleled success—three straight World Series championships—

while the Giants finished well off the pace in the National League West during the same years. He lost at the gate as well; in 1974 and 1975 the Giants' home attendance was the lowest of any season since the team moved west, barely clearing the five hundred thousand mark each year.[53] To add to all of the other distractions, his real estate venture in Casa Grande, Arizona—a project he hoped to turn from a spring training site into a golf resort with adjacent homes—was stalled, diverting precious capital from the running of the ball club, "soaking up money as the quickly as the desert soaks up the rain," as one Giants front office employee put it.[54] After the 1974 season, Stoneham announced a $1.7 million loss to the stockholders of the National Exhibition Company.[55]

There was no longer any way to gloss over the obvious: the Giants were in trouble and Stoneham simply did not have the resources nor perhaps the resolve to solve the club's problems. In the spring of 1975, he approached the other owners in the National League with grim news. He had enough money to meet only two months of payroll and needed a loan from the league to finish the season. At the same time, he announced his intentions to sell the team, hoping to find a local buyer to keep the Giants in San Francisco.[56] With this announcement, Stoneham gave notice that a fifty-seven-year family connection to Giants baseball had ended. A new era was about to begin, but the future looked anything but secure for the San Francisco Giants.

In the end, it may have been that the game Horace Charles Stoneham was overseeing as the Giants' owner had passed him by. As he wrestled with the ball club's calamitous predicament during the early 1970s, he appeared out of touch with the new realities of the business side of baseball. He admitted as much in a 1973 spring training interview.

> Years ago when the owners held meetings most of the talk was baseball. Now you run into corporations that control stock. There are accountants and lawyers and corporation officials and so much of the talk is legal. Now it's how and why before you can get to the players on the field.[57]

For an owner who cared first and foremost about his players, and who was loyal to them almost to a fault, this commercial and legal emphasis was a trying adjustment.[58] Once he made his decision to sell, he seemed relieved of the pressure and in some ways began to enjoy the game again, savoring his last days with the Giants. This deep-rooted affection for the game was something that Roger Angell recognized when he sat with the Giants' boss for a game at Candlestick Park in the summer of 1975. Aware that Stoneham was selling the team after such a long association (the chief reason for the writer's visit), Angell viewed the Giants' owner rather nostalgically, as if granted a fleeting glimpse of a vanishing species, "the last of the pure baseball men, the owners who owned nothing but their team and cared for nothing but the game."[59] Angell read Stoneham as a baseball traditionalist with a historical bent, a man who cast his mind on other days, more comfortable recalling the exploits of McGraw, Mathewson, Terry, Ott, Hubbell, and, yes, Mays, than discussing the storm of problems that passed through his organization over those past few years and put him in his current predicament. Stoneham's one remaining task as owner would be to find a suitable buyer for his ball club.

BOB

Now that the Giants had been part of San Francisco life for almost twenty years, Horace Stoneham assumed that he would have a few offers from locals who would want to keep the team where it is. While he would have to sell the team, he had not given up on the connection between the city and baseball, despite the latest attendance dips—the 1974 and 1975 attendance numbers at Giants home games were the lowest in the league. These seasons could be temporary, he reasoned, and a new owner might reverse all of that by bringing new energy to the ball club.

Stoneham was only half right. The city still had a connection to the ball club, but there was no rush of local offers to buy the team. Recent events and certain conditions had dimmed the attraction of owning the Giants. Sportswriters argued that the conditions at Candlestick, coupled with the team's mediocre play in the early 1970s, might be discouraging fans from coming to the ballpark. Another view suggested that the unusual confluence of social and political unrest in the city beginning in the late 1960s was threatening the fans' attraction to baseball. The turmoil growing out of the free-love drug culture of 1967–68 Haight-Ashbury, and the subsequent disturbances, sometimes violent, in the racial and gay activism of the 1970s, unhinged the city and unsettled ordinary citizens.

New leadership was about to challenge those assumptions, but it would come from city hall rather than from a prospective big league owner. When George Moscone took office as San Francisco's mayor in January 1976, he was determined to restore a sense of calm and normalcy to the city. Nor did he think that baseball was irrelevant in any restoration plan; rather, he saw it as an important part of the city's cultural identity. When he learned that Stoneham's decision to sell the team might result in San Francisco losing its baseball team, the mayor acted quickly by moving to find a local owner to prevent the team from leaving town.

SEVEN

"Bobby Thomson Lives!"

It would be difficult to imagine a more troublesome time for a base-ball franchise than that of the San Francisco Giants in their dog days of summer 1975. As *San Francisco Examiner* columnist Art Spander put it, the team was caught in a vicious circle. Unable to pay their annual rent to the city for the use of Candlestick Park, in debt to the National League for funds to meet regular payroll, and incapable of going after quality players, the Giants were trapped. Spander observed, "The vicious circle continues. Without money, the Giants can't get the players they need. Without the players, they can't build a team to draw spectators. Without spectators, they can't get the money they need."[1] Owner Horace Stoneham also felt trapped personally when he announced in late spring that the club was up for sale, putting an end to all of the speculation in the press about his future with the team.[2] It was a painful move for Stoneham, but on the advice of his chief legal counsel, James Hunt, he accepted the inevitable: the National Exhibition Company, whose books Hunt had been poring over for almost a year, was insolvent.[3] The Giants had lost three million dollars over the past two years and owed the National League four hundred thousand dollars.[4] Stoneham stated publicly that he preferred a buyer who would keep the team in San Francisco, but he also indicated in other remarks that, given the Giants' urgent financial bind, he would meet with anyone, from anywhere, who was interested in owning the ball club.[5]

Stoneham's remarks shifted newspaper coverage of Giants base-ball from the sport pages to the financial section. The real drama in the Giants' 1975 season was played out in the team's front office with club officials, local attorneys, accountants, and prospective bidders looking to acquire a Major League franchise; the action on the baseball diamond appeared to many as secondary. The sportswriters were particularly perplexed. Various newspaper accounts highlighted the Giants' precarious financial situation and speculated on a change of ownership but also on the possibility that a sale of the ball club might mean that the team would move.[6] Fans reacted to the speculation by forming "Save Our Giants" clubs, organizing attendance drives, and even entertaining plans for a publicly held company that might buy the team.[7]

Even the players were looking over their shoulders. Baseball is a notoriously demanding game to play, made even more so when the team one plays for is in disarray. No doubt it was difficult that summer for the Giants' players to concentrate on hitting, signs, base-stealing, or which base to throw to when stories circulated about the team being unable to make payroll and with no fixed idea about its location for the following season. The Giants finished the season just under .500 at 80-81, but they were never in the division chase, closing out the year a whopping twenty-seven and a half games out of first place. Once the season ended, players faced a winter of uncertainty about both the team's situation and their own. Heralded young pitcher John Montefusco, who loved the Bay Area, was unsure about buying a house, not knowing where he might end up next year. Outfielder Bobby Murcer could not tell his agent whom to contact about his upcoming contract.[8] Dave Rader, who had a contract but wanted it restructured, had no idea whom to call about a discussion.[9]

The quandary over the Giants' future surfaced publicly after a private gesture of friendship and respect. After a National Exhibition Company board meeting in early May 1975, Horace Stoneham pulled aside board member and local real estate magnate Bob Lurie, telling him sotto voce that the team would soon be officially for sale.[10] A year before when there were rumors of an impending Giants sale, Lurie had mentioned to Stoneham in a private conversation that if the Giants were ever up for sale, he might be an interested buyer.[11] Loyal even when facing financial duress, Stoneham wanted to honor that conversation and his relationship with Lurie by offering him the inside track.[12] True to his word, Lurie began exploring possibilities of ownership immediately. He made it clear to Stoneham, however, that while interested, he would need time for detailed consideration and a chance to firm up a partnership; ever the prudent businessman, he had no plans to make an immediate offer to buy the ball club.[13]

One person whom Lurie approached concerning ownership was Chub Feeney, whom he had befriended while serving on the Giants' board of directors. Their conversations were informal and private, focusing mainly on ideas about the logistics of buying a Major League franchise.[14] Local newspapers got wind of Lurie's connection with Feeney and projected a quick solution to the Giants' current dire straits, based upon a perfect partnership: Lurie would establish local ownership with the necessary capital, and Feeney would provide a historical connection to the ball club and significant experience in the business of baseball.[15] What sounded too good to be true, however, proved exactly that: the partnership never materialized. Lurie admitted to having preliminary discussions with Feeney about the Giants franchise but insisted that there was no formal agreement between them, and certainly no official joint offer made to Stoneham.[16] In mid-May, less than two weeks after the rumor of a Lurie-Feeney partnership broke, with pressure coming from National League owners anxious about the future leadership of the league, Feeney felt the necessity to issue a formal statement about his intentions.[17]

> It is common knowledge that I am a friend of Bob Lurie, a member of the Giants' board of directors, who reportedly may make an offer to purchase the club from Horace Stoneham. At this time, I wish to clear the air and state that I am not now involved with Lurie or any group in the possible purchase of the club. As president of the National League, a position I enjoy, it is my hope to continue in this position for as long as my presence in this office is desired by the owners of the 12 National League clubs.[18]

Once Feeney made his announcement, Lurie changed his course of action. After suggesting that he might be more inclined to buy the ball club if he had the Bay Area to himself, he put his activity as an active buyer on hold and remained in the background for the next six months as an interested bystander, biding his time, with an eye out for a suitable partner.[19]

If Stoneham wanted to test the market discreetly and informally for a buyer with local renown, Bob Lurie was a good first choice. Born in San Francisco, educated at nearby Menlo School and then at Northwestern University, where he earned his bachelor's degree in business, Lurie learned the ins and outs of both the corporate world and San Francisco society from his father, Louis Lurie, a preeminent real estate magnate. The Lurie Company was one of the most successful and prosperous businesses in the city, and the elder Lurie was one of the distinguished figures in the city's cultural and social circles. In addition to being an astute businessman, Louis Lurie was well appointed politically and a generous philanthropist. His daily lunch table at Jack's Restaurant on Sacramento Street attracted actors, singers, writers, movie stars, politicians, and local celebrities.[20] As one local columnist put it, in Boston there are the Cabots and Lodges; in San Francisco there are the Luries.[21]

Returning to San Francisco after college in the early 1950s, Bob lived in his father's shadow as he learned the family business, gradually taking on more responsibility in property management; he also became active in social and cultural events in the city. After the Giants came west in 1958, the younger Lurie was asked to join Stoneham's board of directors, most of whom were easterners, to provide local perspective as someone familiar with the city's corporate and social culture. It was in his role as a board member that Bob Lurie developed a business relationship with Stoneham and a friendship with Chub Feeney. By the time of the Giants' arrival, he had taken a more active role in the Lurie Company's activities and was well known in the city's business and finance circles. When Louis Lurie died in 1972, Bob had, in effect, been running the business for a number of years. Stoneham's approach to Lurie about the impending sale grew naturally from their relationship and from the respect the Giants owner had for Lurie's position in the community.

Lurie's initial interest cheered Stoneham, despite the fact that it did not lead to an immediate offer to purchase. It was early enough in the sales process that Stoneham might hope for a good outcome with Lurie as the future team owner. This was certainly the thinking of the local press, which was well aware of the prominence of the Lurie Company. Stories about the Lurie family as the obvious choice to buy the team if Stoneham were to sell surfaced as early as 1972.[22] Given Lurie's history with the ball club, it was not unreasonable that the press would conjecture about a Lurie ownership. He was known to the local press not only as a member of Stoneham's board, and therefore familiar with the Giants' organization, but also as a fan who attended games and had some affection for the team. Moreover, he was well connected in sporting circles as an avid golfer, playing annually in the Crosby Pro-Am tournament at Pebble Beach and at various local courses in and around the city. For Lurie himself, interest in owning a baseball franchise reflected a sense of independence and self-assertion, a sign that he was willing to consider taking a risk in venturing beyond the traditional real estate interests of the Lurie Company.

Once Lurie made it clear that, while interested, he would move deliberately on any purchase of the Giants, the press's initial presumptions about a quick and smooth solution to the Giants' problem quieted. So too did the momentum from other local buyers, an indication that the sale of the Giants would likely be a lengthy process. Not surprisingly, the lack of a quick fix only increased the press's interest in the drama of the ball club's impending sale. Over the summer, while Lurie remained in the background as uncommitted, prompting "will he or won't he" speculation from local writers, other occasional suitors would make their intentions known, energizing the press. Robert Post, a financier who owned the Beverly Hills mortgage company American Funding, contacted the Giants about purchasing the team and, presumably, keeping it in San Francisco.[23] After checking the books, however, Post decided that the Giants were a poor investment and withdrew from the field. The books would continue to vex Stoneham as buyers would cool once they took a glance at the Giants' financials. One serious feeler came in late July from a group of investors from Japan, interested not only in the baseball team but also in Stoneham's real estate holdings in Arizona.[24] A few weeks later, citing financial complications with their domestic holdings, they had a change of heart.[25] Old Giants manager and Stoneham pal Herman Franks expressed fleeting interest but wanted the baseball team without the bundled real estate properties.[26] A few other local groups made informal queries about the Giants, but by late fall the activity of summer had fallen off considerably.

In an attempt to drum up local interest, Giants vice president Jerry Donovan made clear Stoneham's desire to keep the team in the city. "If it is to a San Francisco group, I think he would sell quickly. Horace does want to keep the team here."[27] There were no new offers, however, especially not from the local front. Meanwhile Stoneham came back to the league for more funding to meet expenses, borrowing against the projected proceeds of his eventual sale. At a special September meeting, league owners authorized another five hundred thousand dollars to see the Giants through their year-end expenses if they were unable to conclude any sales of the franchise or the real estate holdings.[28]

Then, in late November, activity began to quicken, the start of a furious finish toward new ownership. In a curious marketing ploy, Stoneham and the Giants' front office gave outright and unconditional releases to manager Wes Westrum and his coaching staff.[29] This dramatic house cleaning was intended to entice a new owner who would be open to rebuilding. Some offers began to surface, though it remained unclear whether the absence of a coaching staff was a factor. Lurie reiterated his interest in buying the team and that he would do so without hesitation if the Oakland A's left town, something that Charlie Finley would never agree to do.[30] Entertainer Danny Kaye and his partner, Lester Smith, spoke of their interest in buying the Giants and moving them to Seattle. When asked about this possibility NL president Chub Feeney remarked that while Kaye and Smith would make good owners, they had yet to make an official offer. Feeney also added that the league was making every effort to keep the team in San Francisco.[31] Other offers trickled in. Former Giants pitcher Mike McCormick headed a group that made an offer, as did Alan Murray, a Marin insurance executive and the president of the San Francisco Giants booster club. But in the end neither of these groups could satisfy the asking price of the National Exhibition Company.[32]

The National League winter meetings provided the owners with plenty to talk about, including speculation on Dodgers pitcher Andy Messersmith's and retired Expos pitcher Dave McNally's challenge to the reserve clause and a threatened suit from the City of Seattle objecting to the transfer of the 1969 Pilots to Milwaukee; their primary focus, however, trained on the Giants' situation in San Francisco.[33] The league appointed a "San Francisco Committee," headed by Dodgers owner Walter O'Malley, joined by John Galbreath, the Pittsburgh Pirates owner, and Charles Bronfman, the principal owner of the Montreal Expos, to study the situation, collect information, and report back with recommendations to the general body.[34] The owners were aware of three possible offers on the Giants franchise, one from the McCormick group, another from former Washington Senators/Texas Rangers owner Bob Short, and a third from an investment group in Toronto. Since none of these met Stoneham's asking price, the league did not consider taking any action for approval. The Toronto group's petition appeared the most promising but did not allow for sufficient compensation to the City of San Francisco for the relocation to Canada, an essential component of that bid.

The deficiency of these offers and especially the possibility that the Giants might leave San Francisco, an explicit condition in the Toronto bid, gave the owners pause, slowing their deliberations. Seizing the moment as an opportunity, O'Malley and his committee cautioned the owners against losing the Bay Area market to the American League. With his eye on the Los Angeles–San Francisco rivalry—Giants series always sold out at Dodger Stadium—O'Malley wanted to maintain the California connection between the teams; he was the leading advocate among the owners for keeping the Giants in San Francisco.[35] A motion came before the owners that if no bona fide offers for the Giants materialized by mid-January, the league would take over operations of the team and keep it in San Francisco until a suitable local owner could be found. The motion was tabled and, as events played out, would never have to be voted on by the membership.[36]

Everything completely changed in early January 1976 when a serious offer suddenly materialized. Yet another group from Toronto, this one headed by Labatt Brewing Company, expressed casual interest in the Giants and contacted Stoneham to begin formal negotiations.[37] After private conversations and a thorough look at the club's books, the Labatt group made an official offer to Stoneham: $8,000,000 for the ball club and $5,250,000 additional payment in escrow to cover any legal fees. On January 9 Stoneham announced that the National Exhibition Company had agreed in principle to the Canadians' offer.[38] Key to the bid was the additional compensation to the city for breaking the Candlestick lease with the team's relocation to Canada. With his acceptance of the offer, Stoneham signaled that, given his dire economic straits, he could no longer wait for local money to keep the team in San Francisco. He knew that it was the intention of the offer from the Labatt group for the Giants to start the 1976 season in Toronto. Giants counsel James Hunt explained Stoneham's mixed feelings to the local press. "Horace Stoneham won't be happy to see San Francisco lose the team, if the deal with Toronto goes through. . . . But it was so much the best offer he's had."[39] The press accepted Hunt at his word and all but conceded that San Francisco would lose its baseball team. "GIANTS MOVING TO TORONTO" ran the headlines in the *Examiner*.[40]

A few days before the Giants announced their agreement with the Labatt group, a new mayor, George Moscone, took his oath of office at city hall. One of his first public statements revealed the seriousness with which he regarded the Giants' situation. Assuming a "not on my watch" posture, he vowed that he would do all he possibly could to avoid becoming the mayor who lost the city's baseball team.[41] His first tactic, taken on behalf of the city's taxpayers, was to direct city attorney Thomas O'Connor to apply to the court to block the sale on the grounds that, in accepting the conditions of the Canadian offer to move the Giants to Toronto, Stoneham would be breaking an agreement he signed in 1958 for a thirty-five-year lease on Candlestick Park, thus depriving the city (and the taxpayers) of income. On January 14, 1976, a temporary restraining order was entered, effectively freezing all action on the sale. The Giants' fate would now be a matter of legal procedures and judicial review, in which the city's interests would be pitted against those of the National Exhibition Company. For good measure, the city's petition before the court also included a request for an injunction against the National League for its part in the impending sale of the Giants to the Toronto group. Meanwhile, Hunt was granted a two-week continuance by Superior Court judge John Benson to prepare the National Exhibition Company's case for selling the club to Toronto. Lou Hoynes, the attorney for the National League, advised the owners that while the restraining order was in place, there could be no decisions on the Labatt group's offer and the Giants' presumptive relocation.[42]

George Moscone's keen interest in the Giants is reminiscent of that of one of his mayoral predecessors, George Christopher, who brought the Giants to San Francisco in 1957. And like Christopher's, Moscone's efforts on behalf of his city went well beyond maintaining a Major League franchise. Born and raised in the city, Moscone attended Saint Ignatius High School, where he was an all-city basketball star in 1947. He went on to the University of Pacific in nearby Stockton, graduating in 1952. After a three-year stint in the U.S. Navy, he attended the University of California's Hastings Law School in San Francisco, paying for his tuition by working as a night janitor with his fellow law student and future San Francisco mayor Willie Brown (the city's first African American mayor). Born to be a politician, as many of his close friends claimed, Moscone was elected in 1964 to the city's board of supervisors and two years later to the California state senate, where he was voted Democratic majority leader. His 1975 mayoral campaign espoused a progressive and liberal platform, promising most of all transparency in city politics and access to the city's services for everyone, especially those who had been marginalized. Once in office, he began working for fair housing, decriminalizing marijuana laws, and making the city a safe place for African Americans and gays. He would pay the ultimate price for his inclusive politics almost three years later, on November 27, 1978, when he was shot and killed in his office at city hall by a distraught former member of the board of supervisors who opposed his agenda.[43]

The legal continuance granted to Hunt and the Giants, while temporary, gave Mayor Moscone some precious days to redouble his efforts to keep the team in San Francisco. During the delay effected by the Giants' continuance, he took full advantage. On January 14, Moscone flew to Phoenix to attend the NL winter meetings in order to make his case before the owners. By all accounts he made a favorable impression. Art Rosenbaum of the *Chronicle* pronounced the mayor's performance a great success, both politically and oratorically.[44] Moscone informed the owners of his plans to find local ownership, or at least an owner who would be willing to keep the team in San Francisco. He assured the league that he had learned of at least three viable buyers: Bob Short, a former baseball owner; Marge Everett, the owner of Hollywood Park race track who unsuccessfully bid on the San Diego Padres franchise; and a San Francisco group, headed by Jack Levine, Raymond Murphy, and Frank Pierce, who wanted to organize a public company.[45] He also mentioned that he knew of at least one other local individual engaged in preparing the financing to make an offer. Without naming anyone, Moscone had Bob Lurie in mind.[46]

During his time at the NL meeting, Moscone detected interest among a significant number of owners, especially Walter O'Malley, John Galbreath, and Buzzie Bavasi of San Diego, to keep the team in San Francisco, giving him some needed encouragement.[47] His spirits somewhat buoyed, he flew back to San Francisco and directed his assistant, Corey Busch, to contact Bob Short, whose initial offer was too low, and Raymond Rossi, owner of the Pizza Hut national chain, who had his eye on Stoneham's real estate holdings. He hoped that a partnership might blossom between the two. Moscone had decided that Short, when partnered with Rossi, presented a more promising option than Everett and the McCormick group. After some hopeful deliberation, however, Rossi backed out on the assumption (a correct one, as it turned out) that the NL owners were not enamored with Short's history of sports franchise ownerships.[48]

With Rossi out of the picture, Moscone then turned to Bob Lurie, whose interest in the Giants had never faltered but whose attempts at finding a local partner had thus far proved unfruitful. Lurie's latest effort was a failed meeting in Chicago with Bill Veeck, who appeared to be interested only in Lurie's financial backing rather than in a true partnership.[49] After the Veeck meeting, a somewhat discouraged Lurie informed the mayor's office that his attempts to find a partner were going nowhere. Nonetheless, he would put up half of the purchase price, if they could find an interested party to join him.[50] A few days later, the mayor suggested a meeting with him and Short, and Lurie agreed. Short flew to San Francisco and the mayor facilitated a discussion between Short and Lurie about a plan to keep the Giants in San Francisco. Both men appeared willing and committed. With Lurie's local connections, Short's baseball experience, the financial resources both men held, and their mutual willingness to keep the team in San Francisco, Moscone felt he had a strong alternative to the Labatt group's offer.[51] Facing an impending deadline, Lurie and Short brokered a partnership and agreed to become co-owners; they would match the Labatt group's offer of eight million dollars to buy the team.[52]

On February 11, 1976, the day the temporary restraining order was due to expire, Moscone entered Judge John Benson's courtroom, flanked by Lurie and Short. Prior to the Moscone party's dramatic entrance, the atmosphere in the courtroom was described by one San Francisco writer as funereal: almost everyone present assumed the Giants would be leaving for Toronto.[53] Since the day the temporary restraining order had been entered no local offer had materialized, despite all the optimistic talk coming from the mayor's office. Speaking on behalf of the Giants, James Hunt put forth in unsentimental language the club's predicament. "We've no alternative but to proceed with the sale to Toronto. We thought we might have heard something more. Maybe we will. But this is the way it's been for months. Nobody wants to put up money."[54] Given this situation, Judge Benson would have no option but to clear the sale to Toronto for the National Exhibition Company. He had made that point at an earlier hearing, that the temporary restraining order was just that, and unless a serious local offer developed soon, he would lift the order and the Giants would be Toronto bound.[55]

With a flair for the dramatic at precisely this moment in the deliberations, Moscone told Judge Benson he had a local party ready to make a legitimate offer to buy the Giants, and he introduced Short and Lurie. Judge Benson asked both men about their intentions and if they were prepared to act immediately. When Short and Lurie answered that they were prepared to make an immediate five-hundred-thousand-dollar "good faith" deposit in escrow and an offer to the National Exhibition Company that would match the terms of the Labatt group, Judge Benson, who would not be upstaged in his own courtroom, responded emphatically with his own sense of drama, issuing a preliminary injunction preventing the team from leaving San Francisco.[56]

> At this particular point, however, the court is convinced by virtue of the offers that have been made here today in open court, that the equities overwhelmingly are on the side of the city, and the preliminary injunction will be granted. . . . I don't care who owns the Giants. The facts of the matter are that this court has granted a preliminary injunction with respect to the Giants' obligation to the City and County of San Francisco.[57]

The mood in the crowded courtroom abruptly shifted to celebratory delight. When those in attendance responded to the ruling with applause and cheering, Judge Benson sternly remind those in attendance that they were not at Candlestick Park. A beaming Moscone, with Lurie and Short at his side, met the press outside. Revealing the knowledgeable baseball fan behind the consummate politician, the first words out of the mayor's mouth were "Bobby Thomson lives!"[58] The mayor got it just right. It was a great victory for all of the Bay Area's Giants fans, a come-from-behind, bottom-of-the-ninth win, as dramatic in its own way as the one on October 3, 1951, when the Thomson home run beat the Dodgers and took the Giants to the National League pennant. Reflecting on Moscone's phrase, one baseball historian observed, "It was indeed a bottom-of-the-ninth miracle. But unlike 1951, this one satisfied the Dodgers too."[59] Like Moscone, so too could Walter O'Malley breathe easier; the San Francisco–Los Angeles rivalry would stand. All that remained for Moscone, Lurie, and Short was the approval of the NL owners who, under O'Malley's influence, were predisposed to keep the Giants in San Francisco. Everything appeared settled.

As it turned out, however, Moscone's Bobby Thomson moment was short lived. A special meeting of the NL convened on February 24 whose sole purpose was to approve the sale of the Giants. With Short in a Minneapolis hospital recovering from a bad fall, Lurie and Moscone attended the meeting and Moscone made a presentation before the owners during which he assured the league of the validity of the offer before them and the stated interest of both the city's chamber of commerce and its business community in keeping the Giants in San Francisco.[60] After the brief presentation, the mayor and Lurie waited outside the meeting room for what they assumed would be a pro forma approval. It was with some surprise when the owners' deliberations took longer than expected. When the owners finally came back to Moscone and Lurie, their approval had a big string attached. It was in fact a conditional approval of the sale, and the condition would prove unbearable for the partnership. The owners, troubled by Short's history as an American League owner, preferred to deal only with Lurie, as a fellow owner. They not only objected to Short's flamboyant manner and his reputation as a wheeler-dealer, buying and selling sports' franchises in relatively quick order; they also were leery of his audacious and creative financing as owner of the Washington Senators, when he moved the team to Texas.[61] Therefore, they demanded as a condition of the sale that Bob Lurie would act and function as the primary owner, the one who would vote at

NL meetings, effectively putting Short in a secondary role in the partnership.[62] An editorial in the *Sporting News* condoned their action.

> National League owners could scarcely be blamed if they examined Short's part in the proposed [Giants'] financing with extreme caution. . . . Short's performance in Washington and Texas hardly recommends him as the answer to the Giants' prayers.[63]

It did not take Short long to respond to the conditions of the approval of the sale and the demand from the NL that Lurie be the voice of the franchise. He immediately and emphatically rejected the league's condition. Conversations over the next few days to reach some understanding and agreement between him and Lurie left both of them at an impasse.[64] On March 2, Short sent a telegram to Lurie with a brief message dissolving the partnership. With a reference to some of his financial backers in Minneapolis, he nonetheless revealed his insistence on being the voting owner at NL meetings as the chief reason he backed out.

> We have discontinued our efforts to adjoin you in keeping the Giants in San Francisco. . . . The club's baseball operations should properly be under my control because of my baseball experience. Good Luck in your efforts to get others to join you in keeping baseball in San Francisco.[65]

Short also sent telegrams to Moscone, Judge Benson, and Chub Feeney repeating his thinking that, given his long experience as a Major League executive and Lurie's limited exposure to the business of baseball, if he couldn't function as the primary voice of the Giants, then he was out of the partnership.[66] Just like that, Short walked away from the agreement. Suddenly, the dramatic moment Moscone likened to the Thomson home run seemed more like a called third strike with the bases loaded.

What happened next belongs in a melodrama. On the afternoon of March 2, a stunned Lurie placed a call to Chub Feeney asking for a forty-eight hour extension to find a new partner among the city's business community. After contacting the owners, Feeney told Lurie that the league would grant him five hours. He explained that the owners were too anxious about the proximity of spring training and league play to wait any longer for ownership issues. As Lurie was scrambling to find another local partner, Corey Busch, the mayor's secretary, received a phone call from Phoenix. Someone named Bud Herseth, a cattle dealer unknown to anyone in the mayor's office, or to baseball for that matter, was on the line asking about the sale of the Giants and whether he might get involved as a partner. He had read about Bob Lurie and the difficulties of the sale and was interested in becoming an owner. Busch was astounded, put Herseth on hold, and broke in on the mayor's meeting. The mayor got on the line and after a few minutes decided that Herseth was serious and worthy of a follow-up. He told Herseth that someone would contact him within the hour.[67]

Immediately Moscone called Lurie, who then placed a call to Herseth. After a forty-five minute conversation, they agreed in principle to form a partnership, with Herseth providing half of the eight-million-dollar selling price. There would be no disagreement about who would be voting at the NL meetings; Herseth was fine with Lurie as the chief owner who would represent the business side of ownership. All that remained was for Herseth's finances to be vetted. When the NL owners were satisfied with Herseth's reliability and financial legitimacy, they approved the new partnership. The headlines the next day in the *Chronicle*'s sport section proclaimed the news: "BEEF KING SAVES LURIE, GIANTS."[68] One writer, with Moscone's allusion to the Thomson home run still in mind, called it "the greatest save in Giants' history."[69] A breathless Lurie gave his account to the newspaper.

> Yesterday I was $4 million shy of the agreed sale price. Then I heard about Bud. . . . I called him and he said he had $4 million. I informed Feeney of this beautiful development. Chub called the owners and we got unanimous approval. . . . It's all set, we own the Giants.[70]

Lurie's head was swimming, but he prevailed. He was a new owner of the Giants and the team would remain in the city.

The next day, Herseth flew to San Francisco to meet Lurie for the first time, face-to-face, and to sign the agreement. Later that evening, Mayor Moscone honored both of the new owners at a civic reception at the Jack Tar Hotel, where Herseth captivated the local press with his cowboy manner. When asked by one reporter whether his one-day decision to invest four million dollars in the Giants didn't worry him, Herseth responded, "I've made cattle deals involving 3 or 4 million in 5 minutes."[71] Another writer asked about the demands of owning a Major League Baseball team. Herseth explained that Lurie would do the heavy lifting. "I've been at the cattle business for 27 years, seven days a week. I bought the Giants for recreation. I load meat at the plant. I feel I'm entitled to a little diversion."[72] Later, in one of their first conversations, Chub Feeney asked Herseth how he came to be interested in baseball. Herseth answered that he had a long-standing interest in the sport: every year he loved betting on the World Series. A suddenly uneasy Feeney quickly shot back that Herseth wouldn't be doing that anymore. A month or so later on a trip to Phoenix, Lurie asked his new partner what he liked to do for fun. Herseth remarked that when things got slow in cattle buying, he liked to get in his pickup, drive out in the desert, and shoot rattlesnakes.[73] The urbane Lurie swallowed hard and pondered silently the brave new partnership that he had forged in order to save the Giants.

1. Stoneham, O'Malley, and Congressman Emanuel
Cellar before the summer 1957 congressional
hearings on baseball's antitrust exemption.
Unlike O'Malley, Stoneham was explicit in his
testimony that he intended to move the Giants to
California. National Baseball Hall of Fame Library,
Cooperstown, New York.

2. (*Above*) Two hundred thousand people turned out in downtown San Francisco to welcome the Giants to the city in early April 1958. San Francisco History Center, San Francisco Public Library.

3. (*Opposite top*) Considered the jewel of Minor League ballparks, Seals Stadium was home to the Giants for the 1958 and 1959 seasons. In their first year in San Francisco, despite the stadium's limited capacity of just under twenty-three thousand, the Giants doubled their 1957 New York attendance. © S. F. Giants Archives.

4. (*Opposite bottom*) Major League Baseball's first game on the West Coast, Seals Stadium, April 15, 1958. Giants pitcher Ruben Gomez faced Dodgers hitter Gino Cimoli, with Valmy Thomas catching and Jocko Conlan the home plate umpire. © S. F. Giants Archives, Dick Dobbins.

5. Builder Charles Harney welcomes Horace Stoneham to Candlestick Park, late March 1960, both men are wearing what would become essential clothing for most games at the ballpark: overcoats. National Baseball Hall of Fame Library, Cooperstown, New York.

6. Candlestick in 1960 showing the parking facility that Stoneham desired. © S. F. Giants Archives.

7. Among the many dignitaries who came for the opening of Candlestick Park was Vice President Richard Nixon, welcomed here by Stoneham and San Francisco mayor George Christopher. © S. F. Giants Archives.

8. The San Francisco Giants were pioneers in Major League Baseball in recruiting and developing Latino players, thanks in large part to the scouting organization in Latin America headed by Alex Pompez, shown here with his recruits at the spring training facility in Florida. © S. F. Giants Archives.

9. Juan Marichal had some great years under skipper Alvin Dark and had a good working relationship with him, as this 1963 photo with Stoneham suggests. But after the 1964 season Stoneham fired Dark for his inability to connect with Latino players, among them Orlando Cepeda and Matty Alou. © S. F. Giants Archives.

10. The elements, especially the wind, wreaked havoc on ballplayers at Candlestick, as seen in this shot of Willie Mays on the base path. © S. F. Giants Archives.

11. A notorious moment in the Giants-Dodgers rivalry came in August 1962 when manager Alvin Dark ordered groundskeeper Manny Schwab to water around first base at Candlestick to keep the Dodgers speedsters from stealing bases. The Dodgers protested and the umpires ordered Schwab to improve the conditions. Schwab raked in peat moss, which made the footing worse. The Dodgers stole one base in a three-game series, which the Giants swept. San Francisco History Center, San Francisco Public Library.

12. (*Opposite top*)All five of these Hall of Famers played together in San Francisco from 1962 through 1965, but during that time the Giants could not win a world championship. Willie McCovey and Willie Mays, *seated*; Orlando Cepeda, Juan Marichal, and Gaylord Perry, *standing*. © S. F. Giants Archives.

13. (*Opposite bottom*) New owners Bob Lurie and Bud Herseth, whose 1976 purchase of the Giants assured that the ball club would remain in San Francisco, led the spring 1976 celebratory parade in downtown San Francisco. © S. F. Giants Archives.

14. (*Above*) Lurie's hiring of Al Rosen and Roger Craig in September 1985 marked a big turn of fortune for the Giants. © S. F. Giants Archives.

15. Roger Craig brought to his managerial style a great optimism and the Humm Baby brand of baseball. © S. F. Giants Archives.

16. Roger Craig and Al Rosen inaugurated the Humm Baby era based on hustle and hard-nosed play. Under their leadership the Giants went to the postseason twice and won the National League pennant. © S. F. Giants Archives.

17. In an effort to play down the infamous windy conditions at Candlestick, Lurie tried a number of promotions and events. One of them was having the great tightrope walker Karl Wallenda traverse Candlestick Park in between a doubleheader with the New York Mets, May 8, 1977. © S. F. Giants Archives.

18. Crazy Crab, the legendary anti-mascot, had a very brief full-time career, lasting only for the 1984 season. Intended to be the target of fans' insults as they vented their frustrations, the crab eventually was hit with material objects, including flashlight batteries and golf balls. As appearances grew more dangerous for the crab, he retired in September 1984 and now appears only occasionally at Giants home games. © S. F. Giants Archives.

19. The Loma Prieta earthquake hit in the late afternoon on October 17, 1989, stopping the World Series and causing massive destruction in the Bay Area, as is evident from this image of the Marina district in San Francisco. Sixty-three people died and there was over six billion dollars in damages. Both teams in the World Series—Oakland and San Francisco—had their neighborhoods and infrastructure damaged. San Francisco History Center, San Francisco Public Library.

20. The Baker-Bonds era that began in 1993 ushered in a successful period in Giants baseball. In the ten seasons leading up to and including the 2002 season, after which Baker left, the Giants were 777-642, went to the postseason three times, and won the 2002 National League pennant. © S. F. Giants Archives.

21. From 1997 through 2002, Jeff Kent followed Bonds in the batting order, giving the Giants a devastating one-two punch. © S. F. Giants Archives.

22. The 1996 campaign for the new stadium stressed employment opportunities and that the stadium would be built with private money. © S. F. Giants Archives.

23. Giants officials were attentive to the progress of construction on the new ballpark, visiting the building site often. Chief managing partner Peter Magowan paid a visit in the spring of 1999. © S. F. Giants Archives.

24. Prior to the new ballpark's opening in April of 2000, Peter Magowan and his executive vice president Larry Baer hold up the headlines from the 1992 *San Francisco Examiner* announcing that the team was leaving for Florida. © S. F. Giants Archives.

25–26. The proximity of the new ballpark
to the downtown and the San Francisco
Bay are two of its charming features.
© S. F. Giants Archives.

27. The Giants' opening game at PacBell
Stadium, April 11, 2000, was against the
Dodgers. Kirk Rueter threw to Devon White,
Doug Mirabelli was catching, and
Ed Montague was the home plate umpire.
© S. F. Giants Archives.

EIGHT

Learning Curve

Bob Lurie had little time to savor his efforts in keeping the Giants in San Francisco. Nor did he have the leisure to apply his considerable business experience in real estate and property management to his new role in running a baseball team. He was joining the world of baseball ownership at a time of considerable turmoil, and he would become immediately and directly involved in its problems. The game was facing a crucial change, one that threatened the owners' essential and traditional modus operandi. In the winter of 1975, Andy Messersmith and Dave McNally challenged baseball's time-honored reserve clause, which stated that if a player refused to sign a contract for the coming season, the team had the right to renew the contract, effectively making it perpetual. The Major League Baseball Players Association, on behalf of Messersmith and McNally, argued that a one-year contract was just that, and a player could become a free agent for the following year.[1] The arbitration panel handling the grievance ruled in favor of the players on a 2–1 vote, shocking the owners and provoking a storm of protests among them. They fired the independent arbitrator, Peter Seitz, who voted in favor of the players (the other two members of the panel were representing the players' union and the owners, respectively), sued in federal court, and appealed in the United States Court of Appeals but to no avail; the players won at every level.

In a fit of pique, the owners in both leagues voted to lock the players out of all spring training practice facilities, effectively cancelling the 1976 Grapefruit League and Cactus League play.[2] The lockout lasted for almost three weeks, during which Lurie primarily played the role of an observer, watching and learning about the politics of Major League Baseball from an owner's perspective. He was especially impressed with Walter O'Malley, whose leadership became apparent when, after eliciting the support of a few crucial owners, he persuaded baseball commissioner Bowie Kuhn to open spring training camps on March 17.[3] O'Malley, always the businessman, argued that the owners could not reverse the players' gains in court and were missing out on important revenue.[4]

The troublesome lockout, however short in duration, provided, paradoxically, some personal benefit: it gave Lurie a chance to adjust to his new role as owner. He had much to consider. In addition to dealing with problems common throughout baseball, Lurie had his own house to order. During the three-week hiatus, he could concentrate on urgent matters close at hand rather than on the more far-flung events of spring training. More or less dormant the past four months over the uncertainties of the club's future, the Giants' organization was in desperate need of attention and revitalization. With no manager and no coaches, with players' contracts to settle, with front office staff in transition, and with the season only one month from opening, Lurie was getting a crash course on the business of baseball. His days were long. Mornings were spent dealing with Lurie Company business downtown; after lunch, he headed out to Candlestick Park and the Giants' offices, working into the evening.

Fortunately he had an experienced hand close by in Spec Richardson, who was assigned to the Giants by the NL during the last six months of the Stoneham ownership and who remained with the club while the legal transfer to Lurie and Herseth took place. The owners reasoned that in loaning money to Stoneham's National Exhibition Company to meet payroll and operate the ball club, they could demand oversight on the use of the funds. They installed Richardson as a kind of chief financial officer pro-temp, to adjudicate any Giants expenditures, including operational costs and player salaries. Lurie's first decision as owner, with a green light from Herseth, was to hire Richardson, who had initially earned his spurs as the general manager of the Houston Astros from 1967 until 1975. With Richardson as the Giants' general manager, Lurie gained both experience and insight. In addition to understanding Major League Baseball's culture, Richardson also knew the Giants' financial situation thoroughly, giving Lurie an informed perspective both in budgetary matters and in planning for player acquisitions, development, and expenditures.

Lurie then turned to the problem of the team's manager. As he was negotiating with Moscone, and planning with Short and then with Herseth, he had in mind his old friend Bill Rigney, who was the Giants manager when the club first moved west in 1958. Rigney, well known to Bay Area fans, could provide tradition at a time of change for the Giants. The only drawback was that Rigney had his eye on retirement. He told Lurie privately that he would manage for only one year, helping the club transition with the new ownership.[5] Nonetheless, it seemed a good choice for Lurie, not only because of their friendship but also because Rigney brought a sense of stability in his connection to Giants history and considerable managerial experience to the job, easing any worries Lurie might harbor about the day-to-day running of a ball club.

With Richardson and Rigney aboard, Lurie looked to his front office administration, rehiring Jerry Donovan, longtime Giants executive under Stoneham, whose local baseball experience went back to his employment with the San Francisco Seals. Donovan helped Lurie with the transition of the administrative staff needed to handle ticket sales, stadium contracts, media coordination, and public relations. In a matter of two weeks, at a furious pace that *San Francisco Examiner* sportswriter Art Spander claimed made up for six months of languor, the Giants rehired key people from Stoneham's administrative staff like John Taddeucci and Arturo Santo Domingo, conducted player personnel reviews, and re-signed players like Bobby Murcer and John Montefusco whose contracts needed attention.[6] Rigney took full advantage of the lockout, seeing it as a blessing in disguise, giving him more time to hire his coaches.[7] Richardson was particularly active, tidying up the remaining contracts and reviewing the farm system. With things moving almost at warp speed and everyone in the organization scrambling, and before Lurie could get comfortable at his owner's desk, spring training was coming to a close, and the Giants would soon open their 1976 season on April 9 at Candlestick Park against the Dodgers.

Opening day was hardly a moment for Lurie to celebrate as a new owner. He had yet another significant problem on his hands. A strike of San Francisco municipal workers that had shut down all public transportation, all refuse service, and even plumbing service, threatened the scheduling of opening day.[8] Worried about the home opener attendance, as well as about the services that would be affected, Lurie was nonetheless resolute in his notion that the show must go on. "Of course we are hoping the strike will be settled so that we can have a normal opening, but nothing is going to stop us. . . . If the strike continues we will have curtailed services, but we will open as scheduled."[9] Mike Marshall, the player representative for the Dodgers, saw things differently and tried to get Lurie and the Giants to cancel the series in deference to the union workers. His counterpart, Giants pitcher Jim Barr, polled the San Francisco players, who unanimously favored opening the season on schedule. "We feel that this team in particular and the Players Association in general had a lot to overcome this spring and we are not going to shut down the season now. The new owners have given us a fresh start and we are not going to ruin it at the outset."[10]

The show did indeed go on as scheduled and, considering all of the impediments, had to be viewed as a smashing success, as 37,261 showed up for the game, the largest opening-day crowd in ten years, even with the difficulties of the strike. Both Lurie and the hometown fans went home happy. On a sunny, almost windless day, Montefusco baffled the Dodgers for 7⅓ innings, Gary Lavelle closed out the game and the Giants came away winners against their rivals, 4–2. The food concessions were limited to three stands, there was no hot water in the clubhouses (forcing the visiting players to shower at their hotel), and, with no municipal transport, the parking lot was packed with private vehicles, making the regularly clogged and prolonged egress from the ballpark even worse.[11] But spirits remained high, the buzz was back to baseball in San Francisco, the players responded, and the

Lurie era began with a victorious first step. Giants left fielder Gary Matthews explained. "Last year we'd get 6000 people in the park . . . and you didn't have the feeling anyone was there. But when there's 37,000 you can feel the buzzing all around. I really feel the city's excited over the team, what with everything that happened[,] . . . you know, nearly losing the Giants."[12]

After sweeping the Dodgers at home, the Giants took to the road, where they lost regularly, establishing a pattern that would prevail throughout the season: a few wins against greater losses. In their first forty games they were 13-27, a fitful start they could never overcome. They finished 74-88, in fourth place in the NL West, 27½ games back. A crucial move by Richardson midseason brought Darrell Evans to the Giants from Atlanta in exchange for the disgruntled Willie Montanez; Evans would prove to be a Giants stalwart at third base for the next seven years. There also appeared a shred of a silver lining in Lurie's first year with the 1976 attendance figures, up over 100,000 from the previous year but at 626,868 still last in the National League. After the season, Rigney kept to his promise in the spring by announcing that he was calling it quits after eighteen years of big league managing. His departure speech included the stock reason for leaving—the desire to spend more time with the family—but he had never intended to stay with the Giants more than one season. Addressing Rigney's departure and the team's disappointing first year, Lurie stated that when he and Bud Herseth bought the team, they agreed upon a three-year plan to turn the franchise around, and Rigney helped them through the first year.[13]

In November, the Giants announced that Joe Altobelli, a relatively unknown manager of Triple-A Rochester, would replace Rigney for the 1977 season. Over the winter, Richardson helped Altobelli by re-signing longtime favorite Willie McCovey, who had been languishing in Oakland during the last part of the 1976 season.[14] Back in a Giants uniform, the thirty-nine-year-old McCovey found new life, with 28 home runs, 86 runs batted in, and a .280 batting average, garnering the 1977 NL Comeback Player of the Year award. Unfortunately for Lurie's rebuilding plan, the '77 Giants could not follow McCovey's lead, posting another losing record at 75-87, almost an exact replica of their previous year's showing. A glimmer of optimism could be discerned, again, in the attendance figures, which grew slightly from the previous year to 700,056 although still remaining last in the NL.

Bob Lurie continued to tell the local press he was a patient man and was in for the long haul.[15] He was also active himself with promotion, going where his predecessor Stoneham would never go, attending meetings at the Kiwanis, the Rotary Clubs, luncheon groups, and dinner clubs, selling the Giants. With the help of his new promotions director, Pat Gallagher, he tried pregame rock concerts, Frisbee contests, even a high-wire spectacle between games of a doubleheader, when Karl Wallenda defied the Candlestick winds and, suspended above the playing field, walked across the stadium.[16] Lurie also made it a point to sit among the fans at Candlestick, getting their views on the game but also demonstrating an indifference to the weather, hoping to lead by example.[17] He hired the Maxwell Arnold advertising agency, who created commercials and marketing schemes including special day giveaways with caps, T-shirts, helmets, and even jackets.[18] With the fans in mind, he brought back longtime Giants radio broadcaster Lon Simmons to call the games.

Meanwhile Richardson appeared to be a man with little patience. With an intent to fashion the Giants as a winning team sooner than later, he continued making changes in the lineup, some of them radical. Once he reacquired McCovey, he then struck a deal with the Cubs to send headliner Bobby Murcer, who had been vocal about how much he disliked the conditions at Candlestick, in exchange for two-time NL batting champ Bill Madlock. After the 1977 season, Richardson decided to commit to the promising young power hitter Jack Clark, installing him as the Giants' permanent right fielder. Just prior to spring training in 1978, Richardson worked a monster trade with Charles Finley, getting Oakland's left-handed ace Vida Blue for seven players (some of them prospects) and cash.[19] Richardson also traded Derrel Thomas to San Diego for Mike Ivie, a player whose versatility as both a first baseman and a catcher made him especially valuable.

All of this activity paid great benefits. The 1978 season was a banner year for the Giants and one of great satisfaction for Lurie. With veteran leadership from McCovey, batting stars Madlock, Evans, Ivie, and second-year power hitter Clark, whose team-best 25 home runs and 98 RBIs combined with a twenty-six-game hitting streak, the Giants led the NL West into the second week of August. Fan-favorite Blue would have a dominant year for the Giants, going 18-10, with a 2.79 ERA, 9 complete games, and 171 strikeouts; he was selected for the NL All-Star team, joining teammate Clark. Left-hander Bob Knepper was also outstanding, going 17-11 with 16 complete games and 6 shutouts. The Giants' downfall came in the crunch time of early September when they dropped seven games in a row and finished the month under .500 at 12-16. They finished a respectful and competitive 89-73, good enough for third place in the NL West, six games behind the division-winning Dodgers.[20]

What might have been viewed as a mediocre or even disappointing year for perennial contending clubs like Cincinnati, St. Louis, or Los Angeles, a third-place finish for San Francisco meant winning baseball, a significant achievement for both the players and the fans; the Giants were big news throughout the city.[21] The real measure of success for the 1978 season came in the attendance, at least as far as Lurie was concerned. The Giants drew 1,740,477, the second-largest in team history since the Giants moved to San Francisco.[22] They drew especially well against Los Angeles; the nine Dodgers games at Candlestick brought in 413,606 fans, just under 24 percent of the season total.[23] For his efforts in putting together the team that surprised the league, Spec Richardson was named NL Executive of the Year.

It was a pivotal year for Bob Lurie in more ways than one. The great success both on the field and at the turnstiles reassured him about his decision to get into baseball ownership. The season's attendance provided a manifestation of fan enthusiasm that Lurie sensed when he bought the club in 1976; he was gratified that after two disappointing seasons he could see positive signs. His first two seasons were discouraging not only in the standings but financially as well; the Giants had lost money both years. As a businessman, Lurie was conscious of the bottom line. Nonetheless, he and Herseth stated at the beginning of their partnership that it would take three years to get the Giants back to both winning (and therefore profitable) ways. The surprising turnaround in 1978 suggested that his timetable was not far off. For at least one season, it appeared that things were moving in the right direction, both in the standings and on the balance sheet.

Certain problems lingered however. Lurie and the Giants were still struggling with the problem of proximity to the A's. After the 1977 season, Charlie Finley began making noises about leaving Oakland and selling the team to Marvin Davis, who wanted to establish a Major League team in Denver. Both the AL and the NL were involved in the discussions, as well as the commissioner, Bowie Kuhn. The A's were not drawing well in Oakland and all parties agreed that it would be in the best interest in baseball if only one team called the Bay Area home. It was generally assumed that the team that would stay would be the Giants. Various plans circulated to facilitate Finley's move, among them financing from the leagues, and a separate contribution from the Giants, to help the Denver ownership acquire the team. To ease the blow, Lurie offered to play forty home games in the Oakland Coliseum, and the San Francisco Board of Supervisors and the Parks and Recreation Committee both agreed to the plan. In the end, however, the dealing and the voting came to naught. Finley became inflexible about the price of his ball club and the City of Oakland refused to cancel the A's' lease, especially after the NFL's Raiders, the Coliseum's other tenant, left town for Los Angeles.[24] Meanwhile, with the fans packing Candlestick Park on a regular basis during the 1978 season, Lurie reconsidered his offer to play forty home games in the East Bay.[25] It appeared that for the foreseeable future, the A's would be staying put in Oakland and the Giants might indeed survive in spite of it.

In addition to his perennial problem with the proximity to the A's, Lurie faced increasing difficulty in his partnership with Bud Herseth. The novelty of the first year's relationship and the distance between them—Herseth traveled only occasionally from Phoenix to San Francisco to see home games during the season—allowed Lurie to remain amiable and professional with his partner. But it was clear from the outset that in temperament and cultural background, the two men had very little in common, something that would eventually strain their working relationship. Herseth consistently explained that he deferred to Lurie in matters related to baseball, but that did not stop him from speaking his mind to the press. Initially, Lurie accepted the notion that his new partner was something of a character and even a loose cannon. His cowboy manner, apparent at their first joint press conference at the Jack Tar hotel the day they were introduced as partners, amused everyone, including Lurie.

Eventually, however, Herseth's sense of humor and country manner began to wear on people, especially those with the San Francisco press. A few thought he might do well to take a Dale Carnegie course on winning friends and influencing people. These writers concurred that Herseth's self-perception was off; he thought of himself as funny, but his humor was based on insults and slurs.[26] Moreover, his behavior could be boorish. During a spring training game in Phoenix, he burst into the stadium radio booth shouting about an idea he had for a promotion—he had just bought a prize bull for four thousand dollars and wanted to circulate a picture of the bull with a Giants cap on its head—causing Lon Simmons, who was broadcasting the game, to try to quiet him. Herseth loudly guffawed and in what one reporter who heard it called "barracks language" exited saying he would take his idea up with someone else.[27] Meanwhile Simmons was forced to cut himself off the air, creating long moments of silence lest he run afoul of the FCC for broadcasting profanity.[28] Herseth then wandered through the stands greeting fans. One of them voiced great enthusiasm for Herseth's colorful Hawaiian shirt, whereupon Herseth removed it on the spot and swapped it for the fan's shirt.[29]

Another incident, a discussion between Herseth and baseball writer Roger Angell, took place during a spring training game in 1976. The topic was the failure of a radio station to live up to the terms of its contract for broadcasting games. Angell was impressed enough with Herseth's colorful speech to quote him generously.

"I damn well don't understand that!" Herseth said loudly. "We make a deal, and now they go and change their mind. I'm glad I don't buy cattle that way. I buy three, four thousand head at a time, and nobody has to worry if I'm going to pay off. My word is my bond. . . . I pay off like a slot machine. I know what these radio people are. I won't say it, though, because there are ladies present. I'll just write it down here on my program." He wrote something and showed me on his program. He had written "S. O. B."[30]

Moments like these, while unthinkable for the mannerly, sophisticated, and essentially shy Bob Lurie, could be passed off as harmless rustic behavior. But what grated on Lurie and eventually crippled their working relationship was Herseth's propensity to speak his mind on Giants business or policy in off-the-cuff remarks to the press. On another occasion in the fall and winter of 1977, during a crucial and delicate stage of negotiations with the Oakland Coliseum over the possibility of the Giants playing some of their home games there, Herseth began to give interviews with the press criticizing A's owner Finley, Mayor Moscone, and the AL owners for their handling of a potential sale of the A's to Denver. At the same time, complaining that he needed to spend more time with his Arizona cattle business, Herseth told the press that he was thinking of selling his half of the team to Emil Bernard, an East Coast financier, who wanted to move the Giants to Washington DC. In both cases, Herseth's remarks took Lurie by surprise, prompting him to engage in some quick diplomatic correction. With respect to Herseth's intention to sell to Bernard, Lurie announced that he would oppose any sale that would involve moving the team; he was insistent that the Giants were not leaving San Francisco.[31] After Bernard was quoted as having lost interest in the Giants, Herseth said that although he had no firm buyer in sight, he still wanted out of baseball and would work something out with Lurie about dissolving the partnership.[32] His interest in selling did not stop him from explaining what the Giants needed to improve; in an interview with a Phoenix columnist he announced his intention to instill a more "Leo Durocher type" attitude in the Giants' play. "Lurie and I have agreed that anybody who does not go all out will be on the next plane to the farm team." Lurie denied the story in a tactful way, commenting that he wished that Herseth would not speak for him.[33]

Fortunately for Lurie, the partnership with Herseth was initially structured so that either side had the right of first refusal to buy out the other in the event the partnership would dissolve. As Herseth became more public about his willingness to get out of the partnership, Lurie responded.[34] In the spring of 1979, Giants attorney James Hunt began working with Herseth's son Ed to buy the additional half so that Lurie would own the team himself, independently and outright.[35] By late spring, the paperwork completed and the funds released, Lurie severed ties with Herseth and became sole owner of the team. It was perhaps inevitable, given the "odd couple" nature of their relationship, even though throughout the process of the buyout each spoke respectfully of the other. In the end, Herseth seemed to have tired of baseball culture, its decorum, and its traditional and customary ways of doing business. Nonetheless, despite his unconventional fit among the owners, he should be remembered as an important contributor at a crucial time in the story of Giants baseball in San Francisco. One could speculate that without his dramatic eleventh-hour entry into the 1976 sale of the Giants, the team might have moved to Toronto after all.

After Herseth's departure, Lurie devoted his attention to improving his ball club. Things turned sour after the breakout year in 1978, both on and off the field. Richardson traded a disaffected Bill Madlock halfway through the 1979 season, a move that sent reverberations throughout the clubhouse. By September, both Blue and Montefusco were threatening reporters, and players in general were at odds with Altobelli. Lurie and Richardson felt that drastic action was needed, and they fired Altobelli with four weeks to go in the season and replaced him with Dave Bristol.[36]

The change in manager may have quieted the clubhouse, but it did little to change the fortunes of the Giants on the field. They were 71-91 in 1979, eighteen games worse than in 1978. They struggled again in 1980, finishing fifth in the NL West, seventeen games out of first place. Again, Lurie changed his leadership, this time both his manager and his general manager, hoping for some success. For the 1981 campaign, he replaced Bristol with Frank Robinson and, midseason, Spec Richardson with Tom Haller, a former Giants player in the 1960s. The Giants signed free agent Joe Morgan in February and traded Mike Ivie to Houston for outfielder Jeffrey Leonard in early April; they brought up rookie Chili Davis to give them depth. The moves provided almost instant results on the field, as the Giants began playing winning baseball again. In the 1981 strike-shortened seasons the Giants were 56-55. But it was in the 1982 season that the team showed dramatic improvement.

The 1982 ball club featured a good mixture of veterans in future Hall of Famer Joe Morgan and former Dodger Reggie Smith—both of them frequent All-Stars—and young players like future All-Stars Chili Davis and Atlee Hammaker. The fiery, no-nonsense Hall of Famer Frank Robinson, the first African American to manage in the big leagues, was a great competitor and a proven winner; he won two world championships in his playing days, and he was named MVP of the NL as a Cincinnati Red in 1961 and MVP of the AL and of the World Series with Baltimore in 1966.[37] His reputation preceded him, and he infused an attitude among the players to compete, play hard, and hate losing. His leadership style was infectious. The Giants surprised the league, contending the entire season, going down to the wire in the NL West, finishing two games out of first place, with a 87-75 record.

Hank Greenwald, the radio voice of the Giants through most of the Lurie years, noticed the change in team chemistry on the 1982 team almost immediately, especially with the management style of Robinson and the influence of veterans like Morgan and Smith on the younger players. "These were guys who were used to something better, who were used to winning, who had played on championship teams. They made the other players change their attitudes, and even their style of play. This certainly had an effect on the Giants' standings."[38]

Attitudes changed no doubt for 1982, but the lack of sufficient talent remained. Morgan and Smith were aging stars and would soon retire.

Robinson's intense managerial style strained relationships among the younger players who, less talented than their mentors, were pushing and struggling to succeed. After 1982, the Giants would revert to their losing ways. The 1983 team went 79-83, finishing fifth in their division, twelve games out of first place. The 1984 team was worse, starting poorly—by June 7, they were 17-36—and never recovering, causing a desperate Lurie to fire Robinson midseason in 1984, replacing him with interim manager Danny Ozark. The replacement had no effect in the win column, as the Giants finished 66-96. Hoping to stop the bleeding, Lurie brought in old-time Giants favorite Jim Davenport for the 1985 season. Davenport, one of the original San Francisco Giants, played his entire career with the Giants and worked as a Giants coach after his retirement in 1970. His popularity and Giants bona fides did not help him as the team's manager, however. During his tenure the Giants hit rock bottom, losing one hundred games for the first time in all of Giants history, both in New York and San Francisco.

Despite all of these moves—six managers and two general managers in Lurie's first ten years—the Giants were mired near the bottom of their division year after year. For all of Lurie's attempts to improve his organization, he could count only two regular-season winning records since he bought the club.[39] A frustrated Lurie was at his wits' end. In mid-August of 1985, he decided to seek advice from an old friend, Al Rosen, a man he had come to know well over the years at various baseball meetings. He admired Rosen's intelligence and his experience in the game but also his candor.[40] Lurie knew that his friend, a former All-Star third baseman for Cleveland and the American League MVP in 1953, a former stockbroker, and an experienced baseball executive with the Yankees and with the Astros, would speak to him openly and honestly about the business of baseball in general, and about the Giants in particular. In reaching out to Rosen, Lurie gained considerably more than sound advice. The move would prove to be of monumental significance, resulting in profound changes, not only for Lurie personally but also for the future of the Giants organization.

NINE

The Humm Babies

"You Gotta Like These Kids!"

In early September 1985, when Bob Lurie placed a phone call to Houston Astros general manager Al Rosen, he hoped to get some advice on what had become for him a worrisome topic: the future of the Giants in San Francisco. First and foremost, he was discouraged by the performance of his team in the current NL West division race. The Giants were in the last month of what would become the first one-hundred-loss season in their storied history. While that number was staggering, it was not in itself the chief source of Lurie's dissatisfaction; rather he was vexed by the persistent climate of losing during his ownership. With only two regular-season winning teams over the past ten years, he had grown weary of finishing at or near the bottom of the division. For once, he would like to enjoy the excitement of postseason play, something he had not experienced in all of his time as owner.

Though paramount, winning was not Lurie's only concern. He was increasingly aggravated by his team's venue, Candlestick Park. Although he had accepted its deficiencies as inevitable when he bought the team, especially its inhospitable weather and the lack of any charm, he grew more convinced with each succeeding year of the effect of Candlestick on both the Giants' performance at home, and, as a consequence, the attendance. At first, he tried cosmetics, including better food choices, pregame entertainment, and some promotions invented by Pat Gallagher, the Giants' marketing director. Fans who braved the elements and remained for extra innings of a night game received the "Croix de Candlestick" button with an iced-over

SF logo and the inscription "Veni, Vedi, Vixi" (I came, I saw, I survived), worn as a badge of honor by those fans who received them. Perhaps the most outlandish promotion Gallagher introduced was the Crazy Crab, who premiered in April 1984. Intended as an anti-mascot to satirize other ball clubs' mascots and give the fans a focus for their disaffection (the Giants lost eighty-three games in 1983 and would lose ninety-six in the '84 season), Crazy Crab was a notorious success. The promotion encouraged the fans to project their frustrations toward the Crab and boo him. Within weeks, however, the boos turned dangerous. Fans began throwing things at the Crab, the hostility increased, and the promotion had to be dropped.[1]

In addition to addressing food and promotions, the Giants also attended to the building itself, making improvements where they could. Restrooms were painted and refurbished and concession stand access made more efficient. A plan for space heaters had to be rejected because of the prohibitive costs. Yet all the efforts at improving atmosphere at Candlestick could not disguise the fact that the place was at root both unsuitable for baseball and inhospitable for fans. Lurie yearned for a new facility closer to downtown.

As Lurie wrestled with his ballpark woes and considered possibilities for a new venue closer to downtown, he also fretted over his organization. Drawing on his business experience, he attempted improvement at almost every level of the administrative team, from player personnel to front-office staffing; yet his actions had little effect on the club's performance. Lurie began his restructuring at the very top. In 1979, after severing ties with Bud Herseth, he was able to make changes more easily as the sole owner. Building and rebuilding the team through post-Herseth trades and promotions brought little success in the standings, however. Lurie then looked at his management, both team managers and general managers, making changes when he thought it might do some good. After five years with Spec Richardson, he hired Tom Haller to become his GM. He also changed field managers at an astonishing pace, six in his first ten years as owner. By midsummer 1985, however, his efforts had borne only occasional success. From 1976 to 1985, the Giants finished near or at the bottom of their division, with only occasional rises to the middle as a winning team, once in 1978 and again in 1982.[2] The last time the Giants had reached postseason play was in 1971, when Stoneham was nearing the end of his ownership. Lurie hoped to end the playoff drought by reorganization, but despite his best intentions, nothing worked. Some conjectured that the frequency of change in the Giants organization might have made matters worse.[3]

Aside from organizational problems, Lurie felt the Giants had to address a public relations issue and their connection with the fan base. San Francisco had become a football town. The city was obsessed with the recent success of the 49ers, who won two Super Bowl championships—one in 1982 and another in 1985—and whose players and coaches were household names among Bay Area residents.[4] One writer argues that the city's obsession with the football team was therapeutic, transforming a cultural malaise. David Talbot, in his history of the social upheaval in San Francisco from the late 1960s to the mid-1980s, describes the city at the end of the 1970s as downtrodden, its spirit crushed by the social unrest and sensational violence of the times.[5] Talbot argues that the 49ers of the 1980s offered the city a chance for "a sense of ecstatic communion," allowing it "to exorcise its demons" by giving its citizens something to cheer about.[6]

> The 49ers were no longer the property of the Faithful. The team was starting to be embraced in every corner of the city. There was something about brainy, brooding Coach Walsh and his band of misfits that struck a chord with the city. Walsh's 49ers seemed like an only-in-San Francisco phenomenon, but in the best possible way.[7]

No mention of the role that the 1982 Giants played in bringing joy to an unsettled and saddened community appears in Talbot's account, although many of the sportswriters commented on the excitement that the team generated among Bay Area fans that year, enough to merit some mention of a contribution to the idea of communal well-being.[8] His slight of the Giants notwithstanding, Talbot's sense of the city's connection with the 49ers cannot be denied. Certainly Lurie was aware of the 49ers' appeal, and it brought even more pressure to improve his ball club so he could compete for a share of the sports market in a town that loved a winner.[9]

All of these concerns were on Lurie's mind when he turned to his friend Al Rosen for some advice and a sense of direction for the future.[10] Lurie sought out others as well, fellow owners he had befriended such as Bud Selig and Jerry Reinsdorf, but he had a special interest in what Rosen might say, given his unique background as a player, a baseball executive, and a businessman. Lurie explained that he planned to make a change at general manager, replacing Tom Haller, and asked Rosen about possible candidates. Rosen suggested some names; they also discussed the importance of instilling a winning philosophy in the organization and of finding the right individuals to foster that attitude. After the call, Lurie reflected on the importance of the new direction that Rosen raised but also on the recognition that there would be hard work ahead in finding the right individuals to facilitate change.[11]

Lurie's and the Giants' fortunes changed definitively a few days later when national newspapers reported that Houston Astros' owner John McMullen wanted to clean house and take his organization in a new direction.[12] Lurie read that Al Rosen, as the GM of the ball club, would be among those likely to be swept up in the housecleaning. The same day, it was Lurie's turn to receive a phone call from Rosen. The message Rosen delivered was simple and succinct: "Don't forget about me."[13] Those words suggested not only Rosen's availability for Lurie's opening but also his interest in the Giants' position.

The next forty-eight hours were packed with furious activity. On September 13, McMullen announced that Dick Wagner would replace Rosen as the Astros GM.[14] Lurie moved quickly. In Houston, ostensibly to be with the team on a road swing but in actuality to interview Rosen, Lurie received permission from McMullen to talk to his former GM.[15] At their meeting Lurie offered Rosen the joint position of president and general manager of the Giants. In what amounted to a significant organizational reshuffling, Lurie would serve as chairman of the Giants, deferring to his new president in all matters about baseball with one caveat. Whenever Rosen made a deal, Lurie wanted to be informed personally; he didn't want to read about it the news-papers.[16] Rosen was happy to accept.[17]

The working relationship between Chairman Lurie and President Rosen would remain smooth, straightforward, efficient, respectful, and friendly throughout their time together running the Giants orga-nization. Their first move was emblematic of their successful collab-oration. On the morning of September 14, the two men called Roger Craig, a person whom Rosen admired for his leadership, his com-petitive spirit, and his record as a player and coach. They offered Craig the job of Giants manager.[18] Craig said he would consider it but needed to talk to his wife, and that he would give them his deci-sion in twenty-four hours. Only a few hours later, Rosen was back on the phone again, telling Craig that he wanted him to start at once, so that the two of them could use the remainder of the 1985 season to do some evaluations for the makeup of the 1986 team. Craig agreed to come, even though it meant that he would begin his career as Giants manager with a losing ball club.

Craig flew out to San Francisco with Rosen, was introduced as the new manager, and immediately started working.[19] His first day on the job was September 18, at a night game at Candlestick in which the Giants beat the Padres 9–6, before a crowd of 2,668. His Giants would finish 6-12 for the remainder of the season. He did very little managing. He introduced himself to the players, turned in the lineup card each game, and spent most of his time observing. Bob Brenly, the everyday catcher for the 1985 Giants, remembers the effect of Craig's persona. "He was a formidable presence, big, imposing, and he was looking at everyone as a player. You had a sense that you were playing for your future."[20] Every night until the season ended, Craig and Rosen would review the game, evaluate players, and discuss the potential composition of next year's team.[21]

With this double-hire, Lurie ushered in one of the most successful, entertaining, colorful, and popular eras in San Francisco Giants his-tory, a period from 1986 to 1992 that would be designated as "Humm Baby" baseball. Rosen and Craig formed a great partnership, and both men were in complete agreement about the kind of baseball they expected from their players. It was the kind of baseball that they themselves had played. Rosen was a tough, tenacious power hitter and infielder for Cleveland in the late 1940s and early 1950s, a time when the Indians were regularly pushing the Yankees for supremacy in the American League. He played as though he carried a chip on his shoulder, due to his highly competitive nature, his aggressive play, and, perhaps to some degree, having to endure anti-Semitic remarks aimed at him. Rosen grew up in Miami, in Little Havana, in the only Jewish family in the neighborhood. He learned to be tough from an early age defending himself against ethnic slurs. Nor did this stop when he got to the big leagues. On a famous occasion, Rosen, who had been heckled as a Jew during a game by the opposing team, went over to their dugout and challenged the speaker to a fight. No one emerged and the remarks stopped.[22] Craig was also a proven winner, at every level of his baseball career. He won three world championships as a pitcher—two with the Dodgers, 1955 in Brooklyn and 1959 in Los Angeles, and one with St. Louis in 1964—and was the pitching coach on the 1984 Detroit Tigers world championship team. Rosen and Craig believed in playing hard-nosed baseball and expected their players to be like-minded.

The Giants of 1986 started spring training with a sense of the new. The first day of camp opened with words from Al Rosen about winning, hustle, commitment, and turning adversity into an asset. Twenty-five years later, Rosen clearly recalled his message at his first team meeting with the Giants. "I told the players that I didn't come here to lose[,] . . . that I wanted players who felt the way I did. Roger and I had to let the players know what was expected of them and what they could expect from us. Once we got that straight, everything changed."[23] It was then left to Craig, as manager, to put Rosen's remarks into practice and to impart his own blend of enthusiasm and competitiveness to his players, a blend of wily veterans like Jeffrey Leonard, Bob Brenly, and Mike Krukow and rookies like Will Clark and Robby Thompson. Craig's method was to marry instruction and advice with optimism and encouragement. He always stressed the positive side, particularly in his observations of excellent play. When he saw one of his players do something spectacular or noteworthy, he would let everyone know about it with a special call, "Humm Baby!"

By the second week of camp, players were becoming accustomed to hearing their manager single out great play and hustle with a loud "Humm Baby!" Robby Thompson, a rookie that year, recalls that the phrase caught on through Craig's continuous and ubiquitous application.

> Roger was always using the phrase whenever there was a good play or a good effort, a humm baby hit, a humm baby catch, a humm baby slide, a humm baby throw. And it even referred to players; so-and-so was a humm baby. Soon we all were trying to live up to the Humm Baby standard. Once in spring training he spotted a good-looking girl in the stands and he called over to me, "Hey Thompson, that's a humm baby sitting over there behind third."[24]

Sportswriters covering spring training eventually wanted to clarify matters with Craig about his pet phrase. A group of them gathered around his desk after one of the early spring training games to ask what exactly did "Humm Baby" mean. His answer didn't explain much.

> I'm not sure what it really means. I just say "That was a 'humm baby' play" after a guy breaks up a double play. It can mean anything. It exemplifies the kind of players I have. He might not have the most ability, but he gives 180 percent.[25]

While Craig's explanation left the writers to puzzle out meaning, and perhaps attempt to fathom the concept of 180 percent, there was no confusion among those who followed the Giants that spring about the change in attitude among the players, nor about the hierarchical nature of the Humm Baby philosophy, from Lurie, who gave Rosen free rein; from Rosen, who gave Craig the authority on the field; and from Craig, who brought the Humm Baby spirit to the players. The organization seemed transformed. Nor was there any mistaking the change in the players' performance. Rookies and veterans alike were playing good, hard-nosed, intense baseball and having fun doing it. Looking back on that time from the vantage point of twenty-five years later, Mike Krukow, one of the veteran pitchers on the Giants, saw the Humm Baby atmosphere as a unique moment of spontaneous combustion. "Once in a while, a group comes together and commits to one another. The chemistry started in the managers' ranks—Al Rosen sparking Roger Craig, who is so upbeat that he changes attitudes."[26] Outfielder Brett Butler who joined the Humm Babies in 1988 after seven years in the big leagues had no trouble accepting Craig's philosophy because it translated into wins. "It was not about individuals; it was about the team."

"Humm Baby" may have denoted the team collectively, but there was, according to Craig, a single genuine Humm Baby player. His name was Brad Gulden, and he was a well-traveled journeyman player who came to the Giants' spring training with only a sliver of a chance to make the club. Gulden broke in with the Dodgers in 1978, played with the Yankees (1979–80), the Mariners (1981), the Expos (1982), and the Reds (1984). When he signed with the Giants in December of 1985, he knew that his playing career was nearing the end. He also sensed that as a backup catcher, he had only a remote chance of sticking with a club that had Bob Brenly as the regular catcher and Bob Melvin as his replacement. Nonetheless, Gulden went to spring training to compete for a job and to go all out in the process. It came down to the last day of spring training, when he was summoned to Roger Craig's office. Gulden recalled that Craig told him he made the team and that he was the Humm Baby![27]

Craig explained that Gulden was the perfect exemplum of a Humm Baby player and that was why he got that designation.

> He was a gutsy player and really hustled. He wasn't the most skilled of the players, but Brad worked hard and always gave it his all. When I called him in at the end of spring training to tell him he made the ball club I said "Brad you made it, you are the real Humm Baby." The guy symbolized what I meant by Humm Baby: he didn't have all the talent, but he had attitude and hustle.[28]

It turned out that Gulden's Humm Baby days with the Giants were brief. He played in only seventeen games, going 2-22, although he had a memorable Humm Baby moment on April 11, 1986, at Dodger Stadium, singling in the winning run with two outs in the twelfth inning of a 9–8 game. Besides his connection to the Humm Baby tag, he also features as a baseball trivia anomaly: he was traded for himself. In November 1980, the Yankees sent Gulden and some cash to the Mariners for a player to be named later. The following May, the Mariners sent Gulden back to New York as that player.[29]

The Humm Baby attitude and play stuck with the Rosen-Craig Giants, even if Gulden did not. As might be expected, rookies like Will Clark, Robby Thompson, and, a year later, Matt Williams, players with no big league history, quickly accepted the Humm Baby style as normal, but even seasoned veterans like Jeffrey Leonard, Bob Brenly, Mike Krukow, and Greg Minton bought in. Craig knew he would need veteran support for his idea and approached Leonard. He was also looking for a clubhouse leader and thought Leonard, whose reputation as a no-nonsense player preceded him, would be an ideal choice and could set the tone for hard-nosed hustle that was the hallmark of the Humm Baby mode. It turned out to be a great move on Craig's part. Leonard responded well to Craig's faith in him as a leader, and other veterans followed; the transition to the new Humm Baby attitude among the seasoned players went very smoothly.[30]

As the new season opened, Craig didn't have to apologize for his Humm Baby manner to either the players or the press. The 1986 Giants came out of the gate playing winning baseball and continued to do so throughout the season, especially in September, going 16-11, a good omen for the future. Under Rosen and Craig, the Humm Babies would finish 1986 at 83-79, third in their division, improving dramatically from the hundred-loss season the previous year. More reassuring for Lurie, the Giants drew 1,528,748 fans in 1986, nearly doubling the attendance from the disastrous 1985 season.[31]

As the Humm Babies developed and defined their style of play, the phrase began to resonate among Bay Area fans. Seizing the moment, Pat Gallagher launched a shrewd marketing plan for the Giants, identifying "Humm Baby" with a new brand of Giants' baseball. He developed the phrase "You gotta like these kids," referring not only to rookie standouts like Will Clark and Robby Thompson but also to the fresh, exuberant style of play redolent in the Humm Baby phrase, something one might hear in sandlots or at youth baseball all over the country. Promotions of Humm Baby gear gave the Giants visibility all over town. There were t-shirts, of course, in many versions of the Humm Baby logo. Caps and hats complete with the Humm Baby phrase were also occasional giveaways at homes games, as were posters featuring various players, underscored with the Humm Baby motto. There were pins, buttons, and even a bright orange kazoo, all of them prominently embossed with the words "Humm Baby." As the Giants continued to win over the next few years, the Humm Baby paraphernalia, including bumper stickers, spread through the Bay Area. Gallagher could sense a shift in fan enthusiasm not only in the attendance but also in a growing demand for Humm Baby gear.[32]

The turnaround season of the 1986 Humm Babies marked the beginning of a great run for the Giants in what would be Lurie's remaining years of ownership. The year 1987 proved even better, finally ending a sixteen-year playoff drought. The Giants settled into first place on August 15, never relinquished their position, and won their division by six games. They would lose the divisional playoff to St. Louis in an exciting back-and-forth seven-game series. Nonetheless, the Humm Babies had sent notice to the rest of the league that winning baseball was back in San Francisco; they also felt, throughout the organization, that their best was yet to come. It didn't take long for them to prove their point. After another winning season in 1988—going 83-79 but with a fourth-place finish, eleven games behind division leader Los Angeles—the Giants were poised for a breakout year and Lurie's crowning moment as an owner.

When he was interviewed for Ken Burns's epic history of baseball for PBS television, Roger Angell singled out 1989 as "the worst year in baseball." Angell's reasons for his dour view included the Pete Rose betting scandal and his subsequent ban from baseball, the death of Commissioner Bart Giamatti in September (viewed by some as a result of stress brought about his decision on Rose), and the Loma Prieta earthquake that disrupted and delayed the World Series in the

Bay Area, all of which he felt brought great harm to the game.[33] With the inclusion of the last example, it would be difficult for Bay Area fans to agree with Angell on the 1989 season. Certainly, Loma Prieta put baseball in perspective. Sixty-seven people lost their lives during the quake on October 17, 1989; the destruction of homes, buildings, bridges, and freeways totaled over five billion dollars in damages.[34] The quake also forced the World Series into a strange two-part play-off, the third and fourth games in San Francisco separated from the first and second games in Oakland by twelve days. Nonetheless, for Bay Area fans, the 1989 baseball season that led up to the World Series was the polar opposite of Roger Angell's view of "worst year"; rather, it was truly magical. For the first time since baseball came west in 1958, two teams from the same metropolitan region would be playing for a world championship.[35] It also proved to be the highpoint of Humm Baby baseball, bringing great satisfaction to Rosen, Craig, and especially Bob Lurie.

In what turned out to be a monumental year not only for the ball club but also for individual players, 1989 marked the second time in their San Francisco history that the Giants would win the NL pennant. As is often the case with pennant-winning clubs, many of the Giants' players had their best years, including Kevin Mitchell, who led the league with 47 HR and 125 RBI and was the 1989 NL Most Valuable Player; Will Clark, who finished second to Mitchell in the MVP balloting and second in the NL batting race; pitcher Scott Garrelts, whose 2.28 ERA led the NL; and forty-year-old Rick Reuschel, "Big Daddy," who would win seventeen games, with a 2.94 ERA, and be named to the NL 1989 All-Star game. Matt Williams, sent down on May 2 to Triple-A Phoenix to work on mechanics—he was hitting .130 with 18 strikeouts in 54 at bats—was recalled on July 23; he finished the remaining sixty-three games with 16 home runs and 46 RBIS, demonstrating the caliber of play that would make him a future All-Star. It was a great year to be a Humm Baby!

Al Rosen was having a good year as well, actively engaged in the trading game to give his team an edge. In the winter of 1988, he sent Mike Aldrete to Montreal for Tracy Jones. Jones got off to a middling start in 1989, and on June 16 Rosen sent him to Detroit for Pat Sheridan, who would be a regular for the rest of the season. The next day, still in a trading mood, Rosen sent young pitching prospects Dennis Cook, Charlie Hayes, and Terry Mulholland to the Philadelphia Phillies in exchange for All-Star closer Steve Bedrosian. Bedrosian proved to be the reliable closer needed for the stretch run, saving seventeen games for the Giants. Besides working the trading lines, the tireless Giants GM was keeping his eye on the farm system in Phoenix, monitoring especially the progress of Williams, who appeared to be terrorizing Triple-A pitching. After a trip there in mid-July, Rosen decided Williams would be back in San Francisco before too long. He also was watching baseball's waiver wires, and when Toronto released former Giants catcher Bob Brenly, Rosen pounced. Brenly was signed on September 2, primarily to provide leadership, knowledge, and perspective as the Giants edged closer and closer to a divisional title, which they secured on September 27.

Bob Lurie celebrated his second divisional title in three years, but the best was yet to come. In the NL playoffs, the Giants faced the Chicago Cubs, against whom they had split the season's head-to-head games, 6–6. In a tense series, the Giants won in five games, 4–1, two of them decided in the last innings, by one run. For the second time since coming to the West Coast, and after a twenty-seven-year wait, the Giants were going to the World Series. Lurie was giddy over his Humm Babies.

The 1989 World Series, initially dubbed "Bays Ball," opened in the Oakland Coliseum, home of the AL Champion Oakland A's. With two teams from either side of San Francisco Bay, it had the feel of those many "subway series" in New York City when either the Giants or the Dodgers would cross the river to play the Yankees. After Oakland took the first two games, the scene shifted to Candlestick Park and San Francisco, where the Giants would be the home team. At a few minutes after five o'clock on October 17, just prior to game three, everything changed. The Loma Prieta earthquake struck Northern California, sending violent tremors throughout San Francisco and

Oakland, causing widespread destruction, rendering even the idea of a World Series game inconsequential.

Much has been written about the "earthquake series"—the term "Bays Ball" no longer appropriate given the turn of events—from so many perspectives that Loma Prieta is perhaps the most documented of any American natural disaster. Set up for World Series coverage, television gave instantaneous pictures as the event unfolded, especially of the stadium and those in it, even though the actual fifteen seconds of the quake compromised the transmission. The concentration of journalists in and around Candlestick Park for the game assured that the disaster would receive significant attention. The nation watched an exodus of players and officials from the two ball clubs, stadium workers, and over sixty thousand spectators from Candlestick Park, which survived the quake with only the slightest of damage. Sports-writers shifted their baseball coverage to the wider destruction of neighborhoods in San Francisco and freeways and bridges in the East Bay. Newspapers were full of articles and pictures; local radio commentators carried on-the-spot reporting on some of the hard-hit buildings and roads and the Bay Bridge.[36]

For the next twelve days both cities scrambled as they dealt with the destruction; baseball was put on hold. Commissioner Fay Vincent and San Francisco mayor Art Agnos were in constant communication, but it was clear that concern for those who had lost their lives, those who were injured, and the enormous property damage had a higher priority than the rescheduling of game three of the World Series. Ballplayers and team officials on both clubs expressed their feelings about loss and damage, and some became involved in relief work. Dave Stewart, who grew up in Oakland, was among the A's who reached out; Bob Lurie led a contingent, including Al Rosen and Matt Williams, to the Moscone Center to visit some who had been displaced by the earthquake.[37]

After a day or two off, the two ball clubs tried to stay sharp with batting practices and simulated games, but neither had any idea when play would resume again. Finally, after a thorough inspection of Candlestick Park that allowed city engineers to pronounce the building sound, Agnos and Vincent agreed on Friday, October 27, to resume the Series. It was thought by many with the ball clubs, and by city officials on both sides of the bay, that the resumption of the World Series would offer the possibility of a return to routine and normalcy, and even a chance for both communities to heal.[38]

Given the proximity of the damage and the destruction, the games themselves seemed almost anticlimactic. More meaningful and significant was the fact the World Series would be played at all. A crowd of sixty-two thousand filled Candlestick Park and stood in silence at the beginning of game three to honor those who lost their lives and to acknowledge the devastation in both communities. Then, following the lyrics handed out upon entrance, the crowd sang in unison the song "San Francisco," which celebrates the recovery of the city from the 1906 earthquake.[39]

Games three and four at Candlestick followed the script of the first two games in Oakland, showing the dominance of the A's. With the long break between games, A's manager Tony LaRussa reinserted his starters from games one and two: Stewart and Mike Moore. The Giants' pitching staff could not match up. Scott Garrelts was knocked out of game three in the third inning when a Mark McGwire line drive hit him in the elbow. Rick Reuschel was scratched as a game four starter after being hit in the right shoulder by a line drive during batting practice. That left Don Robinson, whose knees and left hamstring were so painful that he had not started a game since September 25. Oakland's bats continued to make noise, while the Giants hitters went quiet. The A's cruised in both remaining games and swept the Giants, who were never in the Series. Afterward, a subdued Roger Craig admitted the A's were better, especially in their pitching.[40] Giants hitting coach Dusty Baker pointed to the obvious: "They were a better team than us; they had better pitching, hitting and team speed."[41]

Roger Angell might have been right about the 1989 World Series, even without the earthquake. It certainly wasn't a competitive Series. Statistical evidence shows that it was among the most lopsided ever played.[42] But there were aspects about the Series that were truly remarkable, as baseball historian Gary Peterson notes.

> The "modest little game" that commissioner Fay Vincent spoke about united people. It healed. It became part of an important discussion on grieving, resilience, and getting back to a normal way of life. It is almost certain that the intense interest in the originally scheduled Game 3 saved lives because countless would-be commuters were in front of their TV sets and therefore not in harm's way.[43]

As it turned out, the 1989 World Series, as one-sided as it was, marked the zenith for Bob Lurie's Humm Babies. The Giants played winning baseball in 1990, a respectable 85-77, but finished in third place in their division, six games off the pace. After five straight years, 1990 would be the last winning season for the Humm Babies. The next two years were filled with disappointments, especially off the field in Lurie's unsuccessful attempts to find a new Bay Area home for the Giants. By midseason 1992, weary of his Candlestick troubles, a frustrated Lurie signaled the end of the Humm Baby era when he announced that he would be open to offers from anyone interested in buying the Giants. Once again, the Giants' connection with the city of San Francisco appeared fragile and tenuous.

While the Humm Babies slumped and slid in their last two years, their overall record was quite impressive. Under Rosen and Craig, Giants baseball from 1986 to 1992 would have to be labeled highly successful, the 1989 World Series blowout defeat notwithstanding. Craig's record as the Giants' manager was 586-566, including his last three weeks in 1985, the year the team lost one hundred games. During that seven-year period, the Humm Babies had more wins in their division than any team except Cincinnati. They were in the postseason playoffs twice and won one National League pennant. More important, they brought the fans back to Candlestick and were able to keep pace with the 49ers for local attachment and loyalty. The Humm Baby Giants drew some of the team's biggest San Francisco crowds. In the pennant-winning year, the Giants drew 2,059,701, the larg-

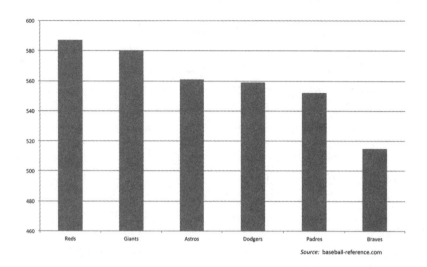

Graph 2. Total Wins: National League Western Division, 1986–1992

Source: baseball-reference.com

est home gate since the Giants moved west in 1958, and home attendance between 1986 and 1992 never dipped below 1,500,000. The
support of the fans during the Humm Baby years would not be lost
on many in the San Francisco business community. The enthusiasm
for Giants baseball, manifested by healthy Humm Baby attendance
figures, would prove to be a crucial factor for local investors when
they learned that the Giants were on the market and Bob Lurie was
looking for a buyer.

TEN

Vox Populi

The success Bob Lurie enjoyed on the field with the Humm Babies was offset by his mounting vexation in trying to solve the dilemma of Candlestick Park. Initially, he pursued the notion that selective renovations and upgrades could be made to resolve nagging problems like the playing conditions and fan discomfort. After a few cosmetic alterations, however, he realized that attempts at improving the facilities could never change the fundamental issue: it was a terrible place to play baseball. Beginning in 1980, he engaged in continual dialogue with the city on how to address his concerns. He would end up joining with three successive mayors of San Francisco over twelve years—Dianne Feinstein, Art Agnos, and Frank Jordan—to work out improvements for Candlestick but could not gain any commitment from city hall on funding. He even tried leaving. He hatched various plans to temporarily locate elsewhere, in Oakland, or in Denver, while working on proposals for a new park downtown or on the Peninsula. In moments of frustration over what he perceived to be the slow bureaucratic pace of city hall, he would announce that the Giants would not play in Candlestick beyond the current season, or that they would move to another venue, or, once more practical matters about moving sunk in, that they would not renew their lease with the city once it expired in 1994.[1] These threats fell on deaf ears. Try as he might, he could never remedy his stadium problem. He felt as if Candlestick were the proverbial albatross around his neck.

Of course, Lurie was not original with his complaints about Candlestick; he was merely one more in a long line of those who had noted its deficiencies. Generations of players had been critical of the place from the time it opened. Sportswriters, too, visitors as well as locals, complained over the years. Even politicians had been critical; when asked why he was against spending city money to improve Candlestick Park, former San Francisco mayor Joseph Alioto once remarked, "It would be perpetuating mediocrity."[2] Some observers, like play-by-play broadcaster Hank Greenwald, who spent sixteen years at Candlestick as the voice of the Giants, dreaded his nights there and suggested the place might be haunted. In a chapter of his autobiography entitled "The Curse of Candlestick," Greenwald muses on an urban legend about Charlie Harney, the man who built Candlestick Park.[3] As the legend goes, when Harney learned that the stadium he was building would not be named after him, he lost interest in the project, missing deadlines in construction that led to cost cutting in the finishing touches to the building. Because of the rancor that followed—complaints from the city engineers that eventually developed into lawsuits and countersuits—Harney became disgusted with the place. Not only did he never attend a game there, but he also cursed it. Greenwald imagines that those who listen closely to the winds that howl around the ballpark at night can hear Harney's eerie laughter.[4]

Harney's curse is only the most prominent of a number of hexes rumored to have plagued Candlestick. One, called "the Nixon curse," goes back to the very beginning, when then–vice president Richard Nixon threw out the first pitch opening the park in April 1960 and proclaimed Candlestick "the finest ball park in America."[5] Another alludes to classical epic poetry: "the curse of Aeolus," named after the powerful king of the winds in Homer's *Odyssey*, accounts for Candlestick's most infamous elemental feature.[6] In baseball lore, the application of curses like these provides an explanation for any number of things: long periods of misfortune, such as the Giants' woes at Candlestick; players' attitudes, losing seasons, and especially spectacular failures, such as the 1993 division race when, despite winning 103 games, the Giants did not qualify for postseason play; or the only two World Series played at Candlestick (1962 and 1989) being beset by what the lawyers term "acts of God," natural forces so severe as to interrupt or cancel events.[7]

It is unlikely that Bob Lurie—a practical businessman—granted any credence to curses or hauntings.[8] Nonetheless, he was certainly tormented during his time at Candlestick. It wasn't simply the Giants' futility in playing there that bothered him; rather, it was his inability to solve Candlestick's challenges that posed the single most exasperating problem during his ownership. He also understood that moving out of Candlestick would not be easy. With the long-term lease with the city that he inherited when he bought the team, he could not leave without the involvement and ultimate approval of the mayor and the board of supervisors on behalf of the San Francisco taxpayers. To build a new ballpark, he knew that he would have to go before the voters.

He started to address the ballpark's problems in occasional talks with San Francisco mayor Dianne Feinstein, who had succeeded George Moscone after his assassination. Their conversations ranged from improvements at Candlestick to proposals for a new playing venue somewhere closer to downtown. Feinstein, while sympathetic to the Giants' situation, had difficulty moving the ball club's needs beyond the discussion stage with the board of supervisors. Nonetheless, she made some attempts to do so. The Giants released a commissioned report on Candlestick to the mayor's office in May 1981 that labeled the facility "unfit for baseball."[9] After receiving the report, Feinstein empaneled a task force to study the observations and to make recommendations to the board of supervisors.[10] The task force came up with two suggestions: one was a plan to dome the stadium, and the other was the construction of a new ballpark. The latter would cost almost $135 million and require the city to find a suitable parcel of land. The former, pegged at about $60 million, included a massive remodeling concept to accommodate both the Giants and the 49ers.[11] The dome/remodeling concept was met with owners' disapproval; Lurie rejected the dome idea as too costly, and 49ers owner Eddie DeBartolo refused to invest in any remaking of Candlestick, calling it beyond repair.[12] Feinstein floated the possibility of a new facility near the Bay Bridge (1985) or near Moscone Center south of Market Street (1986), but both of these would fail due to more pressing demands on the city's coffers.

Lurie was also in conversation with San Mateo County officials, hoping to get approval for a new ballpark near the Bay Meadows Race Track, even though this would take the Giants farther south, fifteen to twenty miles from downtown San Francisco. San Mateo County offered a twelve-acre parcel for a new ballpark where parking could be shared with the racetrack. In the end, however, the San Mateo County Board of Supervisors rejected the proposal.[13] While they liked the idea of hosting the Giants, county officials could not reconcile themselves to the necessary changes to roads and highways that a new ballpark would demand.[14]

Undaunted, Lurie continued to explore options. During the summer of the dismal 1985 season, he flirted with selling to Peter Stocker, owner of the Pacific Union Company, offering a portion of the team if he could secure a downtown San Francisco venue that would allow the Giants to leave Candlestick. Stocker proposed acquiring land in the Rincon Hill district west of the Embarcadero and financing a new ballpark.[15] If Stocker could make headway, Lurie would propose leaving Candlestick prior to the 1986 season and playing for a "rent-out" period in Denver for three years while the new stadium was under construction.[16] Mention of this scheme brought some NL heavyweights to town, including President Chub Feeney and an advisory subcommittee consisting of owners Peter O'Malley (Dodgers), Ballard Smith (Padres), and Bill Giles (Phillies) to consult with the Giants on their stadium problems.[17] As it turned out, the league's input was unnecessary. In early November the agreement between Lurie and Stocker fell apart over Stocker's financing sources. His funding for the construction of the ballpark relied heavily upon the sale of fifteen thousand box charter seats, revenue that would be unavailable for operational expenses for the ball club. Lurie rejected the proposal out of necessity. In all likelihood NL owners would have done the same, since Stocker's funding source would have cut into the visiting team's share of the gate.[18]

Lurie's failure with Stocker kicked the proverbial can down the road to be dealt with later. The Giants would play the 1986 season in Candlestick Park. Some in the San Francisco baseball community, however, saw an encouraging sign in the otherwise disappointing Stocker affair. One writer reminded his readers that Lurie saved the team once by stopping it from moving to Toronto; now his efforts with Stocker demonstrated that same hometown loyalty. Rather than shop the team to out-of-town (or even out-of-state) buyers, Lurie chose to work with Stocker specifically because of his pledge to keep the team in San Francisco.[19] The decision to stay put in Candlestick after the Stocker partnership collapsed was further proof of that loyalty.

Putting the Stocker disappointment behind him, Lurie launched an idea of playing his home games in Oakland and sharing the Coliseum with the A's, primarily in the hopes that the San Francisco Board of Supervisors might feel some sense of urgency and take action on a new downtown ballpark. With the Giants across the bay, the City of San Francisco would be out the rent from Candlestick that the team's home games provided. The Oakland transfer, proposed with no specific date in mind but rather in the "near future," was merely a feint on Lurie's part since it carried serious impracticalities: its implementation would require compromises and adjustments on the part of both baseball and the municipal city governments. After a brief consideration, the Oakland Coliseum board of directors rejected Lurie's proposal as too complicated an adjustment to accommodate both the A's' and the Giants' schedules.[20] Meanwhile, Lurie announced that he would play "the next few seasons" at Candlestick while he looked into other options.[21]

Lurie's first genuine breakthrough came in August 1987 when Mayor Feinstein agreed to take the Giants' proposal for a new downtown stadium before the board of supervisors. After a lengthy debate, Feinstein joined with seven supervisors to put "Proposition W" before the voters in the November election. The sole purpose of Proposition W was to seek funding to support the construction of a new ballpark at Seventh and Townsend Streets.[22] At the press conference after the board of supervisors vote, both Feinstein and Lurie unveiled the design for the forty-two-thousand-seat stadium, explained the advantages of having baseball closer to downtown, and outlined a plan for repayment, chiefly from baseball revenues, which would minimize taxpayers' risk. The move showed considerable nerve on Feinstein's part, given the political risks. As one columnist described the climate around City Hall,

> Feinstein has some obvious problems in dealing with a downtown stadium. She faces an electorate that is lukewarm about baseball, and a Board of Supervisors that could not achieve a quorum if describing the shape of a baseball were a requirement.[23]

The campaigning for Proposition W followed predictable routes. Most of the coverage in the newspapers favored the proposal as both a solution to Candlestick and a chance to keep the Giants in San Francisco.[24] The *Chronicle* editorial board recommended a yes vote, as did the *Examiner*.[25] Most of the sportswriters of both papers favored the measure, as did the San Francisco Chamber of Commerce. Political reactions were more complicated. Mayor Feinstein, who was not running for reelection, backed Prop W, but some of her fellow politicos, including mayoral candidate Art Agnos, opposed the measure chiefly because of the Seventh and Townsend location, favoring instead a Third and Mission site, closer to downtown. The Sierra Club lined up against Prop W, as did neighborhood coalitions who varied in their objections, some against public funding for ballparks, others because they believed the Seventh and Townsend location lacked planning in regard to traffic. The election result was disappointing for Lurie and the Giants; Proposition W went down to defeat by a 53–47 percent margin, losing by eleven thousand votes.[26]

On the field, meanwhile, the Giants were enjoying great success and the fans were showing keen interest in the Humm Baby style of baseball. During the 1989 pennant-winning season, buoyed by fan enthusiasm and high attendance at home games, Lurie decided to go before the voters a second time with a new downtown stadium referendum, this one with the backing of newly elected mayor Agnos, who was pushing his favored site at Third and Mission for the Giants' ballpark. At a joint press conference on July 27, Mayor Agnos and Lurie announced plans for a forty-five-thousand-seat stadium in

China Basin, at Second and Berry Streets.[27] With the help of Supervisor Wendy Nelder, a strong supporter of keeping the Giants in town, Agnos got the board of supervisors to approve Proposition P for the November election.[28] During the campaign, Lurie got an important concession from the board of supervisors when they approved a change in the Giants' lease at Candlestick, making it a year-to-year agreement rather than long term through 1994.[29] This change would prove to be important in allowing the Giants to leave town after a season, giving Lurie crucial leverage with the city. Those who favored Prop P used the new ruling to suggest that San Francisco might lose its team if the measure did not pass.

The campaign during the fall was helped by the successful run of the Giants, who won the NL pennant. World Series fever gripped the town, and the city warmed to its baseball team; those who favored the measure argued that its passing would ensure that the Giants would be around for a long time. Again, the newspapers touted their support for Prop P, so too the chamber of commerce, the League of Conservation Voters, the downtown business association, and a number of politicians, none more enthusiastically than Mayor Agnos, who gushed about how the new ballpark could be another of San Francisco's great tourist attractions.

> It won't just be a field with stands around it. . . . It'll be something unique to San Francisco with a great view of the bay, a fabulous place to go whether you are crazy about baseball or not. It'll be a spectacle.[30]

Other groups, considerably less enthusiastic than the mayor, opposed the measure. The Harvey Milk Lesbian and Gay Democratic Club rejected Prop P because the location would cut into possibilities for public housing. San Francisco Tomorrow, an environmental organization, argued against the construction of a ballpark that would add more congestion to an already crowded part of the city. Some neighborhood associations worried about property values in the south of the Market region.[31] Despite the opposition, however, polls taken in early fall indicated that the measure had a slight chance of passing.[32] In the hopes of strengthening the chances for approval, Lurie repeated his dissatisfaction with Candlestick, saying the Giants could not continue to play there.

The Proposition P campaign, along with everything else in the Bay Area, was radically transformed on October 17, 1989, at 5:04 pm. The Loma Prieta earthquake, centered about ten miles northeast of Santa Cruz and measuring 6.9 on the Richter scale, immediately changed the discussion about city budgeting and the construction of ballparks. Damage in the billions of dollars to roads, buildings, and infrastructure around the Bay Area, especially in both Oakland and San Francisco, would demand new priorities on public expenditures.[33] Agnos diverted most of his "Yes on P" campaign workers to the Red Cross for relief work, but he did not give up his support for the proposition. On the contrary, he insisted that the new ballpark was needed now, more than ever, both for economic reasons and for civic morale. In an open letter to the citizens of San Francisco he explained,

> I need to stimulate the economy. And construction of a new ball park will do that. And this election (Proposition P) will send a signal to the rest of the world that we believe in our future.[34]

A few days before the vote, a story broke about some underhanded opposition to Prop P that gave Agnos new talking points. Gregg Lukenbill, a wealthy Sacramento businessman, made a substantial contribution of $12,500 to the "No on P" organization. A few years earlier, Sacramento was considered as a possible home for the Giants if things did not work out in San Francisco. Agnos cried foul. He saw some deviousness in Lukenbill's political donation. The mayor cautioned the San Francisco electorate to be wary, suggesting that Lukenbill's activities could signal that Sacramento might again be considered as a possible home for the Giants if Prop P were turned down. The story had a short life in the press, where some picked up on the idea that Sacramento was trying to steal the Giants. Agnos simple repeated how important it would be to pass Prop P.[35]

On the evening of the election, the biggest surprises were the size of the voter turnout and the narrow difference in the decision. Despite the pressing needs of earthquake relief, over 173,000 San Franciscans voted and the margin was slightly fewer than 2,000 votes. Unfortunately for Lurie and the Giants, the "No on P" votes prevailed by a slim margin of 50.5 percent to 49.4 percent (86,592 against the measure, 84,618 for it). The results became clear late in the evening; Agnos and the "Yes on P" group conceded defeat four hours after the polls had closed. The vote marked the second time in three years that San Franciscans would say no to spending their tax dollars on a baseball stadium. A discouraged Lurie made a short exit speech at the campaign headquarters before heading home.

> Candlestick Park cannot stand as a long-term home to the Giants. I can say we'll stay at Candlestick next year, as planned. But after that, I cannot say. There are hundreds of thousands of fans who are deeply disappointed by the outcome. The Giants and their fans now face an uncertain future.[36]

No doubt intended as a perfunctory statement after an unfavorable result at the polls, Lurie's words were nonetheless remarkable in two ways: they served as a farewell to San Francisco in that they implied an end to further attempts to work with city hall to keep the Giants in town, and they were prescient about the team's "uncertain future." In what was surely a difficult moment, given his emotional investment in pursuing a downtown ballpark, Lurie gave up on his native city and turned his sights to where he knew there was enthusiasm over the Giants.

Both San Mateo and Santa Clara counties had expressed interest in getting the Giants to relocate in the South Bay. But Santa Clara County, of late, had shown particular interest. County representatives had lobbied Lurie prior to the Prop P campaign about the possibility of moving the Giants south by discussing specifics for a new stadium in the city of Santa Clara that would include acreage for parking. There were also overtures from the city of San Jose.[37] A key strength behind this interest was the recognition of the demographics of Giants fan support; almost 50 percent of those attending games at Candlestick came from the Peninsula.[38] Lurie had put the possibilities in Santa Clara on the backburner as he concentrated of the

Prop P campaign; his first choice for relocation was always down-town San Francisco. But now having been turned down again by the San Francisco voters, and desperate to move from Candlestick, he found new interest in returning to discussions with the Santa Clara contingents. He would not have long to wait.

Once the results of Proposition P voting were final, the South Bay communities and county officials moved quickly. Led by Larry Stone, former Sunnyvale mayor, a South Bay coalition of business and com-munity leaders contacted Lurie in the hopes of bringing the Giants to Santa Clara.[39] The coalition introduced their plans for a proposed 1 percent countywide utility tax to finance the construction of a new ballpark in a northern section of Santa Clara, near the Great America amusement park. The cost of the stadium would be $125 million and it would seat forty-five thousand. One small degree of irony about the location was the weather. The afternoon winds at the Great American park recorded regimes that were similar to Candlestick; once the sun went down in Santa Clara, however, the winds died off.[40]

For their part, the Giants were quick to respond. By mid-spring 1990, they had approved the design and agreed in principle to the move, pending a successful outcome of the financing. Corey Busch, the Giants' vice president, assured the local officials that Lurie wanted to keep the team in the Bay Area and thought that the South Bay would be a great place given the solid fan base there. Busch also reassured the Santa Clara contingent that the Giants were not talking to any-one else about moving.[41]

The various municipalities began procedures for approval of a ref-erendum to be placed before county voters in a November election. The city councils of Sunnyvale, Milpitas, Mountain View, and San Jose approved the 1 percent utility measure for the ballot. In early August, the city of Santa Clara joined the others.[42] Palo Alto decided not to join but would be subject to the vote nonetheless. Over the next three months the campaign followed predictable polemics, one side extolling the benefits of having Major League Baseball in the com-munity while the other criticized higher taxes to pay for the privilege. There were some on the anti-tax side who pushed an objection used in the two failed San Francisco measures, that Bob Lurie was a rich man who did not need public support to further his business interests. The November balloting followed similar patterns to those of the 1989 Prop P campaign: the results were terribly close—50.5 percent to 49.5 percent, with fewer than three thousand votes separating the sides—and the utility tax measure was defeated, making it the third ballot measure in four years that the Giants would lose.[43]

In a curious footnote to the disappointing Santa Clara vote, the Giants could declare a type of Pyrrhic victory that would loom large in future years in a territorial dispute with the Oakland A's. While preparing for the Santa Clara vote, Bob Lurie sought and received permission from A's owner Walter Haas to move to Santa Clara County.[44] Haas's permission would allow the Giants to claim Santa Clara County, and with it the city of San Jose, as their territory, a claim that was reinforced by Major League Baseball on four subsequent occasions.[45] Nonetheless, this claim of territorial rights would remain a bone of contention between the Oakland A's and the Giants for years to come.[46]

One of the anomalies of the Santa Clara countywide election was its complexity. Many municipalities took different sides of the debate on the funding of the proposed ballpark, and the results reflected those discrepancies. Voters in the northern part of the county, in Palo Alto and Mountain View, rejected the utility tax measure by a wide margin—61.2 percent to 38.85 percent—but those in the San Jose area narrowly favored the proposal.[47] Moreover, in the San Jose election, Susan Hammer, a pro-ballpark advocate, won the mayor's race. She believed that having Major League Baseball in San Jose would make the city "big league." Noting the approval rates for the utility measure in her district, Hammer moved immediately to pursue the Giants. In the first hundred days after her inauguration, she formed a twenty-nine-member commission on Major League Baseball for the city of San Jose. She then approached a subdued Bob Lurie about her ideas for a new stadium for the Giants in San Jose.

After some intense persuasion on the new mayor's part, aimed at convincing a wary Lurie about her enthusiasm for a campaign, the

Giants' owner agreed to a deal with San Jose. The proposal called for a $185 million stadium with the city paying $155 million; the Giants would pay the remaining amount plus any overrides in construction costs. The referendum, called Measure G, would impose a utility tax of 2 percent on San Jose residents. In March, the San Jose City Council agreed to place the measure before the voters in a special June election. Support for Measure G came from high places: baseball commissioner Fay Vincent, knowing Lurie's time at Candlestick was almost up, urged San Jose fans to pass the referendum and keep the team in the Bay Area. "The San Francisco team cannot play in Candlestick much longer. The Giants are going to play somewhere else. Candlestick is not a hospitable place for baseball."[48] Hammer's commission formed interest groups and raised money to advertise on behalf of the measure. Those objecting spoke against the use of public funds for sports facilities and pointed to the adverse effect the new ballpark would have in displacing those who lived on or near the proposed building site. After three months of campaigning and discussion, the voters rejected the measure by a wide margin, 54.5 percent to 45.5 percent.[49] For the fourth time in five years, Lurie and the Giants lost out at the ballot box.

There can be no real measure of how frustrated and disheartened Bob Lurie was by the results of the fourth and final public vote to find funding to keep his team in the San Francisco Bay Area. With all of the attempts to win over public support, with the time spent in meeting with various mayors, boards of supervisors, and city and county councils, and with campaigning on behalf of the measures and referenda, attending luncheons and rallies, he was completely exhausted both physically and emotionally. Moreover, acknowledging the results of all the elections took a personal toll. Lurie had taken a financial risk seventeen years ago, buying the team to save it from moving. In recent efforts to find a new location for a ballpark, he gave high priority to keeping the team in the Bay Area. He did both of these in large part because he felt the Giants were a community asset, valued by those who lived in the city and on the Peninsula. Now, after four successive defeats at the polls, it appeared that he might have saved himself the effort. Discouraged and drained, he could no longer continue the struggle to relocate the Giants in the Bay Area. It was time to let go. With the results of the San Jose election behind him, he made his decision to sell the team.[50]

III

PETER

It wasn't a question of whether Bob Lurie would sell the Giants but when. He no longer had the patience nor the will to deal with the Giants at Candlestick Park. He also was too discouraged to consider another attempt for a new stadium. Word leaked out that he was willing to hear from buyers, but no one from the local community came forward. Lurie's hope was that the team would remain in the Bay Area, but he would consider the first serious offer, regardless of where that buyer lived.

As events in the summer of 1992 unfolded, Lurie's dilemma would become more difficult than he thought possible. Once touted as a local hero for saving the Giants from leaving, he would find his position completely reversed. Nor would his situation be made any easier after political moves within Major League Baseball in late August delayed all movement on the Giants' sale. At the end of the 1992 season, when Lurie had hoped to be out of baseball, he was still the owner of the Giants. It appeared for the foreseeable future that he would have to draw on what little patience he had left.

ELEVEN

"It's Déjà Vu All Over Again"

After the disappointing results of the San Jose vote, a stunned and dejected Bob Lurie kept a low profile while he considered his next move. Parts of the stadium campaigning touched a personal nerve and Lurie felt it. Some voters took exception to a baseball owner with substantial personal wealth asking the public to fund a ballpark for his team. Others felt that this objection clouded the essential issue of the referenda: the Giants could not continue to play in Candlestick and be successful. Giants broadcaster Hank Greenwald, for one, argued that Lurie's personal story should never have been part of the conversation. The ballpark was a community asset, Greenwald pointed out, and would remain so long after Lurie had sold the team.[1] San Francisco supervisor Wendy Nelder said as much in the build-up to the 1989 Proposition P vote.

> It seems to me that there has been too much focus on Bob Lurie. It's easy for people to get mad at the idea of building a stadium for Bob Lurie. But it is not about that. The Giants are basically a city resource, and we need to remember that.[2]

San Francisco Chronicle columnist Glenn Dickey lamented that taxpayers saw the vote for a ballpark as providing public welfare for a wealthy individual rather than as something for themselves and their children.[3] Lurie himself tried to clarify that it was not his stadium or ballpark, that it belonged to the city, or to the community, and as such was a public resource. Nonetheless, rightly or wrongly, there could be no doubt that "Lurie, the wealthy businessman" figured into the debates of all four referenda, sometimes in the form of direct questions to the owner at town hall–type meetings asking why, with his assets, he wouldn't build the ballpark himself.[4] It is not difficult to imagine when faced with moments like these that Lurie would take the negative results at the polls in such a personal way.[5]

A day after the San Jose vote, Mayor Frank Jordan spoke by telephone with Lurie about a new plan to build a downtown stadium.[6] The mayor had been feeling some pressure to have a proposal ready if San Jose voters turned down the measure for a new ballpark, or at the very least to give Lurie some indication that city hall wanted the Giants to remain in San Francisco. The most pointed request came in early May 1992, in a letter to Jordan from James Lazarus, vice president of the San Francisco Chamber of Commerce and a nonvoting member of the board of supervisors' Ballpark Task Force. Lazarus repeated an assumption held by some San Francisco political insiders that the San Jose measure would not pass and, as a result, Lurie would more than likely sell the team, possibly to out-of-town interests. Lazarus therefore urged the mayor to be ready to contact Lurie the day after the election. "If you support a downtown ballpark, I believe you must make that support known on June 3."[7] When the mayor reached out to Lurie, the Giants' owner was apprehensive, to say the least. He listened politely to the mayor's professed interest in keeping the team in San Francisco, even though he had been down that road before. His part of the conversation was circumspect and noncommittal, especially about his intentions for the future of the Giants.

A few days after their telephone conversation, an astonished Lurie read in the local press that the Giants had agreed to an exclusive arrangement with the city on location, in effect giving local buyers first shot at a sale.[8] He quickly responded with a letter to the mayor, correcting the record and explaining that he would be meeting in New York with Commissioner Fay Vincent and National League president Bill White "to discuss the Giants' situation." Lurie was especially adamant that the Giants would not restrict themselves initially to dealing with San Francisco interest groups.

It has been reported that I indicated to you that I would not talk to any other communities about relocating the Giants until I talk to you about plans to keep the team in San Francisco. That is clearly not our position, and I know that in our conversation I never made that statement to you. . . . Frank, as you know, the Giants have been involved in numerous efforts over the past many years to find a way to keep the team in the Bay Area. These efforts have been at considerable expense to the Giants in terms of both time and money. While I have always resisted those who have made overtures to move the Giants from the Bay Area, I believe that the Giants must now consider those alternatives.[9]

Lurie's letter to Jordan ended any speculation about whether the Giants were willing to entertain offers to move outside of the Bay Area. It was now crystal clear that they would do so. Lurie also explained to Jordan that under no circumstances would the Giants get involved in any further ballot measures.[10]

Once he, Al Rosen, and Giants vice president Corey Busch returned to the Bay Area from their New York meeting with Vincent and White, Lurie felt much clearer about his situation. In dealing with the Giants' dilemma, Vincent applied a standard that consisted of four criteria developed by baseball in 1990 to govern franchise movement: the organization has been losing money over a substantial period; there has been declining attendance over a period of three years; the stadium is inadequate or unsuitable for baseball; and the team resides in a community that has demonstrated a lack of interest in baseball by vote or otherwise.[11] Vincent reiterated these criteria to the press and added that the Giants met all of them "squarely."[12]

I think the history of transfers leads one to the conclusion that baseball ought to be careful, but I think there are circumstances under which I am prepared to acknowledge that a transfer should be looked at. . . . San Francisco has my permission to look at these options.[13]

While he would subsequently refashion his meaning of "options," Vincent initially gave all indications to Lurie that the Giants could pursue moving out of Candlestick to remedy their present situation. At the press conference immediately following his meeting with Lurie, the commissioner confounded the issue somewhat when he added that this permission did not mean that the Giants had "automatic approval to move."[14] In stressing this last point, Vincent undoubtedly had baseball protocol in mind; all franchise sales and transfers are subject to approval by owners in both leagues. The ambiguity of Vincent's position would, however, become a bone of contention later in the year when offers came in to buy the Giants. Nonetheless, Lurie, Rosen, and Busch left the June meeting with Vincent feeling they had been given a clear go-ahead to shop the team and consider relocation. As Busch explained it, the commissioner had, in effect, granted them "a hunting license."[15]

Meanwhile, the mayor's office began to stir to life. Jordan, knowing that Lurie would be shopping the team, turned to close advisor and friend Walter Shorenstein, a prominent figure in Democratic political circles and a local real estate tycoon rumored to own over 25 percent of San Francisco's downtown commercial properties, including the iconic fifty-two-story Bank of America tower.[16] Shorenstein, for his part, assembled a group of the city's insiders and powerbrokers, including investment banker and philanthropist Warren Hellman. They, in turn, drafted Stanford business professor H. Irving Grousbeck, a close friend of Hellman's, who had made his fortune not as a college professor but as the cofounder of Continental Cablevision.[17] Grousbeck, a lifelong baseball fan, had a standing interest in owning a team. He looked into purchasing the A's and the Angels in the mid-1980s and in fact had expressed some interest to Lurie at the time that he might be interested in the Giants.[18]

While the discussion and planning among the Shorenstein-Hellman-Grousbeck group remained provisional, it was clear to everyone involved that Grousbeck would be the principal investor. He met with Lurie in mid-June, for informal discussions; the meeting was cordial and respectful. Grousbeck made known his interest in the Giants and explained that there would be a small, informal group of investors joining him in exploring a possible purchase.[19] For the moment, however, there would be nothing definitive, not even an understanding of a right of first refusal. As far as Lurie understood, the meeting was an exploratory, informal conversation between two businessmen. In mid-July Grousbeck telephoned Lurie and asked to see the Giants' financials, which Lurie agreed to send. For Grousbeck, seeing the books was a crucial step in the buying process; he had told Shorenstein and Hellman that, while interested in pursuing the Giants, he was not doing so out of civic pride. He intended to run the franchise as a successful business and needed all the information he could have to determine that. But he was far from ready to make any offer.

Aside from Grousbeck, all other locals remained on the sideline, biding their time. In a July interview with the *Chronicle*, Lurie explained that there had been no local offers, and while he had hoped the team would remain in the Bay Area, he could not remain a "good guy" and go bankrupt. Reliable people have expressed interest in the Giants, he went on to say, but only from outside the Bay Area.[20] The lack of local offers may not have been pure coincidence. According to those who studied the local business front, the operative game plan among prospective San Francisco buyers appeared to be watchful waiting. Shorenstein, in particular, urged patience among the investors, thinking that Lurie might not sell, or that if he did Major League Baseball wouldn't give final permission for the Giants to move. By waiting, Shorenstein reasoned, local investment groups might see a more favorable price for the ball club.[21] This strategy did not go unnoticed among some in the press who urged local buyers to act soon, lest the Giants leave town.[22] Grousbeck certainly adhered to a "move slowly, if move you must" program, proceeding at his own deliberate pace and in a tight-lipped manner, not going public with his intentions until late July, and then only to say that he was exploring the possibility of an offer.[23] Meanwhile, Corey Busch was on the road, testing the waters in certain key communities. By the end of July, he had a strong bite from a Florida group in Tampa–St. Petersburg, who wished to bring Major League Baseball to their region. One advantage that St. Petersburg had over many locales was a crucial one: a new stadium. Taxpayers in the Tampa–St. Petersburg area had approved funding for the Suncoast Dome in order to attract a big league team. An indoor arena completed in 1990, the Dome had a capacity of forty-three thousand.

Busch returned home and reported to Lurie and Rosen that the St. Petersburg group was keenly interested and appeared to be prepared financially for big league baseball. Lurie then settled into steady but secretive discussions with St. Petersburg city manager Norm Hickey; assistant city manager Richard Dodge; and a group of six investors headed by Vincent Naimoli, former chairman of Anchor Glass, and Naimoli's friend Vincent Piazza, a businessman from Pennsylvania whose son Mike would have a stellar Hall of Fame career as a catcher for both the Dodgers and the Mets.[24] Initially, the Florida group offered Lurie eighty-five million dollars, a price commensurate with contemporaneous purchases of Major League franchises like Detroit (eighty-five million dollars) and Seattle (ninety million dollars). Lurie countered, however, explaining that because of the Giants' storied history as one of the preeminent teams in baseball, he expected a higher price.[25] Naimoli made a counterproposal, and negotiations developed rapidly over a series of daily phone calls to the point that both parties felt the necessity for a face-to-face discussion in San Francisco.

The Lurie-Floridian summit meeting took place under a cloak of secrecy, complete with covert travel and transfer arrangements. On Thursday morning, August 6, the St. Petersburg team of Hickey, Dodge, Naimoli, and two other investors, Jack Critchfield, St. Petersburg utilities chief, and Mark Bostick, a Tampa businessman, arrived in San Francisco by corporate jet and were whisked away in private cars to the seclusion of Bob Lurie's office on the fifty-first floor of the Bank of America building. The group then holed up with Lurie and Rosen for a tense six-hour marathon session, with offers and counteroffers passing back and forth between the parties. There was a short break for a catered lunch. By late afternoon, the two parties had hammered out an agreement in principle. The Giants would be sold to Naimoli's group for $113 million and would move to St. Petersburg and play the 1993 season in the Suncoast Dome. In keeping with the strictly hush-

hush procedure, the two parties also agreed that the announcement would be delayed one day to allow the visitors to return home when there would be a coordinated press conference in the two cities. As a final measure of good will, Lurie agreed to not consider another buyer "until the St. Petersburg offer had run its course."[26]

The joint announcement on Friday, August 7, that the Giants were sold to a Florida group triggered responses on both coasts that ran the gamut in extremes. "TAMPA BAY HAS GIANT DEAL" proclaimed the headline in the *St. Petersburg Times*.[27] The Tampa–St. Petersburg community broke out in enthusiastic euphoria, an expression of joyful relief in finally landing a Major League franchise for their Suncoast Dome investment. Having failed numerous times before in attempts to acquire a big league team, they now had some satisfaction with the catch phrase that had motivated the spending of their tax dollars: "if you build it, they will come."[28] The Suncoast Dome hosted an impromptu rally, attracting several thousand people, St. Petersburg Giants t-shirts went on sale, and a local radio planned to broadcast the remainder of the Giants' 1992 games.[29]

There could not be a greater contrast of emotional response in the other bay area. The headlines in the *San Francisco Examiner* the day after the press conferences announced the grim news: "GIANTS: BYE-BYE, BABY." Articles over the weekend in both the *Examiner* and the *Chronicle* expressed shock, surprise, even outrage. Mayor Jordan held a hastily arranged press conference vowing to fight back. "This is not a done deal by any stretch of the imagination," the mayor assured those present. He then announced plans to start a "Save Our Giants" campaign and to promote the sale of season tickets.[30] Herb Caen, in his characteristic manner, disagreed and wrote in one of his columns that it would take a miracle to save the Giants "unless the Seventh Calvary, led by Gen. Walter Shorenstein, rides in with a bid of $113,000,001. . . . And the chance is thinner than a 19 cent hamburger."[31] Caen was even more pessimistic two days later. "Speaking of gloomsville, if you go to the last baseball game of the season at the 'stick, save the stub as a memento. It might be the end of an era."[32] Many others, apparently blind to the fact that no local offer to buy the team had surfaced since the June 3 ballot defeat in San Jose, blamed Bob Lurie for turning his back on his native city.[33]

The whirlwind activity conducted in the front office and speculation on the team's future had a strong effect on the Giants' 1992 season. Before the San Jose ballpark vote on June 3, the Giants were 27-23, in second place in their division, one game behind the leader; the day after the San Jose results they opened a home stand before a paid admission of 8,850, not exactly a show of fan support. They went on to lose seventeen of the next twenty-four games, falling into fourth place, from which they never recovered.[34] In the particularly turbulent and eventful month of August when the sale to St. Petersburg was announced, the Giants had a woeful stretch, managing to win only nine games. They finished 72-90, in fifth place in the NL West, twenty-six games behind division-winner Atlanta.

In the midst of franchise transformation or personnel changes, players often speak of being professionals, playing every day regardless of the business side of baseball. Some contend that playing the game offers an escape from its sometimes harsh economic realities. But players are not ignorant of their club's circumstances; they learn about them from many sources: clubhouse gossip, the press, and radio and television talk shows. Moreover, the business of baseball often intrudes on an individual's personal, human side and daily life with trades and reassignments. Not surprisingly, Giants players felt the shock waves of the club's turbulent predicament during the 1992 season. Speaking after the season was over, pitcher Jeff Brantley was blunt: "The whole thing just kind of burned us up, a major distraction. . . . The focus on the second half of the season wasn't on winning; it was on where we were going to play."[35] Infielder Robby Thompson, a native Floridian, said all of the confusion about location was unsettling.[36] Hitting coach Dusty Baker said it was frustrating. "It was hard to stay focused on baseball. All the questions weren't, why didn't you hit a home run, or strike someone out, but what do you think of the move?"[37] Manager Roger Craig could have been speaking for everyone on the ball club when he observed, rather philosophically, that uncertainty puts one's life on hold. "As far as my situation is concerned, I have no idea where I stand."[38]

Meanwhile, the business side of Giants baseball continued apace. Undeterred by the news of the Florida sale, Irving Grousbeck studied the Giants' books and remained the single local knight in shining armor, poised for a rescue. But with the St. Petersburg price tag now a matter of public knowledge, Grousbeck could not reconcile the figures and dropped out of the bidding. In a press release on August 12, he explained that his view of the finances could not support an offer to buy the team. "I tried nine ways to Sunday to make the numbers work, something that even a half-way reasonable person would invest in; I just couldn't do it." Grousbeck went on to say that his study of the books confirmed what Bob Lurie had been saying all along, that the Giants would lose between ten to twelve million dollars a year playing at Candlestick. Grousbeck also added that he had no confidence in the prospects of a new downtown stadium. He concluded on a note of sadness: "I am disappointed for both Giants fans in the Bay Area and for myself. I was very optimistic when I started but now I am discouraged."[39]

With Grousbeck out and the only offer coming from the St. Petersburg group, hopes sank in the Bay Area. For the second time in less than twenty years, it appeared that San Francisco might lose its baseball team. The situation looked like an eerie repetition of the winter of 1976 when Stoneham agreed to sell the team to a Toronto group. In that case, Stoneham waited for a local group to make an offer before he agreed to out-of-town-interest. The 1992 situation appeared to follow the Stoneham script: the locals did not respond to the news that the Giants were for sale. One of the Giants officials stated, "Bob Lurie is not standing in the way of any deal. If somebody makes a legitimate offer . . . and would keep the team in San Francisco, Bob would cash that check tomorrow."[40] Back in 1976 Stoneham felt the same way. As Yogi Berra would have said, it was déjà vu all over again.

With no viable local offer in sight, the mayor's office went into overdrive, searching desperately for another credible group that could present an alternative to the Florida bid. Baseball owners were scheduled to meet in St. Louis in early September, and the St. Petersburg offer would be one item of business for consideration. A show of popular support from the home front at the meeting might give San Francisco a fighting chance to keep the Giants. Ron Blatman, the economic development officer on Mayor Jordan's staff, got word that George Shinn, the owner of the NBA Charlotte Hornets, might be interested in buying the Giants. Blatman followed up with a phone call and spoke with Shinn's assistant, Spencer Stolpen, who confirmed his boss's interest. This confirmation put in motion a response that took on greater urgency once Grousbeck's decision became public. Blatman contacted his old friend Larry Baer, a native San Franciscan working for CBS in New York but who nonetheless kept in touch with people in San Francisco; moreover, Baer, a former team executive during Lurie's ownership, was a keen Giants fan with an interest in keeping the team from leaving town.[41] At Blatman's urging, Baer traveled to Charlotte and invited Shinn to come to San Francisco. The hope was that Shinn might replace Grousbeck and partner with local investors to present an alternative proposal to the Florida bid. In late August, Shinn agreed to travel to San Francisco with Baer for preliminary discussions.[42]

When Shinn arrived in San Francisco on August 24, he was welcomed with a great sense of optimism and hope. Here was an interested buyer with significant capital, enough to hold a local partnership together. Moreover, the fact that he came with a sports ownership background sat well with the San Franciscans. Shorenstein's second group of potential buyers (minus Grousbeck and Hellman), including investment magnate Charles Schwab, Gap clothier owners Don and John Fisher, philanthropist Richard N. Goldman, and a new member, Safeway boss Peter A. Magowan, were eager to sit down with Shinn and discuss his ideas for a purchase of the Giants.

Magowan was a crucial new addition to the group. A lifelong Giants fan who grew up in New York City and saw the Giants play in the Polo Grounds when he was a boy, he served on Lurie's board of directors for eleven years, giving him deep knowledge of the ball club's operations and familiarity with baseball's culture. Once he gave strong thought to joining with Shorenstein's partnership, he resigned from the Giants' board. Magowan also had a friendship with Larry Baer, who, increasingly, was working behind the scenes pulling various individuals together who might join in a counteroffer to keep the Giants in town. It was Baer who invited Magowan to get involved with Shorenstein and the others.[43] Magowan's agreement to join the group would turn out to be of great significance and consequence for the future of the Giants in San Francisco.

The local investors were particularly pleased that Shinn, as an experienced NBA executive with the Charlotte Hornets, would run the franchise, something none of the other investors wanted to do. The initial meeting, however, was not without its intense moments, and Shinn remarked later that the encounter with the San Francisco investors was akin to a proctology exam with Shorenstein as the chief proctologist.[44] After the meeting, Shorenstein proclaimed Shinn to be in good condition, enough for the group to go ahead in its planning. Shinn agreed to guarantee half of the offer to buy the Giants, with twenty million dollars in cash and the remainder in loans. The other investors would make up the remaining for a total of around ninety-five million dollars. It looked promising. The press, aware of Shinn's background in professional sports, saw him as the final piece that would form an alternative group to the Florida investors. The mayor's office felt that with someone of Shinn's stature and experience in sports ownership, the city would have a strong bargaining position. Even the fans saw Shinn as the savior of the home team, cheering and greeting him as he walked around Candlestick at a Giants game, decked out in the home team's cap and jacket for the occasion, with Mayor Jordan and his entourage in tow.[45]

The evening visit to Candlestick turned out to be the high point of Shinn's involvement with the Giants, although not everyone there that night was so sanguine. Up in the owner's box, a disgusted and livid Bob Lurie called Shinn's triumphal strut around the ballpark a cheap publicity stunt, and a dishonest one as well, raising the hopes of fans without having the capability to deliver. Lurie is on record as remarking, correctly as it turned out, that Shinn was so severely leveraged that he would be unable to hold his own in the partnership. Lurie punctuated his view by saying "Shinn was so in hock he could not buy the bats and balls."[46] Busch, who sat next to Lurie that night, was blunt in his own criticism, calling Shinn's showboating at the ballpark disrespectful, not only to the game of baseball but also to Bob Lurie.[47]

The investor group eventually discovered the same annoying truth about Shinn. As the negotiations developed over the next three weeks, primarily in telephone conversations and faxes between Shinn and the locals, Shorenstein, Magowan, and company became increasingly uneasy, and not just over money. One of Shinn's demands, a buyout clause that if triggered might allow him to move the team, did not sit well with the San Franciscans and had to be struck from the agreement. Shinn was not pleased. He also had a plan for cutting expensive players to ease the overhead. The locals thought this would diminish chances for good attendance and disagreed. Then the critical financial issue unfolded. As the time was fast approaching when the San Francisco group was to go before the baseball owners with an offer of their own, Shinn became increasingly enigmatic about the source (and the amount) of his capital. Finally, facing an eleventh-hour deadline and realizing that Shinn's liquidity was suspect, the local group cut him out of the partnership.[48]

In retrospect George Shinn's role in saving the Giants for San Francisco might be described as the triumph of failure. His part in the story of the Giants' turbulent history proved to be a necessary detour in the process of sustainability among the partners. Though it was Bob Lurie who first pegged him correctly, others soon discovered the truth—Herb Caen described Shinn as "barefoot boy with cheek but no checkbook"—and his dubious financial status eventually led to his rejection as a legitimate partner. Nonetheless, he provided the San Francisco investors with two things they desperately needed: a sense of optimism and the chance to buy some time in the process of countering the St. Petersburg offer.[49] Dealing with Shinn brought the local investors together, forging a coalition that would prove essential down the stretch run in late fall toward a purchase.

The San Francisco group also benefited from a curious twist in Major League Baseball politics. In late August, a majority of the owners banded together in an 18–9 vote of no confidence in Commissioner Vincent. The anti-Vincent forces were critical of the commissioner's stand on labor issues, the realignment of teams, and his handling of the Giants' sale, especially his ambiguous signal to Lurie that he could accept an offer for the Florida group without the approval of the league.[50] Vincent stood his ground and refused to resign, saying he was acting within his authority as commissioner of baseball, and on the matter of the Giants' sale he insisted that he did not give Lurie permission to accept an offer, only to look for one. While there continued to be various interpretations about what was said to Lurie and the Giants about selling the team, the other issues were serious enough that a majority of the owners wouldn't budge from their position that Vincent should step down. After a tense week of struggle between the commissioner's office and the owners, Vincent decided to comply with the owners' wishes "for the good of the game" and resigned from office on September 7, 1992.[51] Suddenly the agenda of the September 9 meeting shifted to a single issue affecting the core of baseball's governance. All other business, including concerns over franchise transfers and ownership sales, would have to be postponed. This meant that for the moment at least the St. Petersburg offer to buy the Giants was off the table.

The resignation of the commissioner vaulted NL president Bill White into greater authority until a new commissioner could be named. In one of his first decisions, White added another layer of complexity to the Giants' sale by announcing on September 9 that, on behalf of the league, he would consider a competing offer from a San Francisco group. "The window is open," White said, effectively giving the San Francisco partners a new opportunity to buy the Giants. He explained that he, rather than Lurie, could accept another offer on behalf of Major League Baseball.

> Bob Lurie is a man of his word. He has given the Florida people his word that he will not take any other offers, but I will accept an offer from the people in San Francisco, and the league will decide on what to do with the Giants.[52]

He informed Mayor Jordan that the so-called window would not be opened indefinitely; he would expect a serious and complete offer from the local group in a few weeks' time.[53]

With White's deadline fast approaching, the investment partners met in Shorenstein's office on Saturday, October 10, to confront two major crises. One had to do with the calendar. White's time limit for a competing offer was October 12. That gave the San Franciscans two days to prepare their submission. But with a change in the partnership a new financial structure was needed to make up for the loss of Shinn's share. Shorenstein made one or two calls and raised a bit more capital. Magowan and Baer called Kevin O'Brien of KTVU, the longtime telecaster of the Giants, and got another contribution.[54] Shorenstein also urged the general partners to up their individual antes. In a matter of hours, the group had a substantial base of capital to go forward.[55]

The other crisis came in the form of a difficulty that tugged at the very identity of the group, leading to an overwhelming question: with Shinn gone, who among the city's movers and shakers assembled that day in Shorenstein's office would take on the role of chief managing partner and run the franchise? There are many accounts of how this question was answered. Most describe the practicalities, that most of the partners—Shorenstein, Schwab, Goldman, Don, and John Fisher, for example—did not have the time or the inclination to run a baseball team and asked Magowan if he would do it.[56] Another account has it a bit more dramatically. "All at once, as if by divine providence, the heads of everyone at the meeting turned in the direction of Peter Magowan, the 51-year-old chairman of Safeway, Inc."[57] Magowan's own, more secular version suggests that he was drafted, chiefly by Shorenstein and Baer, to secure the progress that had been made, and that if he did not accept the position, all of the group's effort would be wasted.[58] By any account, however, the move turned out to be a momentous one, solidifying the group and providing strength in leadership. Magowan was an experienced executive, but he also brought to the group a deep love and understanding of baseball and a lifelong connection to the Giants. This affection for both the Giants and the game of baseball would energize him in the short-term for the negotiation ahead with an offer for the Giants, and it would prove in the long-run to be a powerful guide in his role as head of the Giants franchise for years to come.

Armed with an agreement cobbled together over the weekend, Magowan, as newly designated chief managing partner of the San Francisco investors, flew to New York Sunday night, October 11, accompanied by Larry Baer. The offer that landed on President White's desk the next day totaled ninety-five million dollars and represented San Francisco's official counter to the St. Petersburg bid. White accepted it with little comment or fanfare, explaining that he would present it to the NL owners in the near future. With Shinn out, the offer was more strongly representative of the San Francisco community, as Magowan explained to the press after he met with White. "It is a strong credible offer from a strong group of investors, made up almost entirely of local people."[59] In an ironic twist, one of the locals was none other than Bob Lurie himself, whose ten-million-dollar short-term loan to the partnership, the same provision he had extended to the Florida group, made him in effect the largest single contributor.[60] Magowan added that he expected a decision from the baseball owners within a month.

The delivery of the competing bid did little to quiet the drama connected with the Giants sale. On the contrary, it had the opposite effect. First there were cries of foul play coming from the Floridians, saying that White, an ex-Giant after all, was hardly a disinterested party. Next came waves of lawsuits, beginning with one from the City of San Francisco alleging that Bob Lurie broke the Candlestick lease, followed by the St. Petersburg investors against the San Francisco investors and Major League Baseball, claiming that theirs was the only legitimate bid, since Bob Lurie, the Giants' owner, agreed in writing to deal only with them. Not to be outdone, the City and County of San Francisco sued St. Petersburg for interference with the contract Bob Lurie held with Candlestick Park. Tampa Bay responded, this time by naming Mayor Jordan. San Francisco then filed a counterclaim, seeking legal fees from the Tampa Bay investors and the City of St. Petersburg because they both had signed indemnification agreements with Major League Baseball against any damages or claims that might occur in the process of buying or selling a franchise. Law Professor Jeffrey Brand explained that the indemnification with Major League Baseball would stop all the litigation in its tracks, since all of the parties—the Floridians, Bob Lurie, and the San Franciscans—signed agreements with MLB.[61] Moreover, any future development of franchise location in either city would effectively end the legal wrangling.[62]

The drama over the Giants sale did not confine itself to the courtroom. It also played out in a bizarre incident involving forces from beyond the grave. A few days before the owners would vote on the sale of the Giants, a letter from Horace Stoneham's widow appeared, explaining that it was the wishes of her late husband that the Giants remain in San Francisco.

> When my late husband brought the club out to San Francisco, he had every intention of the club remaining in the city permanently. . . . If I could speak to Bob Lurie I would tell him to remember his feelings when he bought the Giants. Although he was somewhat reluctant, he knew it was best for the Giants to remain in San Francisco.[63]

Valleda Stoneham wrote the letter to all twenty-seven Major League owners who would decide the Giants' fate. Or did she? After getting a call from one of Lurie's assistants questioning some of the details in the letter about the 1976 Giants sale, Mrs. Stoneham, who was eighty-nine years old, denied writing it or even understanding it. Then Jaime Rupert, Stoneham's granddaughter, intervened. Rupert, who had power of attorney for her grandmother, explained to the press that her grandmother was ill and confused. Valleda did write the letter, Rupert maintained, although she (Rupert) typed it. In an added twist, Rupert said she signed the twenty-seven letters to the owners on behalf of her grandmother but that her grandmother had signed the original.

Nor was Bob Lurie quiet in the days approaching the owners' vote. He and Corey Busch began a marathon schedule in an attempt to meet with each of the owners to explain the details and benefits of the Florida offer. Much has been made about Lurie's professional commitment to his St. Petersburg buyers, that he had given his word not to consider another offer until theirs had been given its full development. Undoubtedly, this eleventh-hour tour around the league testified to that promise. But there was also the matter of business. The Floridian offer was considerably higher than the Magowan-Shorenstien offer, and owners would appreciate that. Moreover, Lurie pointed out, the San Francisco offer contained some contingencies, such as getting a loan at a financial interest rate acceptable to the buyers, that would put him further at risk.

Two days before the meeting, the San Franciscans strengthened their hand by dropping the three most restricting contingencies, one of them being the condition of an favorable interest rate, and raising their total offer to one hundred million dollars. They also received substantial help from the San Francisco Board of Supervisors. In a letter to Bill White in late October, Mayor Jordan outlined certain concessions the city would give to the Giants regarding Candlestick, including a waiver on stadium rent and the payment by the city of all utility and field management costs.[64] These would considerably ease the costs of playing games at Candlestick and help the Giants' overall bottom line, something that would lessen the concerns of other owners.

At the November 10 meeting of the National League, the owners rejected the St. Petersburg–Tampa bid by a decisive 9–4 margin, the minority votes cast by the Florida Marlins, the Chicago Cubs, the Philadelphia Phillies, and the St. Louis Cardinals. The leading voice in opposition to the sale was Dodgers owner Peter O'Malley, who did not want to lose the Dodgers-Giants California rivalry.[65] The owners' decision freed Bob Lurie from his obligation with the St. Petersburg groups; he was now able to consider other offers for his club. A joint statement issued by Magowan and Shorenstein hinted of optimistic relief. "If Bob Lurie should decide to sell the Giants today, our group is ready to acquire the franchise."[66] Lurie, for his part, was quick to respond, indicating that he would review the hundred-million-dollar offer made by the San Franciscans. For someone who had been through an emotional wringer over the past two months, Lurie sounded remarkably composed.

> I congratulate Peter Magowan, the entire San Francisco group and everyone in the Bay Area who worked so hard to keep the Giants in San Francisco. I know the feeling you have today. I had the same wonderful feeling in 1976. . . . I will not be restrained from expressing my happiness that the anxiety created by the events of the past several months is finally over for Giants fans, whom I have always considered to be the greatest fans in baseball.[67]

Lurie remarked that while he did not expect his review of the Magowan offer to take more than a few days, he wanted to give it his due diligence since he was its largest single investor. Bud Selig, acting on behalf of the owners, said that as soon as Lurie accepted the offer, baseball would vote on the sale, probably at the December meeting.

Reactions around San Francisco ranged from ecstatic to guarded euphoria, in keeping with a city that loves a party but cultivates a sense of cool. At Pat O'Shea's Mad Hatter, the crowd was giddy, with an enthusiastic Mayor Jordan working the crowd and leading the "Let's Go Giants" cheers, hoping to cash in politically on the recent turn in the team's fortune. In fact, unlike some of his mayoral predecessors like Christopher and Moscone, Jordan played a minor role in the latest chapter of Giants history in San Francisco, leaving the heavy lifting to the men of finance and commerce such as Magowan, Shorenstein, and the Fisher brothers. In the "Save Our Giants" movement, Jordan was more facilitator than innovator. At Perry's on Union Street, the champagne was on the house, and orange and black balloons floated along the top of the ceiling; the mood was one of civilized revelry. At a corner of the bar sat Chub Feeney—Horace Stoneham's nephew, former

Giants vice president, and former NL president—a prime witness if there ever was one to the bumpy, twisty path of Giants history, going back even to its New York days. A beaming Feeney raise his champagne glass and announced to those around him, "I am delighted." The celebration spread throughout the city. Bars around the downtown center were jammed. Sports radio talk shows like KNBR's were overwhelmed with happy and relieved fans.[68]

Feelings were reversed in St. Petersburg and Tampa. The frustration of coming so close and then being jilted again grated on fans, bringing back the sour taste of losing the White Sox in 1988. Some said it was more of the same, a lack of respect for Central Florida as a big league venue. Others complained that the rejection was a slight on American values, that Bob Lurie should have been able to sell to the buyer of his choice; they chided the U.S. senators from Florida, Connie Mack III and Bob Graham, for not responding sooner in a challenge of baseball's antitrust exemption.[69]

Mack and Graham were instrumental in scheduling a one-day Senate hearing in early December in Washington DC, but little came of it. Bud Selig, chairman of the owners' executive committee—in effect the acting baseball commissioner—testified in front of the subcommittee on antitrust, monopolies, and business rights, chaired by Senator Howard Metzenbaum. Selig defended baseball's decision to keep the Giants in San Francisco, pointing out that in matters of franchise transfers Major League Baseball prefers to ban relocation except in dire circumstances. Selig also suggested that baseball's unique antitrust exemption creates great stability in the sport, that no individual owner can move his team without the approval from the league owners.

I am very proud of baseball's record on franchise stability. Because of baseball's exemption, it has by far the best record of professional sports in this area. No baseball club has been permitted to relocate since the Washington Senators moved to Texas in 1972. . . . Baseball has not abused its anti-trust exemption. . . . We do not allow a club to relocate simply so that the owner can earn greater profits. Indeed, the National League rejected the move to Tampa-St. Pete despite the fact that it would have netted Bob Lurie an additional $15 million.[70]

California senators Dianne Feinstein and Barbara Boxer expressed the relief and happiness of San Franciscans and Bay Area residents that the Giants would not be moving. The two senators from Florida went on record to register their disappointment about St. Petersburg's loss, but little headway was gained by the hearings. The subcommittee had no intention of challenging baseball's long-standing exemption to antitrust laws, nor of reversing any action by baseball regarding franchise relocation. In hindsight, Selig's point about profit and loss in the Giants' sale seems a bit disingenuous, considering that by rejecting a franchise transfer to St. Petersburg in which they would realize no revenue, the owners would stand to gain several million dollars each in fees once they granted Tampa–St. Petersburg an expansion franchise (which they finally did in 1995).[71]

Despite the jubilation, official business lay ahead. "It is still Bob Lurie's franchise," Larry Baer said.[72] But things were indeed falling into place. After a period of review and consideration, Lurie accepted the San Francisco offer. Then it was a simple matter of bringing the agreement to the owners for their approval. Having given so much time and consideration to the Giants' case, the owners found little to trouble them. The discussion at baseball's winter meeting was largely pro forma. The combined NL-AL assembly voted 27–0 to approve the sale and the transfer of the Giants from Bob Lurie to the Magowan partnership. Once again, at the eleventh hour with a local purchase, the Giants would remain in San Francisco. And once again, under yet another ownership, the franchise faced an uncertain future in the same ballpark that had troubled them for over thirty years.

TWELVE

The Improbable Dream

At the early December 1992 owners' meeting, Peter Magowan and
his executive vice president, Larry Baer, wasted no time in turning
their attention to running a baseball franchise. In fact, in their eager-
ness to hit the ground running they jumped the gun, spectacularly.
Together they hatched a bold plan to launch a new era in San Francisco baseball. They decided to go after the best player in the game
and sign him to a Giants contract. Magowan and Baer approached
Barry Bonds's agent, Dennis Gilbert, and began negotiations. Bonds
was a great choice for a number of reasons. The two-time NL Most
Valuable Player with Pittsburgh was now in the prime of his career
at the age of twenty-eight, and a free agent, willing to test the open
market. He had strong connections to the Giants: his father played
for San Francisco for seven seasons and his godfather was Willie
Mays. Moreover, he had personal ties to the Bay Area. Bonds went to
Serra High School in nearby San Mateo, where he was an outstanding athlete.[1] Magowan thought of Bonds not only as the best in the
game but also as a hometown boy who would be a great fan favorite.

Negotiations with Gilbert went remarkably smoothly and quickly,
especially when Magowan offered to make Bonds the game's best-
paid player with a six-year contract for $43.75 million—$7.2 million
a year—the most lucrative in baseball history. Gilbert and Bonds
were happy to accept. There was only one problem, a big one, as it
turned out. Magowan did not have the legal standing to make such an
offer, or any offer, for that matter. The combined ownership of Major
League Baseball had not yet gone through the formality of approving
the Giants' sale at their winter meeting, which meant that the team

was still Bob Lurie's property. Without his approval, no new contract could be offered nor issued, not to Bonds, nor to anyone else for that matter. Not surprisingly, Lurie wanted no part of any deal involving Bonds. If something went wrong with the impending sale to the Magowan group, or if there were any delay in the owners' approval, he did not want to be saddled with the game's best-paid player.[2]

A highly publicized December 7 press conference to announce the signing was abruptly cancelled and for two days the negotiations with Bonds remained in limbo.[3] Lawyers for both sides got together in an attempt to find language that would overcome the impasse, while Larry Baer assured Gilbert that this was a mere formality before the deal would be finalized. Meanwhile, owners expressed their displeasure at both Magowan's breach of protocol and, especially, at the amount of Bonds's contract.[4] A chastened Magowan made some arrangements to protect Lurie then reported back to the owners. "If we are not approved, Mr. Lurie has the right to decide if Barry Bonds is a member of the Giants. If he winds up with the team, he will not be responsible for Barry Bonds's contract."[5] Magowan then approached Bonds and Gilbert to reassure them that the new Giants partnership would honor the agreement.[6] With assurances formalized by the lawyers, Bob Lurie accepted the terms with Magowan and Bonds became a Giant. Eventually the paperwork that was holding up the owners' vote worked its way through all the channels. On January 13, 1993, the owners formally voted final approval on the sale of the Giants. On January 15, funds were transferred to Lurie's bank, designating the closing of one era and the beginning of another: the Magowan group became the official owners of the San Francisco Giants baseball club, with Barry Bonds in the center of their lineup.[7]

With the anomaly of the Bonds signing behind him, Magowan settled into the running of the ball club. There was much to do and time was of the essence. Believing in a fresh start, Magowan, with help from Larry Baer, began to reshape the organization. Bob Quinn had taken over from Al Rosen as general manager. The new administration, with Quinn involved, then looked for someone to replace Roger Craig as manager and chose Dusty Baker, who signaled a new beginning but also provided stability during a period of transition, since he had served as hitting coach under Craig.[8] To help make that transition even smoother, Quinn and Baker retained Bob Lillis as bench coach, who had served in that capacity under Craig.[9] After the Barry Bonds signing became official, the Giants decided to bring in Barry's father, Bobby, as a hitting coach. Hiring the elder Bonds was important for two reasons: not only to ease son Barry's start on a new team but also to indicate the new ownership's regard for Giants history. Bobby Bonds began his professional career as a Giant, and his reconnection with the ball club was in some part a chance for Magowan to recognize that history. Perhaps the supreme example of Magowan's commitment to the Giants' storied tradition came a few weeks later in late February when he signed Willie Mays to a lifetime contract with the ball club, to be a presence in spring training and to work as a community representative, especially with young people.[10] With Lillis, Bobby Bonds, and Mays secured, Quinn and Baker then began to look at the roster to see where they could strengthen the team for a good run in 1993.

For Magowan and Baer, however, a more serious issue confronted them. Their purchase of the Giants meant that they were necessarily stuck with Candlestick Park, warts and all. With the opening of the 1993 season less than three months away, they had little time to take a soulless concrete structure with its notorious weather and make it attractive and fan-friendly, a task akin to the Herculean labor of cleaning the Augean stables. It was made more difficult from a planning and budgetary perspective because it would allocate precious club assets for what would only be a short-term result. Magowan knew his stay in Candlestick had to be brief. During the lead-up to the purchase of the Giants NL president Bill White pulled Magowan aside to tell him how important a new ballpark was to the Giants' future in San Francisco. "I can't bail you out again," White said.[11] Baseball's governors had indicated in their approval of the sale to Magowan's group that the Giants should find a new home. But before Magowan could begin the important planning for a new ballpark, he had to accept that Candlestick would be the Giants' home for the immediate future.

Knowing there were limits to changes that could be made to the physical structure, Magowan nevertheless did what he could to improve Candlestick's appearance, adding, for example, new paint and refurbished concession stands. All of the grass in the infield and outfield was replaced and upgraded to the highest quality. The chain-link outfield fence was covered with green padding to create a softer look. New bleachers seating fifteen hundred were brought in behind the left-field fence, so that fans could catch home run balls. The food was upgraded with more choices. Cleanliness was a priority, not only in restrooms and near the concessions but also around the park in general, with attention given to periodic sweeps to pick up wind-blown wrappers, paper, and cups.

In addition to altering Candlestick's physical appearance, Magowan had another repair job on his hands: the ballpark's image. For years, Bob Lurie had publicly decried the shortcomings and deficiencies of Candlestick as part of a strategy to find a new ballpark. To counter that negative perception, Magowan gave considerable thought to the experience of being at the ballpark.[12] Drawing on his love of the game—he once said he was a fan first and then an owner—and his background in marketing at Safeway, he applied the idea of customer satisfaction as part of the experience of a day at the ballpark. On the morning of opening day in 1993, he gathered the ushers and stadium workers together for what he called a "little pep talk," reminding everyone that the baseball fan was in effect a customer, someone who should be welcomed and encouraged to come back for another visit.[13] An emphasis was placed on friendly service, being cheerful and polite, greeting visitors as they arrive at the ballpark and treating them as guests. Candlestick employees wore "We're Listening" buttons early in the 1993 season, encouraging feedback and suggestions. Even Magowan wore one as he walked around the ballpark in April 1993.[14]

The fans responded. Attendance soared in 1993, totaling 2,606,354, the highest figure for the forty years the Giants played in Candlestick.[15] There was a huge opening-day crowd of 56,589; the six home games with the Dodgers drew 273,509, and a three-game home series with the Braves pulled in 155,437. Undoubtedly the attention to customer satisfaction brought many fans back for repeat visits. There was also the so-called honeymoon effect with the new ownership, players, and manager. By far, however, what brought fans through the turnstiles in 1993 was the exciting brand of baseball the Giants played, with Barry Bonds leading the way. It was a magical season, what might be termed the last great pennant race (or, more exactly, division race), when winning the division was the only route to the postseason, and when the Giants' fate went down to the final game of the year.

Having lost ninety games the year before, the 1993 Giants were picked by most baseball pundits in their preseason polls to finish fourth in the NL's western division. With offensive firepower from Bonds, who would be voted the 1993 NL Most Valuable Player, and supported by strong pitching from two twenty-game winners, Bill Swift and John Burkett, the Giants broke out in early May and by July 22 were 65-32, ten games in front. They held first place until September 11, when in the midst of an eight-game losing streak they were overtaken by the surging Atlanta Braves. The final three weeks of the season produced a furious finish. In the last seventeen games, the Braves went 12-5 and the Giants 14-3. Both clubs were tied for first place on the final day of the season, October 3, each team with a phenomenal record of 103-58. To heighten what was already a tense dramatic setting for the Giants, they were playing their archrival Dodgers in Los Angeles, having won the first three games in a four-game series. But the odds they were facing were steep; they had not swept a four-game Dodgers series on the road since 1923. A superstitious Magowan, with his deep knowledge of Giants baseball history and looking for any edge for his orange and black, asked Willie Mays and Bobby Thomson to join him at the game.[16] Who better to have next to you on October 3, Magowan reasoned, the same day forty-two years before when Thomson hit his "shot heard 'round the world" to beat the Dodgers for the NL flag? But Thomson's 1951 magic didn't carry, and after the fourth inning the game was never in doubt. The Dodgers scored early and then often, winning 12–1 and sending the Giants home to wait till next year. A stoical Dusty Baker, who would be voted the 1993 NL Manager of the Year, remarked that it wasn't to be. Magowan, who rightly saw some measure of success in a turnaround season, commented, "When people remember the 1993 season, they won't say Atlanta won 104 games. They'll say the Braves and the Giants had 103 wins going into the last day, and then the Braves won."[17]

The 1993 season was an auspicious beginning to new ownership, and to the Bonds era, setting the parameters for Giants baseball for the next fourteen years, into the new century. It was Bonds's team, and he dominated play as few players ever have. In turn, the Giants sculpted their lineup to accentuate his abilities. They were ever alert to protecting Bonds in the batting order with other imposing power hitters. Once Will Clark left in 1994, Matt Williams hit behind Bonds. The Giants eventually traded Williams to Cleveland for Jeff Kent, who from 1997–2003 gave the Giants a wicked one-two punch for seven seasons before leaving as a free agent. They added Ellis Burks in 1998 as another big bat to protect Bonds, who had become one of the game's most feared power hitters.[18] During the ten years that Baker managed the team, through 2002, with Bonds in the center of the lineup, the Giants won the NL pennant, reached the postseason playoffs three times, and were 840-715. Playing winning baseball, they drew respectable crowds and broke two million again in attendance in 1999, the last year they played at Candlestick.

The Bonds era continued for a few more years under Felipe Alou, who became manager in 2003, replacing Baker. In Alou's first year at the helm, the Giants won one hundred games and again reached the postseason, the first time they had back-to-back postseason play since the 1936 and 1937 World Series appearances. The team continued to feature power, with Bonds defining the team. To replace Jeff Kent, the Giants signed Marquis Grissom and Jose Cruz and also added Andres Galarraga, who was closing out a great career as a power hitter and could be used sparingly.

Beginning in 2005, however, things began to change, giving the Giants a chance to imagine and prepare for life without Bonds. The year 2005 was injury-plagued for Bonds, and he played in only fourteen games. After that year, his productivity dropped considerably from the spectacular numbers from 2001–2004, when he was voted the NL Most Valuable Player four straight years. In 2006 he hit .270, with 26 HR and 77 RBI; in 2007, his last year as a Giant, he hit .276, with 28 HR and 66 RBI. The 2007 season was taken up with Bonds chasing Hank Aaron's home-run record, which proved a major distraction to the team, especially with the accompanying accusations of steroid use and the attendant media circus. As he closed in on Aaron's record, Bonds was consistently jeered and ridiculed on the road, especially in Los Angeles; only in San Francisco, where he remained popular, did he receive both credit and adulation for his hitting. After the season was over, Peter Magowan sat down with Bonds to explain that the Giants would not re-sign him for the following season. To his credit, Magowan felt he was the one to do this, since he signed Bonds to his original Giants contract. Magowan made his decision based on forward thinking, not as a punitive reaction to past action; he looked to the future of the Giants rather than to charges of Bonds's alleged performance-enhancing drug use.

> We had just completed our third losing season, and I said to Barry during the termination discussion, "As Branch Rickey once told his best player with the Pirates, Ralph Kiner, 'Ralph, we're in last place with you. We're just as well off in last place without you.'" The Giants at this time were an aging team and getting worse. We needed to go in a new direction with the development of our farm system . . . and the drafts, which quickly landed Lincecum, Cain, Posey, Crawford. The alleged steroid use had nothing to do with my discussion.[19]

A new style of Giants baseball was about to begin with Bruce Bochy at the managerial helm. He would shape the ball club to his liking, away from pure power hitting and more toward pitching and defense.

The strong start to the Baker-Bonds era on the field, playing winning baseball and drawing fans to the ballpark, and the excitement of the 1993 division race gave Magowan a lift. His first season as the team's chief managing partner had gone rather well. Conditions at Candlestick were improved, the fans were back, and the ball club was operating smoothly under Quinn and Baker. At the season's end, Magowan intended to sit down with Larry Baer and give some needed thought to a new ballpark. Before they could begin their stadium planning, however, another round of troubles broke out in baseball, demanding their complete and undivided concentration.

Ever since the 1975 Messersmith-McNally challenge to the reserve clause, labor relations had roiled baseball off and on for almost twenty years. Problems between players and owners finally reached an impasse at the beginning of the 1994 season. The 1990 collective bargaining agreement was due to expire on December 31, 1994, and the owners and the players remained deeply divided on a new pact. The central tension was an old one, created by a single problem: money. The players insisted on compensation that reflected their worth in an open market; the owners resisted, fearing that soaring players' salaries could cripple many small-market teams' ability to meet payroll. Added to this was the claim of a number of owners that the players' salary demands would tip the competitive balance of the game to the few deep-pocket teams in large cities such as Los Angeles and New York.

The 1994 season opened as scheduled, but both sides refused to budge from their respective positions. The owners proposed a revenue-sharing plan to help the small-market teams but coupled it with a salary cap. The Major League Baseball Players Association emphatically rejected any idea of restrictions to salary and set an August 12 strike, in the hopes that the owners would blink, as they had done on previous threats of player walkouts in the late 1970s and early 1980s.[20] This time, however, the owners had amassed a "strike fund" of nearly a billion dollars and were not so easily cowed. They settled in for the long haul and by early September the season was cancelled and with it postseason play, including the World Series.[21] Neither side had expected the other to be so determined.[22]

The owners' next moves were calculated to show that they, too, could play hardball. On December 23, 1994, they unilaterally imposed a salary cap. Then in early January of 1995, they announced that they would open the new season with replacement players.[23] Their intention, some said, was to break the union.[24] The MLBPA responded with two separate complaints to the National Labor Relations Board. In late February, the NLRB found that the owners had illegally imposed the salary cap and forced them to withdraw it. Then, in response to the hiring of replacement players, the NLRB, on behalf of the players association, filed an injunction in U.S. District Court to return regular players to work under the terms of the expired 1990 agreement.[25] On March 31, 1995, Judge Sonia Sotomayor, a future Supreme Court justice, ruled on behalf of the players. Under Judge Sotomayor's decision the owners were compelled to reinstate the terms of the last collective bargaining agreement, and the players, eager to get back to baseball, accepted it. After 234 days the strike was over. An abbreviated spring training followed and the regular 1995 season opened on April 26.[26]

For Peter Magowan the entire process of the strike and its fallout was at once edifying, frustrating, and discouraging. As a new owner among baseball's governors, he adopted a respectful strategy of listening and learning, getting a sense of how baseball dealt with crisis. Magowan, however, was no stranger to labor issues, having dealt often with unions as head of Safeway. He made what he termed "small contributions to the discussion when appropriate" and established a good working relationship with Richard Ravitch, the owners' representative in the strike talks. Magowan also joined in discussions with many of the owners of the so-called mid-market teams like St. Louis, Anaheim, Philadelphia, and Toronto, who were feeling the pinch of the effects of the strike.[27] In the end, given the gravity of the issues surrounding the strike, Magowan's early exposure to the culture of ownership was a kind of baptism by fire. By necessity, he had to learn quickly and adapt.

However he measured his experience at the owners' meetings, he was clearly discouraged about the effects of the strike on baseball in general and on the Giants in particular. He was blunt about his assessment of the Giants' situation at the beginning the 1995 season. "The 1994 strike completely destroyed the momentum of the 1993 season," he remarked.

I was naïve to think that we would bounce back in 1995. In fact we lost half of our attendance from 1993. Revenue was way down. We suffered more than most teams. I got letters from fans saying, "How could you take our game away?" This set us back from any planning. We were trying to survive rather than plan a new ballpark.[28]

The Giant were back to square one when Magowan's group had taken over from Lurie. As they dealt with the realities of poor attendance and bad publicity for baseball in the early months of the 1995 season, planning for a new ballpark seemed light years away.

Once they got through the 1995 season and sensed that a rhythm, however fragile, had returned to baseball, and the press began to restore a confidence in the game, Magowan and Baer could give some attention to the idea of a new stadium. They began first, in conversations in the fall of 1995, musing about their favorite baseball venues and sharing impressions of the parks they had visited. They then moved to more practical considerations to develop a strategy to go forward. Given the recent history of the Giants' failed ballots on public financing, Magowan understood that a new stadium could not be built with public money. As both he and Baer explained the problem, "we needed a new approach; we had to get the community to see the ballpark in a new light. And that meant one thing: private financing."[29] But the new approach would require more than creative thinking; it would require the hard work of diplomacy, working the corridors of city hall and downtown businesses, and diligence in winning over the skeptics in the community. Privately constructed ballparks were a rarity in recent baseball history; the last one to be built was Dodger Stadium, finished in 1962.

The daunting practical side of campaigning for the ballpark was eased somewhat by an accompanying exercise of conjuring up the perfect stadium and of dreaming about what it would look like. Both Magowan and Baer had a penchant for the old, traditional locales like Fenway Park in Boston or Wrigley Field in Chicago. Combining an aesthetic sense with an historical one, they conceived of the ballpark as a special place, reflecting both the uniqueness of the sport itself and the environs where it would be built. They understood what former baseball commissioner A. Bartlett Giamatti described as the evocative power of an urban ballpark.

> When we enter that simulacrum of a city, the arena or stadium or ballpark, and we have successfully, usually in a crowd, negotiated the thoroughfares of this special, set-aside city, past the portals, guarded by those who check our fitness and take the special token of admission, past the sellers of food, the vendors of programs[,] . . . after we ascend the ramp or go through the tunnel and enter the inner core of the little city, we often are struck, at least I am, by the suddenness and fullness of the vision there presented: a green expanse, complete and coherent, shimmering, carefully tended, a garden.[30]

Giamatti's sense of a timeless place of cultivation, perfectly designed for a powerful evocative effect, is reflected in Magowan's and Baer's explanation of their dream park. Their planning grew out of the traditional side of baseball. "We wanted our park to evoke the feeling of the best of the old parks, with Wrigley and Fenway as our models. . . . Both were intimate, grass-field parks. Both had distinct features that let you know where you were."[31]

The Giants had their location; the Port of San Francisco had agreed to lease them a 12.7-acre bay-front parcel in China Basin, south of Market Street but close to the Embarcadero. A sense of this location became a powerful concept for both Magowan and Baer as seen in their instruction to the stadium's architectural team, Hellmuth, Obata, and Kassabaum, Sport, Venue and Event (HOK-SVE) the leading stadium design firm, who built Oriole Park at Camden Yards in Baltimore, Jacobs Field in Cleveland, and the new Busch Stadium in St. Louis.[32] "We contacted the only architect we wanted to work with: Joe Spear of HOK Sport. . . . We urged him to dream and to draw, to create something fitting for the site. What we envisioned was a ballpark more compelling, more distinctive than any other of recent memory."[33]

Magowan and Baer wanted the setting to permeate the design not only throughout the ballpark's façade but also in the playing field.

China Basin is tied to San Francisco's maritime history as a place where nineteenth-century clipper ships sailed to and from China, giving the location its name. By the late twentieth century, the area had evolved from an industrial waterfront to warehouses and offices. The 12.7-acre parcel set aside for the ballpark was bordered on one side by King Street, a major traffic arterial, and on the other by the edge of the bay, what would be called "McCovey Cove" after Giants Hall of Fame slugger Willie McCovey, in the proximity of warehouses and some offices. The location was seen by many in the city as an area primed for development. As Magowan and Baer explained, "The best ballparks . . . are created not by an architect; they're created by a site imposing itself on the architect."[34]

Spear immediately grasped the sense of the local for his design. His intention was to connect the stadium with the bay but also blend it with the neighborhood structures to create a cohesive architectural style. His design preserved the traditional look and feel of the Wrigley and Fenway style ballparks while at the same time expressing something uniquely San Franciscan. One stadium scholar described Spear's design as an example of "urban nostalgia, from the brick-faced façade reminiscent of the area's warehouse and commercial history, to an arched promenade that allows fans to watch games through an out-field fence, to a large old-fashioned glove that adorns a space between left and center fields."[35]

With his deep interest in Giants history Magowan also wanted the design of the park to honor the team's heritage, from its days in New York as well as its time in San Francisco. Spear obliged that interest with countless examples of the ball club's rich and storied history. The recent past is represented in various locations outside the park by a number of nine-foot bronze statues of former San Francisco Giants, all of them Hall of Famers: Willie Mays, Willie McCovey, Juan Marichal, and Orlando Cepeda. Painted on the exterior wall of the right-field façade is a record of world championship titles from both New York and San Francisco, as well as a list of NL pennant years and plaques of various players. There are also plaques set in a large stone by McCovey Cove highlighting great moments in each of the seasons in San Francisco. Inside the stadium on the second level of the grandstand, running chronologically from the right-field corner around the home plate area and out to left field are numerous photos of managers, players, and great moments in crucial games, which taken together constitute a kind of photographic history of the franchise, from John McGraw, Christy Mathewson, and the early New York Giants down to the present. The sense of baseball history extends even to the San Francisco Seals, the old Pacific Coast League team; their beloved manager, Lefty O'Doul, has a plaza named for him adjacent to McCovey Cove.

Magowan also worked with Spear on the interior playing field, especially on how it would be influenced by its location and the dimensions of the site. Just as Fenway has its "Green Monster" wall in left field resulting from its tidy fit within its Boston neighborhood, features of the new park's playing field could evolve from its own small dimensions and the proximity of the water. Magowan thought that the restriction of space could dictate an interesting irregular outfield that would have an impact on how the game would be played. Unlike football or basketball, where the playing dimensions are fixed, baseball, aside from the infield measurements, always had irregularities in the old parks like Fenway, the Polo Grounds, Ebbets Field, and Shibe Park in Philadelphia. At the China Basin site, the right-field dimensions would be restricted by the close proximity of the water, only 309 feet from home plate in the corner, but would quickly run away from the plate toward right-center, which would be 421 feet at its deepest. The left-field foul line would be 339 feet and 399 in straight away center field. There would be sharp angles in both right-center and left-center. The right field wall would be 24 feet high (another historical gesture—an homage to Willie Mays who wore number 24) to prevent easy home runs down the line and also add to the dramatics of "splash hits" that clear the wall and land in McCovey Cove. Magowan's interest in the fan's perspective would limit the dimensions of foul territory as well, since the seating is designed to get the fans as close to the action as possible, especially behind home plate and near the infield.

The dreaming came easily to both Magowan and Baer, as did their collaboration with Spear; now they had to get public support for their planning and then find a way to pay for everything. The first step was to put a ballot measure before the San Francisco voters to gain approval for the construction of the stadium. While the park would be constructed from private funding, the Giants still needed public approval to remove certain restrictions that applied to the Port's China Basin site and to change some of the infrastructure before they could begin construction. The board of supervisors authorized a special March 1996 election in which Proposition B would come before the voters of the City and County of San Francisco. Prop B, as it came to be known, involved only land use restrictions, the most important of which were to increase the limitations on building height from 40 to 150 feet and to waive parking requirements near the ballpark.

In the build up to the vote, Magowan and Baer wasted no effort in cultivating strong citywide support for the measure. While Prop B differed from previous referenda in making no demands for public money to build the park, Magowan and Baer were wary about possible negative residue carrying over from the 1987 or 1989 ballpark ballot defeats. They hired a professional political consultant, Peter Hart, who recommended polling in those neighborhoods that voted "no" in the 1987 and 1989 ballpark referenda. As part of the campaign, they approached three important community leaders in the city to head a "San Franciscans for a Downtown Ballpark" committee, State Senator Quentin L. Kopp, Roberta Achtenberg, and Rev. Cecil Williams, each of whom represented a different constituency in the city's social and political fabric.[36] The campaign then began to solicit support from a number of individuals, who could coalesce into strategic groups and be listed in the official San Francisco Voters Pamphlet. Politicians from the city who supported the measure were grouped strategically at the beginning of the pamphlet: Willie Brown as mayor was listed first, individually and separately, followed by "Former Mayors United in Support of a New Ballpark" that included Joseph Alioto, Dianne Feinstein, Art Agnos, and Frank Jordan. U.S. senators Dianne Feinstein and Barbara Boxer and Congresswoman Nancy Pelosi were gathered together as approving, as were seven members of the board of supervisors.[37] Nonpolitical groups who were pro-ballpark followed in the Voters Pamphlet, including "African-Americans for a New Ballpark," "Asian-Americans for a New Ballpark," "Latinos for a New Ballpark," "Russian-Americans for a New Ballpark," "Lesbians & Gays Part of the Team," "Business Leaders for a New Ballpark," and even a group from the Double Play, the famed historical watering hole on 16th and Bryant Streets, opposite where Seals Stadium used to stand, listed in the pamphlet as "Double Play Patrons for a New Ballpark." Leaving no stone unturned, Magowan and Baer managed to convince nine individuals who voted no on the two previous city ballpark measures to stand as another group in the Voters Pamphlet, entitled "Old Foes, New Supporters of a Downtown Ballpark."[38] Weeks prior to the vote, Magowan and Baer made their way around town with a scaled model of the new stadium, displaying it at prominent venues for voters to see.

All of the planning, organizing, polling, and campaigning paid off for the Giants in a stunning victory at the polls. Proposition B was overwhelmingly approved by San Francisco voters by a substantial margin of 66 percent. The local papers celebrated the news. "GIANTS BALLPARK: HOME RUN" ran the headlines in the *San Francisco Examiner*; "S. F. VOTERS SAY PLAY BALL" was the headline in the *Chronicle*.[39] Politicians, campaign workers, Giants officials, and average baseball fans celebrated all over town, including at the Double Play, where supporters of Proposition B toasted the home team.

Once the vote was approved, Magowan and Baer could get to work on the financing. The projected cost of building the stadium was $357 million. Magowan explained that from the outset the plan to raise capital was multifaceted. The first stage was a brilliant marketing ploy aimed at 1996 season ticket–holders. Over the following winter they received a promotional package in a cardboard box shaped like home plate. Inside was a pop-up view of the new park, a film showing an architect's rendering, information about the design and construction, and a brochure on the charter seat program. One season ticket–holder recalls being extremely impressed.

Inside the front cover was a true masterpiece of marketing. I can't quote it for you exactly because I donated the package to the Hall of Fame, where it has been on display in the Ballparks exhibit for a long time. However, I can give you a very close paraphrase. "Imagine you're sitting in your permanent seat at Pac Bell Park. It's a balmy Thursday afternoon, with a light breeze blowing in off McCovey Cove. A waitress brings your lunch, which you ordered earlier, to your seat, and a little while later the concierge brings a fax from your office. It's another glorious afternoon at the ballpark, and late in the game comes the moment you've been waiting for. Barry Bonds lofts a high fly ball deep to right field. You watch the ball soar toward the 24-foot-high wall, watch it climb, climb, climb, up over the ball and directly into the waters of McCovey Cove. And you say to yourself, 'I'm not in Candlestick any more.'"[40]

The advertising campaign coupled with a sale of charter seats provided much-needed capital. Magowan and Baer were pleased with the results. "We raised $75 million by selling licensing fees at $5,000 for the best seats. Naming rights were $50 million; other advertising brought in $50 million."[41] With this amount of capital commitment, they looked to borrow the rest. Their first choice was Bank of America, an old-time San Francisco bank with ties to the Giants. Walter Shorenstein owned the Bank of America building and Bob Lurie was one of the tenants. But Bank of America said no. They then pursued another bank with a local history, Wells Fargo, but they also said no. Finally, Magowan and Baer travelled to New York City and presented their plan to Chase, who approved the loan. The City of San Francisco also provided some help. Using a tax-increment financing plan, the city provided $12 million in infrastructure (amenities outside the ballpark including road vacation, street lighting, a transit stop, and utilities connections).[42]

Magowan and Baer had accomplished what had been previously thought impossible. They had overcome all the disappointments, false starts, and near misses of recent Giants attempts at trying to build a new ballpark. They had managed to get city hall, the community, local businesses, and neighborhood groups to support the idea of a downtown baseball venue at a location agreeable to all. With public approval and the crucial financing in hand, they now had a "shovel-ready" project. On December 11, 1997, they broke ground at China Basin, and the building of the new park was on its way. Pacific Telephone and Telegraph of California had paid fifty million dollars for the naming rights; the new stadium would be called Pac Bell Park. Magowan and Baer hired Kajima, a Japanese construction management firm, to coordinate the building of Pac Bell. Kajima in a sense "rode herd" on the structural engineers and the construction company, Haber, Hunt & Nichols.[43] The two Giants executives visited the construction site on an almost daily basis to keep up with the progress, a far cry from Horace Stoneham's passive connection to the building of Candlestick.[44] The attention to detail and the superb management of the project paid off. Pac Bell Park opened on April 11, 2000, twenty-seven months after the groundbreaking ceremonies. The Giants finally had their downtown home. Coming full circle from opening day on the West Coast forty-two years before in Seals Stadium, the Giants' opponent in the first game at Pac Bell Park was the Los Angeles Dodgers, a fitting historical echo at the dawning of a new century of baseball in San Francisco.

Epilogue

"The Home Team"

More than owners, managers, players, bad bounces, or clutch base hits, the ballpark has been the single most important factor in shaping the Giants' historical narrative in San Francisco. For forty years Candlestick Park and its infamous conditions determined the fate of the franchise, both on the field and in the stands. Once Pac Bell Park opened in 2000, there was a dramatic shift in attitude, perception, and the team's fortunes. To many in San Francisco it was love at first sight. Players marveled at the playing field and locker room facilities. Taken by the ambience and location, fans flocked to the park, establishing a pattern of sellouts for every home game. Longtime voice of the Giants Lon Simmons suffered through many cold nights at Candlestick; when he first saw Pac Bell Park, he remarked, "Finally the Giants have a ballpark that looks like San Francisco."[1] The neighborhood around the park throbbed with life and activity. Mike Krukow, one of the Giants' broadcasters, noticed the way the ballpark immediately connected with the city's character. "It was an old soul the day it opened. You had the feeling it was in San Francisco even before the bridges."[2]

The coherence and sheer beauty of the new park brought the deficiencies of Candlestick into sharper focus. Everything about Pac Bell accentuated the gap between the new park and the old—the location of the park amidst a thriving neighborhood, the attractive combination of brick and steel in the façade, the proximity of downtown, the views of the Oakland hills from the upper decks, the sight of the Bay Bridge from the right field seats. Even the weather was better, due to adjustments to the stadium's configuration after some wind studies.

There was nothing like any of this at the remote location of Candlestick, ten miles from downtown. After only one month in the new park, players, fans, broadcasters, and sportswriters alike shuddered to think of Giants baseball at Candlestick.

Beyond the stark contrast in appearance and location, the comparison between the fortunes of the home team in Pac Bell and Candlestick was also dramatic. For the forty years the Giants played at Candlestick, they went to the postseason five times; they won division titles three times and the NL pennant twice. They won no world championships. Once they moved into Pac Bell Park in 2000, things changed quickly. In their first four years in the new park, the Giants went to the postseason three times and won a NL pennant. Overall, in the sixteen years that they have played at AT&T Park (the ballpark changed name in 2004 to SBC Pac Bell and then in 2006 to AT&T Park), the Giants have been to postseason six times and have won four NL pennants and three World Series championships.

The team's fortunes have shifted emphatically at the turnstiles as well. During the years at Candlestick the Giants were consistently near or at the bottom in home attendance figures. Only in the first five years, when Candlestick was a novelty and the Giants were at their height during Stoneham's ownership, did the team draw near the top of the NL. After that, through the Lurie years and into the early Magowan years, with only a few exceptions, they were among the lowest in league attendance while playing at Candlestick. Once the Giants moved into AT&T, their attendance soared; eleven times in their first sixteen years they were among the top three in the NL. Only twice during that period did they fail to draw over three million fans.[3]

In explaining the Giants' change in fortune, one historian credits Magowan's efforts in building the ballpark. "Of all the accomplishments of the Magowan era—signing Barry Bonds, . . . saving the team from Florida—perhaps none stands as massive and beloved as what opened as PacBell Park and now goes by the name of AT&T Park."[4] While this is a worthy commendation, it misses Magowan's wider historical intentions for AT&T Park. In the preface to *Splash Hit!*, a collection of photos and essays on the construction of the ball park, Magowan and Larry Baer write about how they envisioned the ballpark. Not content to see it merely as something immediately appealing and addressing a current need, they believed it would endure.

> The ballpark has already gotten praise from fans and critics. We believe it will also pass the most difficult test—the test of time. We're certain that fifty years from now, it will still be beautiful and unique, and by then it will have proudly established what it is only just beginning to create: its own history and tradition.[5]

In their perception of AT&T Park, Magowan and Baer had something in mind that would last, not simply as a venue to play ball nor as a landmark for itself alone but as a kind of identifiable rooted center or hub—what the Greeks called an omphalos—a place where fans might have a long-term connection with their team. They were also thinking of the ballpark in the context of San Francisco Giants history, looking back to a turbulent past when the team almost left town twice and forward to the promise of a future where, in this splendid location, the Giants might find themselves, for a long time to come, the definitive home team.

ACKNOWLEDGMENTS

Over the six years that I have been working on the story of the Giants leaving New York and establishing a history in San Francisco, I have had the help and good wishes of so many people that to mention them all would require an extra chapter. Some have expressed their interest by suggesting that the story of the Giants' move was long overdue; others have said that they didn't realized the Giants came west the same year as the Dodgers; still others, Giants fans to the core, were happy to hear that their team would be the subject of a book-length narrative. All of them were intrigued and enthusiastic about the topic. I was buoyed by their response. There are some, however, who gave special help along the way and deserve particular mention.

I came to this baseball topic after forty years of studying and writing about Anglo-Irish literature, feeling much like a graduate student beginning a new field of study. I was welcomed to the subject of baseball history cordially by seasoned scholars and writers at both the annual NINE conference and SABR. I offer my sincere thanks to them, and especially to the following, whose encouragement, kindness, generosity, and advice have meant much to me: Charles Alexander, Mark Armor, Dick Beverage, Rob Fitts, Steve Gietschier, Rick Huhn, Dan Levitt, Lee Lowenfish, Andy McCue, Lyle Spatz, Steve Steinberg, Trey Strecker, and Steve Treder.

I owe a special debt of gratitude to former Giants owners and their families, and to former chief managing partners. Jaime Rupert and Kim Rupert, granddaughters of Horace Stoneham, met with me, gave me access to family materials, and provided affectionate portraits of their grandfather; they also helped me with dates and family history.

Bob Lurie and his wife, Connie Lurie, have been extremely generous with their time, both in person and on the phone, and in providing access to scrapbooks and photos; they were also helpful in putting me in contact with former players and Giants executives. Bill Neukom was encouraging, especially in the early stages of this project, and readily facilitated my contact with Giants personnel; he has remained interested in the progress of the book. Peter Magowan gave freely of his time on a number of occasions, meeting with me for conversations, responding to follow-up questions in emails and on the phone, and arranging contact with Giants officials; he also made available his collection of clippings, letters, and journal articles. To all of these people I owe a great debt. Their willingness especially to talk about their experiences and time with the Giants has enriched my understanding of the Giants' story in San Francisco. Most important of all, they have offered kindness and encouragement throughout the project.

A high school and college classmate, Gary Hughes, a baseball lifer and legendary super-scout who has worked in ten Major League organizations over the years, made countless phone calls on my behalf and sent out many emails that resulted in my meeting or speaking with former players, current baseball managers, broadcasters, and journalists. His help is greatly appreciated and his friendship cherished.

Certain individuals in the Giants organization have been helpful in arranging interviews and contacts with former players and club officials: Mario Alioto, Staci Slaughter, Bertha Fajardo, Nancy Donati, and Becky Biniek. I want to thank especially Missy Mikulecky, Giants photographer and archivist, who has provided access to team print materials and photographs, who has been cordial in all of our meetings together, and whose conversations about Giants history I have enjoyed immensely.

A number of people kindly read selected individual chapters of this book and offered thoughtful commentary: Dominic Carboni, Michael Curley, Katy Feeney, Christopher Garratt, John Garratt, Ron Garratt, Gary Hughes, Lee Lowenfish, David Lupher, David Smith, Lyle Spatz, Steve Steinberg, and Steve Treder.

Others read the entire book in an early version. The time and the effort they gave were important in sharpening my focus and in helping me avoid some mistakes. I appreciate their willingness to give their time, and I thank them: Cliff Bellone, Barney Deasy, Andy McCue, and especially Pat Henry and Gabriel Schechter.

Steve Steinberg spent a good deal of his time helping me with the preparation of photos. Keith Andrews interrupted a busy schedule to help create and design the graphs. I thank them both for their efforts.

I owe debts of gratitude to a number of people at different institutions, organizations, libraries, and archival offices who have aided me in access to materials and documents. At my home institution, the University of Puget Sound, Peggy Burge has been a godsend over the years I have been at work on the Giants. She tracked down articles and has found items that have been beyond my abilities to locate. The San Francisco Public Library has been a mecca for me, on the fifth floor, in the periodical room, and especially on the sixth floor, the historical collection, where I consulted the papers of San Francisco mayors Art Agnos, George Christopher, and Frank Jordan. The staff has been courteous and very helpful. I want to thank especially Susan Goldstein, who helped me on my first visit there, answered a number of emails, and has connected me with other librarians, especially Tami Suzuki and Christina Moretta. Early in my research I traveled to the Walter O'Malley archival office in Los Angeles. I thank Brent Shyer and Robert Schweppe for their help in preparing materials, for my time with them, and for answering questions in my subsequent emails. Tim Wiles was extremely helpful when I visited the Hall of Fame Library in Cooperstown, New York, for three days of research; he also answered many questions in follow-up emails. I visited the University of Pacific's special collections to consult the collected papers of San Francisco mayor George Moscone. Michael Wurtz and his assistant, Nicole Grady, gave me a gracious welcome and access to the Moscone Papers. Dick McWilliams helped me with the Dobbins collection on my visit to the California Historical Society. During my visits to the New York Public Library and the Library of Congress I received considerable help from the reference librarians and research assistants. Rick Swig gave me access to his extensive collection of Giants memorabilia, magazines, and photos; he also helped me connect with former Giants players.

I want to thank Rob Taylor, my editor at the University of Nebraska Press, for his enthusiasm for this topic and for his encouragement along the way, and to Courtney Ochsner and Sabrina Stellrecht, who guided the book through the final stages of production.

Friends have been supportive and patient over the years I have been at work on this book. Their company and good humor have been important during my research and writing. I thank Doug Branson, Bob and Sonia Cole, Bill Cotton, Steve Givens and Gloria Reeg, Mott Greene, Kent Hooper, Ron and Trish Johnson, Skip Martin and Barbara Warren, Bill Oltman, Andy Rex, Roger Smith, Tony Verdoia, Dick White, George Wickes and Molly Westling, and all of the Brave and Bold Spring Training group.

My entire family has been solicitous and encouraging since I have been at work on this project. Their humor and affection have been heartening at crucial stages in the writing. I appreciate them all. Two family members, however, deserve a special tribute. Research for this book necessitated considerable travel from my home on Whidbey Island to San Francisco. My sister Linda Garratt Slezak provided accommodation, transportation, hospitality, and good company while I was visiting the Bay Area. My wife, Sally, has offered steadfast encouragement from the beginning. She has read drafts of all the chapters and offered numerous suggestions that have been very helpful; she has cheerfully accompanied me on numerous research trips and to baseball conferences. Most of all, she has been patient and understanding of the time it has taken me to finish this project. I deeply appreciate both of these great women for their part in this work; I owe them a debt of gratitude.

AUTHOR'S NOTE

As part of my research for this book, I have had the good fortune and privilege to interview a number of people who have some connection to the Giants in San Francisco. I have enjoyed meeting them; they have been approachable, cordial, and informative. My conversations with them have provided invaluable insight and perspective on the subject of Giants history. Their willingness to speak with me is greatly appreciated. Some have passed away since I began this work and I regret that they will not be able to see their contribution in print.

Giants managers and players: Felipe Alou, Dusty Baker, Bob Brenly, Orlando Cepeda, Will Clark, Roger Craig, Jim Davenport, Dave Dravecky, Monte Irvin, Mike Krukow, Duane Kuiper, Willie Mays, Willie McCovey, Masanori Murakami, Gaylord Perry, Robby Thompson

Giants officials and employees: Jack Bair, Corey Busch, Pat Gallagher, Jim Hunt, Bob Lurie, Peter Magowan, Mike Murphy, Bill Neukom, Al Rosen, Arturo Santo Domingo, John Taddeucci

Broadcasters and journalists: Ron Fairly, Hank Greenwald, Bruce Jenkins, Vin Scully, Lon Simmons, Larry Stone, George Vecsey.

Others: Dominic Carboni, Bill Coles, Barney Deasy, Katy Feeney, Jim Fregosi, H. Irving Grousbeck, Arnold Hano, Gary Hughes, James Lazurus, Peter O'Malley, Andy McCue, Jaime Rupert, Kim Rupert

Interview citations appear in the endnotes in the following format: Name of the individual, interview with the author, date.

NOTES

1. Sunset in New York

1. The Giants drew 824,112 in 1955. Cincinnati drew 693,662 and Pittsburgh 469,397. By contrast Brooklyn drew 1,033,589 and the New York Yankees 1,490,138. See Thorn et al., *Total Baseball*, 107–8.

2. Up until the late 1940s, fans could walk along with the players and umpires, who were heading toward the clubhouses in center field, to reach the gates in left-center and right-center. After an altercation between Leo Durocher and a Brooklyn fan, baseball commissioner Happy Chandler ruled that fans would have to wait until the players and umpires cleared the field before they would be allowed to use the center field exits. See Thornley, *Land of the Giants*, 102.

3. Henry D. Fetter reports that the Giants' number of box seats—3,814—ranked far behind both Brooklyn's 5,562 and the Yankees' 17,836. See *Taking on the Yankees*, 424n39.

4. These would be the cheapest seats in the park, but they were not without their benefits, particularly the camaraderie among the fans. See Arnold Hano's account of game one of the 1954 World Series in *A Day in the Bleachers*.

5. Boutan, "Was Postwar Suburbanization 'White Flight'?" 417–43; Bloom, *Public Housing That Worked*, 87–123. For a focused discussion on "white flight" as it relates to baseball, especially in Los Angeles, see Avila, *Popular Culture in the Age of White Flight*, 2–7, 145–184.

6. *Sporting News*, March 6, 1956.

7. *New York Herald Tribune*, August 25, 1955.

8. *Sporting News*, May 25, 1956.

9. Celler Hearings on Baseball, 1946.

10. *Sports Illustrated*, July 19, 1957.

11. *New York Times*, August 19, 1955.

12. Arthur Daley, reflecting on the project, which would be huge, remarked that there was a limit to "giantism," even for the Giants. See *New York Times*, May 15, 1956.

13. *New York Herald Tribune*, April 12, 1956.

14. For a good summary of Jack's idea see Murphy, *After Many a Summer*, 178–81.

15. *Sporting News*, May 15, 1956. See also *Sporting News*, February 8, 1956.

16. Thorn et al., *Total Baseball*, 76.

17. *Sporting News*, May 30, 1956.

18. *Sporting News*, February 9, 1955.

19. *Sporting News*, May 27, 1957.

20. "Historic Documents," March 23, 1957, Walter O'Malley: The Official Website, http://www.walteromalley.com.

2. Dawning in the West

1. The Seals had a loyal following in San Francisco, with a storied history and wonderful homegrown talent including the DiMaggio brothers Joe, Vince, and Dom. Fittingly, the Seals would win the PCL title in 1957, their last year of existence.

2. *San Francisco Chronicle*, November 4, 1954.

3. San Francisco Grand Jury Report, December 31, 1958, Henry North, Chairman.

4. *Sporting News*, February 9, 1955.

5. *Sporting News*, February 20, 1957. McCarty met first with Hank Greenberg, the general manager of the Cleveland Indians, in July 1955, and then with Calvin Griffith of the Washington Senators in the fall. Neither meeting produced any commitment on the part of the clubs to come west.

6. *San Francisco Chronicle*, September 15, 2000.

7. Flaherty, "The Miracle Move of the Dodgers," 3; Sullivan, *The Dodgers Move West*, 95; Parrott, *The Lords of Baseball*, 11–12.

8. *Los Angeles Times*, February 22, 1957.

9. McCue, *Mover and Shaker*, 141.

10. George Christopher, "How We Won the Giants," *American Weekly*, September 22, 1957, 6–8.

11. *Sporting News*, March 6, 1957.

12. www.walteromalley.com, "Historic Documents," March 2, 1957.

13. Christopher, "How We Won the Giants," 6.

14. Christopher, "How We Won the Giants," 7.

15. In an internal memo dated March 23, 1957, O'Malley records a conversation with Stoneham to the effect that the Giants were ready to leave New York for Minneapolis and did not think much about the possibility of San Francisco. Thus his conversation with Stoneham in early May reflects a new openness to the possibility of San Francisco on Stoneham's part. See "Historic Documents," Walter O'Malley: The Official Website, http://www.walteromalley.com.

16. Christopher, "How We Won the Giants," 8.

17. Frick telegram to Walter O'Malley, May 10, 1957, "Historic Documents," Walter O'Malley: The Official Website, http://www.walteromalley.com.

18. *San Francisco Examiner*, May 11, 1957.

19. Letter from George Christopher to Walter O'Malley, May 15, 1957, "Historic Documents," Walter O'Malley: The Official Website, http://www.walteromalley.com.

20. Christopher, "How We Won the Giants," 7. New York Times, May 29, 1957; Los Angeles times, May 29, 1957.

21. Christopher, "How We Won the Giants," 7.

22. Internal memo, "Historic Documents," Walter O'Malley: The Official Website, http://www.walteromalley.com, March 23, 1957.

23. *San Francisco Examiner*, May 11, 1957.

24. *San Francisco News*, May 11, 1957.

25. Christopher, "How We Won the Giants," 8.

26. For Walter O'Malley's testimony, see Celler Hearings on Baseball, 963–1000.

27. Celler Hearings on Baseball, 1945, 1947.

28. Jack Walsh reported on Stoneham's testimony. See *Sporting News*, July 24, 1957; and *New York Daily News*, July 19, 1957.

29. Thomas O'Toole, *Wall Street Journal*, August 7, 1957. Minneapolis would have charged the Giants $496,000 annual rent; San Francisco was charging $125,000.

30. Letter from George Christopher and Francis McCarty to Horace Stoneham, August 6, 1957, California Historical Society, San Francisco.

31. *New York Daily News*, August 20, 1957.

32. The vote by the board was 8–1 to accept San Francisco's offer. See *New York Times*, August 20, 1957; *New York Herald Tribune*, August 20, 1957; and *San Francisco Chronicle*, August 20, 1957.

33. Goodwin, *Wait Till Next Year*; Golenbock, *Bums*; Kahn, *The Era*, especially 327–38; Murphy, *After Many a Summer*; Fetter, *Taking on the Yankees*; Vecsey, *Baseball*, 131–38.

34. *New York Times*, August 23, 1957.

35. For O'Malley's influence on Stoneham, see, for example, Sullivan, *The Dodgers Move West*, 4; Fetter, *Taking on the Yankees*, 259–79; Zimniuch, *Baseball's New Frontiers*, 8; Kahn, *The Era*, 334; Frommer, *New York City Baseball*, 7–10. For an amusing corrective, see Veeck, *The Hustler's Handbook*, 97, 101–2.

36. Andy McCue explains the problem as a misunderstanding about location. "You will see it repeated again and again that O'Malley persuaded Horace Stoneham to leave New York. He did persuade Stoneham to go to San Francisco, but Stoneham had already made the decision to leave New York for Minneapolis. O'Malley only changed the destination." See *Mover and Shaker*, 357.

37. Kuhn, *Hardball*, 23.

38 Peter O'Malley, interview with the author, September 22, 2011.

39. Bob Lurie, interview with the author, June 5, 2011.

40. Andy McCue, interview with the author, September 10, 2011.

41. Ron Fairly, interview with the author, August 12, 2011; Jaime Rupert, interview with the author, September 17, 2011.

42. Ted Brock, "The Giants Find a Home," *City Sport*, March 1976.

43. Neil Sullivan mentions Fox only once in *The Dodgers Move West* (143–44), and Michael D'Antonio only once in *Forever Blue* (227). Robert E. Murphy mentions

Fox twice, in passing; see *After Many a Summer*, 226, 322. Andy McCue briefly mentions Fox's relationship with Walter O'Malley; see *Mover and Shaker*, 127, 149, 319.

44. Shapiro, *Bottom of the Ninth*, 111; McCue, *Mover and Shaker*, 127.

45. Celler Hearings on Baseball, 2120–22.

46. *New York Times*, June 3, 1964.

47. David H. Ostroff, a television industry historian, claims that both the Giants and the Dodgers were stockholders in Skiatron; see "A History of STV," 371–86. Andy McCue reports that both the Giants and the Dodgers were silent about their connections to the pay TV company; see *Mover and Shaker*, 319.

48. Celler Hearings on Baseball, 2115–32.

49. *Chicago Daily Tribune*, September 5, 1957.

50. Celler Hearings on Baseball, 2117, 2122.

51. Celler Hearings on Baseball, 1957, 2122.

52. *San Francisco Chronicle*, July 22, 1957; *San Francisco Examiner*, July 22, 1957; *New York Daily News*, July 22, 1957.

53. *New York Times*, June 1, 1957.

54. Ostroff, "A History of STV," 374; Mullen, "The Pre-history of Pay Cable Television," 39–56.

3. Reinvention

1. Goldblatt, *The Giants and the Dodgers*, 156; Fost, *The Giants Baseball Experience*, 120; Willie Mays, interview with the author, October 29, 2014; Willie McCovey, interview with the author, May 13, 2013.

2. Barra, *Mickey and Willie*, 256–57.

3. Smith, *Red Smith on Baseball*, 250.

4. *New York Daily News*, September 30, 1957; *New Yorker* article, quoted in Herb Caen, *San Francisco Chronicle*, July 18, 1958.

5. *New York Times*, September 11, 1957.

6. *San Francisco Examiner*, April 14, 1958.

7. *San Francisco Chronicle*, April 20, 1958.

8. *San Francisco Chronicle*, April 15, 1958.

9. Einstein, *Willie's Time*, 111.

10. "Mickey Fans Mays, Mays Fans Mantle," *Esquire*, August 1968. Mays reflected on fan reactions to Mantle and him. "Mickey used to get booed a lot at Yankee Stadium. I didn't have any problem like that until later, when the Giants moved to San Francisco. Then I got booed. It wasn't so much what we were. It was more what we weren't. Neither one of us was Joe DiMaggio."

11. *San Francisco Call-Bulletin*, April 14, 1958.

12. *San Francisco Examiner*, November 3, 1958.

13. Goldblatt, *The Giants and the Dodgers*, 157.

14. This was not the case with the manager and coaches. Alvin Dark, the Giants' skipper, and his coaches, Wes Westrum, Whitey Lockman, and Larry Jansen, all

played on the New York Giants club. But the sportswriters ignored the coaching staff and concentrated on those playing in San Francisco.

15. Einstein, *Willie's Time*, 162–63.

16. Burgos, *Cuban Star*, 182–85.

17. Hirsch, *Willie Mays*, 282.

18. See Garratt, "Horace Stoneham and the Breaking of Baseball's Second Color Barrier."

19. There are many accounts of this episode. See, for example, Einstein, *Willie's Time*, 206–13.

20. Thorn et al., *Total Baseball*, 76.

21 For a sense of Bardelli's culinary style and atmosphere see Simmons and Simmons, *On the House*, 206.

22. Anastasia Hendrix and Julian Guthrie, "Bardelli's, Haven of Fine," SFGate.com, June 20, 1997, http://www.sfgate.com/news/article/Bardelli-s-haven-of-fine-3113939.php.

23. Hogan and German, *The San Francisco Chronicle Reader*, 9.

24. *San Francisco Chronicle*, September 22, 1957; October 16, 1957; November 3, 1957; November 6, 1957; November 27, 1957.

25. See, for example, *San Francisco Chronicle*, January 21, 1958; February 7, 1958; April 9, 1958; April 10, 1958; May 5, 1958; July 21, 1958; December 25, 1958.

26. *San Francisco Chronicle*, January 21, 1958.

27. *San Francisco Examiner*, September 24, 1957.

28. *Sporting News*, July 2, 1958.

29. *San Francisco Examiner*, October 23, 1957.

30. San Francisco Public Library, "PPIE: The City That Knows How," http://sfpl.org/index.php?pg=2000141201.

31. Starr, *Golden Dreams*, 88.

32. Starr, *Golden Dreams*, 91.

33. Starr, *Golden Dreams*, 123.

34. McCue, *Mover and Shaker*, 242–43.

4. Scandalstick

1. Atlas, *Candlestick Park*, 45.

2. *San Francisco Chronicle*, April 11, 1960.

3. *San Francisco Examiner*, April 11, 1960.

4. Dodger Stadium opened for the 1962 baseball season.

5. *San Francisco Chronicle*, April 12, 1960; Peters with Shea, *Tales from the San Francisco Giants Dugout*, 95.

6. Goldblatt, *The Giants and the Dodgers*, 175.

7. *San Francisco Examiner*, April 11, 1960.

8. *San Francisco Chronicle*, April 11, 1960.

9. *San Francisco Chronicle*, April 12, 1960.

10. *San Francisco Chronicle*, April 11, 1960.

11. *San Francisco Examiner*, April 11, 1960.

12. Quoted in the *San Francisco Chronicle*, April 15, 1960.

13. Willie Mays, interview with the author, October 30, 2014.

14. *San Francisco Chronicle*, April 13, 1960.

15. Articles began appearing in both the *Chronicle* and the *Examiner* one month into the season describing the windy conditions and the brutal cold of night games. See especially Dick Friendlich, "The Mystery of Candlestick Park," *San Francisco Chronicle*, June 22–23, 1960.

16. Angell, *Five Seasons*, 263.

17. Peters with Shea, *Tales from the San Francisco Giants Dugout*, 98.

18. *San Francisco Chronicle*, July 9, 2001.

19. *Los Angeles Times*, May 16, 1972.

20. Vin Scully, interview with the author, September 22, 2011.

21. *San Francisco Chronicle*, April 12, 1961.

22. Perhaps the most notorious shortcoming was the failure of the planned heating system in club seating, prompting well-known San Francisco attorney Melvin Belli to sue the Giants successfully to return his payment for season tickets.

23. Ron Fimrite, "Sticking It to the Stick," *Sports Illustrated*, August 29, 1989. Fimrite writes that leaving Candlestick's parking lot after a game was as easy as exiting Manhattan at rush hour. "Candlestick was opened at a time when conventional wisdom held that all new stadiums should be built out of town and near freeways. . . . Candlestick is a monument to that now discredited theory."

24. The 49ers were rarely affected by Candlestick's infamous winds. San Francisco's weather mellows in the fall and the 49ers often played to some glorious Indian summer afternoons.

25. Greenwald, *This Copyrighted Broadcast*, 60.

26. Felipe Alou, interview with the author, March 10, 2012. Alou also mentioned that it was while watching his teammate and fellow outfielder Willie Mays play the ball in the Candlestick wind that he recognized how truly great Mays was as a center fielder.

27. Lon Simons, interview with the author, March 12, 2012.

28. Quoted in Hertzel, "Going for Two," *Pittsburg Press*, July 10, 1984.

29. Robby Thompson, interview with the author, June 15, 2012.

30. Peters with Shea, *Tales from the San Francisco Giants Dugout*, 99.

31. Peters with Shea, *Tales from the San Francisco Giants Dugout*, 100.

32. A general history of Major League ballparks and discussion of each city's stadium can be found in Shannon and Kalinsky, *The Ballparks*.

33. Seals Stadium was undersized and with no warning track in the outfield. Los Angeles Coliseum, the Dodgers' home between 1958 through 1961, demanded a peculiar field dimension with left field only 250 feet away with a screen 40 feet high that stretched well into left-center. Right field by contrast was 440 feet away. See Reidenbaugh, *Take Me Out to the Ballpark*, 143.

34. The most thorough account of the complicated and litigious building of Dodger Stadium appears in McCue's *Mover and Shaker*, 191–271. See also Sullivan, *The Dodgers Move West*, 137–82; and D'Antonio, *Forever Blue*, 291–307.

35. Jim Murray, *Los Angeles Times*, April 1962. Quoted in Goldblatt, *The Giants and the Dodgers*. 177.

36. David Bush, "Strange History of Candlestick Park," *San Francisco Chronicle*, March 19, 1979.

37. Stoneham's remarks are quoted in the report of the Grand Jury of San Francisco, under the foremanship of Henry E. North, December 1958, San Francisco Public Library Archives. They also appear in "The Giants: From N.Y. to S.F.," *The Californian*, June 1960.

38. *San Francisco Chronicle*, July 9, 1957.

39. *San Francisco Chronicle*, August 22, 1957.

40. *San Francisco Chronicle*, March 19, 1979.

41. Report of the SF Grand Jury, December 1958. See Atlas, *Candlestick Park*, 27.

42. Harney had built a number of the highways, bridges, and roads in the Bay Area from the 1930s through the 1950s.

43. *San Francisco News*, August 29, 1957.

44. Christopher, "How We Won the Giants."

45. *San Francisco Examiner*, August 22, 1957.

46. *Sporting News*, August 28, 1957.

47. *San Francisco Chronicle*, April 4, 1958.

48. Bush, "Strange History of Candlestick Park."

49. *San Francisco Chronicle*, September 19, 1957.

50. "How It Was Financed," *San Francisco Chronicle*, March 19, 1979.

51. Bush, "Strange History of Candlestick Park."

52. *San Francisco Chronicle*, August 12, 1959.

53. An account of the Schwab/Harney contretemps appears in Goldblatt, *The Giants and the Dodgers*, 174.

54. Bush, "Strange History of Candlestick Park."

55. Report of the SF Grand Jury Report, 1958. The most comprehensive discussion of the report can be found in Lewis Lindsay, "San Francisco's Baseball Stadium," *Californian*, 10–12. See also, Burton H. Wolfe, "Candlestick Swindle," http://foundsf .org/index.php?title=Candlestick_Swindle.

56. I am indebted to both Bernard T. Deasy, president of Merritt Community Capital Corporation and longtime San Francisco resident, and Bob Lurie, ex-owner of the Giants and a former member of the grand jury, for my understanding of the civic role of the city's grand jury.

57. Report of the SF Grand Jury, 1958.

58. Grieve was one of the most active of the early advocates for Major League Baseball in San Francisco. He was also an enthusiastic supporter of the bond issue. When he died in 1966, the Giants named their press reception area "The Curly Grieve Room."

59. *San Francisco Chronicle*, December 30, 1958; *San Francisco Examiner*, December 30, 1958.

60. *San Francisco Chronicle*, June 2, 1960.

61. Burton Wolfe, "Candlestick Swindle."

62. *San Francisco Chronicle*, October 15, 1959.

63. *San Francisco Chronicle*, February 26, 1960.

64. Nor did he attend any of the ceremonies or public celebrations for the park's opening (John Taddeucci, interview with the author, June 12, 2014).

5. Perennial Bridesmaids

1. 2015 *San Francisco Giants Media Guide*, 425.

2. "The Business of Baseball," *Dun's Review*, May 1964, 44.

3. Shannon and Kalinsky, *Ballparks*, 219.

4. Quoted in Einstein, *Willie's Time*, 242.

5. Vin Scully, interview with the author, September 22, 2011.

6. Vin Scully, interview with the author, September 22, 2011.

7. The Los Angeles Rams played their last season in Southern California in 1994, moving to St. Louis for the 1995 season. The San Francisco Seals, the Oakland Acorns (or Oaks), the Hollywood Stars, and the Los Angeles Angels were mainstays of the Pacific Coast League until the Giants and Dodgers moved west.

8. Ron Fairly, interview with the author, July 23, 2012.

9. Lasorda was manager of the Dodgers from 1976 through 1996. Under his stewardship, the Dodgers went 1599-1439 with four National League pennants and two world championships. In head-to-head competition with the Giants, Lasorda's Dodgers were 192-157. See Schott and Peters, *The Giants Encyclopedia*.

10. I owe this observation to Gabriel Schechter, a former Giants season ticket–holder.

11. Felipe Alou, interview with the author, March 18, 2012.

12. Willie Mays, interview with the author, October 30, 2014.

13. The rivalry was intense due in large part to location. It was the only time in Major League history that two teams in the same city competed in the same league. The feuding between the Dodgers and the Giants in New York is well documented. See, for example, Goldblatt, *The Giants and the Dodgers*, 88–134.

14. Einstein, *Willie's Time*, 242–45; Hirsch, *Willie Mays*, 434–36; Leavy, *Sandy Koufax*, 179–80; Peters with Shea, *Tales from the San Francisco Giants Dugout*, 73–76; Konte, *The Rivalry Heard 'Round the World*, 69–71.

15. Einstein, *Willie's Time*, 242. Einstein quotes the account of the Watts riot and its effects on the game that appeared in *Time* magazine in late August 1965; see Goldblatt, *The Giants and the Dodgers*, 194–95.

16. Hirsch, *Willie Mays*, 434–35; Roseboro, *Glory Days with the Dodgers*, 1–13; Vrusha, *Benchclearing*, 83.

17. Marichal and Freedman, *Juan Marichal*, 120–21.

18. Goldblatt, *The Giants and the Dodgers*, 195.

19. For a thorough discussion of the Marichal/Roseboro incident and how it affected their subsequent relationship, see Rosengren, *The Fight of Their Lives*; for Rosengren's treatment of Marichal's time as a Dodger, see 165–67.

20. Rosengren, *The Fight of Their Lives*, 168.

21. Marichal and Freedman, *Juan Marichal*, 184; Peters with Shea, *Tales from the San Francisco Giants Dugout*, 76; Goldblatt, *The Giants and the Dodgers*, 199; Rosengren, *The Fight of Their Lives*, 186.

22. Vin Scully, interview with the author, September 22, 2012; Willie Mays, interview with the author, October 30, 2014.

23. As was Duke Snider, the only Dodgers player.

24. *The Giants and the Dodgers*, 189. To add to the uncanny repetition, Snider was 2-3 in both games.

25. Roger Angell assesses the importance for the city: "On the evening of the day the Giants won the pennant, the circulation manager of the *San Francisco Chronicle* approached the news editor and said, 'What is the headline?' 'It's "WE WIN"—white on black.' 'How big?' 'Same size as "FIDEL DEAD!"'" See *The Summer Game*, 75.

26. The 1965–68 second-place finish was in a National League of ten teams.

27. The beginning of the end for Dark came with the publication of three articles on the Giants' clubhouse by Stan Isaacs in *Newsday* in late July and early August 1964. Isaacs quotes Dark as questioning the "mental alertness" of "Spanish-speaking and Negro players," whose alleged deficit, he claimed, results in their making more mistakes in the game than do white players. Dark also insinuated that white players have more pride in their performances than do "Spanish-speaking and Negro" players. Later, Dark claimed he was misquoted, but Isaacs stood by the accuracy of the quotations in his articles.

28. For the most complete discussion of the sign-stealing episode, see Prager, *The Echoing Green*.

29. Furman Bisher, *Atlantic Journal*. Quoted in Hirsch, *Willie Mays*, 426.

30. *Sporting News*, January 30, 1965; February 27, 1965.

31. Einstein, *Willie's Time*, 214; Hirsch, *Willie Mays*, 421.

32. The definitive account of Masanori Murakami's career with the Giants is Robert K. Fitts, *Mashi*. I am indebted to Fitts for my synopsis of the Murakami story.

33. Fitts, *Mashi*, 134. For a detailed account of the back-and-forth negotiations over Murakami's contract, see Fitts, *Mashi*, 119–35.

34. "1965 San Francisco Giants Pitching Statistics" (Franchise Encyclopedia, 1965 Pitching Statistics), Baseball-Reference.com, http://www.baseball-reference.com/teams/SFG/1965-pitching.shtml.

35. November 2, 1968. Franks's overall record during his four-year stint as Giants manager was 367 wins against 280 loses.

6. A Perfect Storm

1. *Sporting News*, November 4, 1967.

2. Art Rosenbaum, *San Francisco Chronicle*, October 12, 1967.

3. *San Francisco Chronicle*, October 19, 1967.

4. Jordan, *The A's* 116–17.

5. *San Francisco Examiner*, October 12, 1967; October 14, 1967; October 19, 1967; *San Francisco Chronicle*, October 12, 1967; October 15, 1967; October 20, 1967.

6. *San Francisco Chronicle*, October 19, 1967.

7. *San Francisco Chronicle*, October 12, 1967.

8. *2016 San Francisco Giants Media Guide*, 371; Thorn et al., *Total Baseball*, 107.

9. Shirley Povich, *Washington Post*, February 20, 1973.

10. *San Francisco Chronicle*, October 12, 1967.

11. Jordan, *The A's: A Baseball History*, 121–58; *Sporting News*, October 21, 1967.

12. Boxerman and Boxerman, *Ebbets to Veeck to Busch*, 162–68.

13. John Taddeucci, a Stoneham front-office employee from 1960 to 1976, remarked that Stoneham's interests in promotions were minimal. There were Cadillac giveaways during Fan Appreciation Day at the end of the season (John Taddeucci, interview with the author, June 12, 2014). Arturo Santo Domingo, a Giants front-office employee from 1962 to 1976, reported that Stoneham feared that televising Giants games would keep people from the ballpark. Under Stoneham only Giants away games with the Dodgers were on television (Arturo Santo Domingo, interview with the author, June 5, 2015).

14. *Sporting News*, October 19, 1968. While Oakland outdrew the Giants overall from 1968–75, the differences were small. Only in 1974 and 1975, both title years for the A's, were the margins between the clubs wide: 845,000 for Oakland, 519,000 for San Francisco (1974); 1,075,000 for Oakland, 522,000 for San Francisco (1975). The Giants outdrew the A's in 1971, 1,006,000 to 914,000. See Thorn et al., *Total Baseball*, 108.

15. From 1972 to 1975 the Giants never threatened in National League pennant races, finishing twenty-six games behind in 1972, eleven games behind in 1973, thirty games behind in 1974, and twenty-seven games behind in 1975. See *2016 San Francisco Giants Media Guide*, 245.

16. *San Francisco Chronicle*, August 11, 1974. On September 24, 1974, the Giants drew 748; for a night game in August 1975, they drew 987 (reported in Ted Green, "San Francisco's Giants: Like a Candlestick in the Wind," *Los Angeles Times*, May 20, 1975). The impression that the crowds were small at Giants games was exacerbated by the changes the city made at Candlestick Park to accommodate the NFL 49ers in 1970, increasing capacity to 60,000.

17. In the winter of 1970–71, the city agreed to enclose Candlestick Park to accommodate the NFL 49ers' move there for the 1971 season. The city also added a fifty-cent amusement tax to each admission ticket to the park, further damaging the Giants' finances (Atlas, *Candlestick Park*, 68–78; Walter O'Malley letter to Horace Stone-

ham, January 27, 1971, "Historic Documents," Walter O'Malley: The Official Website, http://www.walteromalley.com).

18. Nonetheless, Franks won more games (367) in his four years as Giants skipper than did any other manager in baseball during the same time period. See *Sporting News*, November 2, 1968.

19. *Sporting News*, August 2, 1975.

20. John Taddeucci, interview with the author, June 12, 2014.

21. R. J. Lesch, "Eddie Brannick," SABR Baseball Biography Project, http://sabr .org/bioproj/person/f0d59a5f.

22. *New York Times*, June 19, 1972.

23. Schott and Peters, *The Giants Encyclopedia*, 103.

24. *Sporting News*, January 6, 1979.

25. *Sporting News*, November 4, 1978. Stoneham lobbied the retired Schumacher to write a history of the Giants, but Schumacher had neither the time nor, perhaps, the inclination.

26. Gary Hughes, interview with the author, August 28, 2015. Hughes, longtime baseball scout, was a close associate of Schumacher during his last years with the Giants.

27. *Sporting News*, December 5, 1969; *Sporting News*, December 20, 1969.

28. *Sporting News*, December 27, 1969.

29. Feeney's mother, Mary Aufderhar, was a National Exhibition Company stockholder.

30. Katy Feeney, interview with the author, August 14, 2015. Feeney, Chub Feeney's daughter, is senior vice president of Club Relations and Scheduling of Major League Baseball,.

31. Wells Twombly, "The Squire: Lonely, Loyal, and Lost," *San Francisco Examiner*, May 13, 1975.

32. Orlando Cepeda, interview with the author, May 10, 2013.

33. Willie McCovey, interview with the author, May 13, 2013.

34. "Mike McCormick" (Encyclopedia of Players), Baseball-Reference.com, http:// www.baseball-reference.com/players/m/mccormi03.shtml.

35. "Gaylord Perry" (Encyclopedia of Players), Baseball-Reference.com, http:// www.baseball-reference.com/players/p/perryga01.shtml; "Hal Lanier" (Encyclopedia of Players), Baseball-Reference.com, http://www.baseball-reference.com/play ers/l/laniehaO1.shtml.

36. Baseball-Reference.com, "Dick Dietz" (Encyclopedia of Players), http://www .baseball-reference.com/players/d/dietzdi01.shtml.

37. The Dave Kingman Website, "1974—San Francisco Giants," http://www.jfkrush .com/davekingman/1974.htm.

38. Einstein, *Willie's Time*, 329.

39. Willie Mays, interview with the author, October 29, 2014.

40. *San Francisco Chronicle*, May 12, 1972; *San Francisco Examiner*, May 12, 1972.

41. *Los Angeles Times*, May 11, 1972; *Boston Globe*, May 11, 1972.

42. *Sporting News*, May 20, 1972.

43. Hirsch, *Willie Mays*, 508.

44. Willie Mays, interview with the author, October 29, 2014.

45. *Boston Globe*, May 11, 1972.

46. *New York Daily News*, May 14, 1972.

47. *New York Times*, May 12, 1972.

48. *New York Times*, May 14, 1972.

49. Quoted in Joe Eszterhas, "A Town Without Willie," *Newsday*, June 11, 1972.

50. *Los Angeles Times*, May 16, 1972.

51. Einstein, *Willie's Time*, 331.

52. *Los Angeles Times*, July 4, 1972.

53. *San Francisco Giants Media Guide*, 495.

54. John Taddeucci, interview with the author, June 12, 2014.

55. *Los Angeles Times*, April 30, 1975; *San Francisco Examiner*, April 29, 1975.

56. *Sporting News*, May 24, 1975.

57. *Newsday*, June 3, 1973.

58. Leo Durocher said, "Horace Stoneham is loyal beyond the point of good business. Personal sentiment should never enter into a baseball judgment but with Horace it always does. . . . He couldn't stand getting rid of a player. . . . Once a trade would hardly be made and he'd be looking to reacquire the man he had just given away. . . . Once you'd been a Giant you could always come back" (quoted in Wells Twombly, "The Squire: Lonely, Loyal and Lost").

59. Angell, *Five Seasons*, 260–79.

7. "Bobby Thomson Lives!"

1. *Sporting News*, July 12, 1975.

2. *San Francisco Examiner*, May 7, 1975; *San Francisco Chronicle*, May 7, 1975; *Los Angeles Times*, May 8, 1975.

3. James Hunt, interview with the author, February 23, 2012.

4. *San Francisco Chronicle*, January 10, 1976.

5. *Sporting News*, May 24, 1975.

6. *San Jose Mercury*, November 20, 1974; *New York Times*, March 8, 1975; *San Francisco Examiner*, April 28, 1975; *Los Angeles Times*, April 30, 1975.

7. *San Francisco Chronicle*, December 18, 1975; *San Francisco Chronicle*, January 9, 1976; *San Francisco Examiner*, January 11, 1976.

8. *San Francisco Chronicle*, January 2, 1976; *San Francisco Chronicle*, February 2, 1976.

9. *San Francisco Chronicle*, January 2, 1976.

10. *San Francisco Examiner*, May 8, 1975.

11. Bob Lurie, interview with the author, October 25, 2011.

12. Wells Twombly, "Stoneham Makes a Noble Gesture," *San Francisco Examiner*, May 8, 1975.

13. Bob Lurie, interview with the author, October 28, 2014.

14. Bob Lurie, interview with the author, April 30, 2012.

15. *San Francisco Chronicle*, May 7, 1975; *San Francisco Examiner*, May 8, 1975.

16. Bob Lurie, interview with the author, April 30, 2012.

17. It was reported that several National League owners, among them Walter O'Malley, wanted to know where Feeney stood with future plans that might affect his duties as the league president. See *San Francisco Examiner*, May 14, 1975.

18. *San Francisco Examiner*, May 14, 1975.

19. Lurie was referring to various stories, none of which had any real validity, about Charles O. Finley moving the Oakland A's out of town. See *Sporting News*, June 28, 1975; Bob Lurie, interview with the author, June 4, 2015.

20. For a developed profile of Louis Lurie, 1888–1972, see the magazine *San Francisco*, June 1968.

21. Quoted in Wells Twombly, "A Look at the Giants' Odd Couple," *San Francisco Examiner*, February 15, 1976.

22. Art Rosenbaum, "Lots of Buyers for Giants," *San Francisco Chronicle*, August 18, 1972. See also, *Los Angeles Times*, July 4, 1972.

23. *Newsday*, May 8, 1975.

24. *Wall Street Journal*, August 27, 1975.

25. *Sporting News*, September 12, 1975.

26. *Sporting News*, August 16, 1975.

27. *Sporting News*, November 8, 1975.

28. Minutes from Special Meeting of the National League, September 24, 1975, Major League Baseball archives.

29. *Sporting News*, December 6, 1975.

30. Bob Lurie, interview with the author, June 4, 2012.

31. *Sporting News*, January 10, 1976.

32. *Sporting News*, December 27, 1975.

33. On the Messersmith and McNally challenge to the reserve clause, see *Sporting News*, January 10, 1976. On the city of Seattle's law suit, see *Sporting News*, January 31, 1976.

34. Minutes from Meeting of the National League, December 10, 1975, Major League Baseball archives.

35. *San Francisco Chronicle*, January 13, 1976; Goldblatt, *The Giants and the Dodgers*, 222.

36. Minutes of the Meeting of the National League, December 11, 1975, Major League Baseball archives.

37. *Sporting News*, November 8, 1975.

38. *San Francisco Chronicle*, January 10, 1976; *San Francisco Examiner*, January 11, 1976.

39. *Sporting News*, February 7, 1976.

40. *San Francisco Examiner*, January 10, 1976.

41. *San Francisco Examiner*, January 11, 1976.

42. *San Francisco Examiner*, January 11, 1976.

43. For a detailed account of Moscone's assassination on November 27, 1978, by Dan White, see Talbot, *Season of the Witch*, 248–66, 313–30. White, a distraught member of the board of supervisors who opposed Moscone's agenda, also killed Harvey Milk at the same time. Milk was the first openly gay man elected to San Francisco's board of supervisors.

44. *San Francisco Chronicle*, January 15, 1976.

45. *San Francisco Chronicle*, January 7, 1976.

46. Before he took office, Moscone knew of Bob Lurie's interest in buying the team. See *San Francisco Examiner*, January 11, 1976; Bob Lurie, interview with the author, August 10, 2015.

47. *Sporting News*, January 31, 1976.

48. *New York Times*, November 22, 1982.

49. Bob Lurie, interview with the author, August 10, 2015.

50. Corey Busch, interview with the author, June 17, 2014.

51. Corey Busch, interview with the author, June 17, 2014.

52. Bob Lurie, interview with the author, July 18, 2011.

53. Wells Twombly, "Giant Miracle: Bobby Thomson Lives!" *San Francisco Examiner*, February 12, 1976.

54. *Sporting News*, February 14, 1976.

55. *San Francisco Chronicle*, February 4, 1976.

56. Lurie's and Short's offer was eight million dollars, the amount specified by the Labatt group for the value of the franchise. There was no need for any additional money to fund lease-breaking since, under a Lurie and Short ownership, the Giants would continue to occupy Candlestick Park.

57. The City and County of San Francisco v. The National Exhibition Company, et al., Superior Court, San Francisco, California, February 11, 1976.

58. *San Francisco Chronicle*, February 12, 1976; *San Francisco Examiner*, February 12, 1976; *Sporting News*, February 28, 1976.

59. Goldblatt, *The Giants and the Dodgers*, 224.

60. Press Release, San Francisco Mayor's Office, February 24, 1976, George Moscone Collection, MSS 328.

61. For a truncated, albeit opinionated view of Short's ownership activities, see Glenn Dickey, "Don't Prolong the Agony," *San Francisco Chronicle*, January 26, 1976.

62. *San Francisco Chronicle*, February 26, 1976.

63. *Sporting News*, February 28, 1976.

64. *San Francisco Chronicle*, March 2, 1976; *San Francisco Examiner*, March 3, 1976.

65. San Francisco Giants Archives, 1976.

66. *San Francisco Chronicle*, March 3, 1976; *Los Angeles Times*, March 3, 1976.

67. Corey Busch, interview with the author, June 17, 2014.

68. *San Francisco Chronicle*, March 3, 1976.

69. *San Francisco Giants Magazine*, 1978.

70. *San Francisco Giants Magazine*, 1978.

71. *Oakland Tribune*, March 4, 1976.

72. *San Francisco Examiner*, March 4, 1976.

73. Bob Lurie, interview with the author, July 18, 2011.

8. Learning Curve

1. I am indebted to Andy McCue for his clarification of the reserve clause (McCue, interview with the author, January 23, 2016).

2. For accounts of the grievances filed by both Andy Messersmith and Dave McNally, the arbitration, and the legal challenges that broke the decades-old reserve clause, see Lowenfish and Lupien, *The Imperfect Diamond*, 17–24; Helyar, *Lords of the Realm*, 177–97; and Angell, *Five Seasons*, 309–27. For a summary that features Walter O'Malley's role, see McCue, *Mover and Shaker*, 344–47.

3. Bob Lurie, interview with the author, August 10, 2015.

4. McCue, *Mover and Shaker*, 349.

5. *San Francisco Chronicle*, April 6, 1976.

6. *Sporting News*, April 3, 1976.

7. *Sporting News*, March 20, 1976.

8. *San Francisco Chronicle*, April 7, 1976; *Sporting News*, May, 1, 1976.

9. *Los Angeles Times*, April 7, 1976.

10. *Los Angeles Times*, April 10, 1976.

11. *San Francisco Examiner*, April 10, 1976.

12. Quoted in Wells Twombly, "A Miracle: It's 'OUR Giants' Now," *San Francisco Examiner*, April 11, 1976.

13. *Sporting News*, March 4, 1978.

14. The Giants traded McCovey to San Diego after the 1973 season, where he spent three years. The Padres traded him to Oakland late in the 1976 season, where he played in eleven games. See "Willie McCovey" (Encyclopedia of Players), Baseball-Reference.com, http://www.baseball-reference.com/players/m/mccovwi01.shtml.

15. *Sporting News*, August 20, 1977.

16. The doubleheader was against the New York Mets, May 8, 1978. See @SFGiants twitter, "Karl Wallenda walks a high wire across Candlestick Park on 5/8/77 #FarewellCandlestick," December 24, 2013, 02:07:39, http://twicsy.com/i/7UbPEe. See also *Sporting News*, August 28, 1976.

17. Bob Lurie, interview with the author, August 10, 2015.

18. *Sporting News*, March 31, 1979.

19. The Giants sent Gary Thomasson, Gary Alexander, Dave Heaverlo, Alan Wirth, John Henry Johnson, Mario Guerrero, and a player to be named later plus three hundred thousand dollars to Oakland for Blue. See *San Francisco Chronicle*, March 17, 1978; *Los Angeles Times*, March 17, 1978.

20. "1978 National League Team Statistics and Standings," http://www.baseball-ref erence.com/leagues/NL/1978.shtml.

21. See for example, William Endicott, "Gloom to Glow," *Los Angeles Times*, August 1, 1978.

22. *2015 San Francisco Giants Media Guide*, 425.

23. "1978 San Francisco Giants: Schedule and Results," http://www.baseball-ref erence.com/teams/SFG/1978-schedule-scores.shtml.

24. *Los Angeles Times*, March 24, 1978.

25. *Oakland Tribune*, July 12, 1978.

26. Jerry Holtzman, *Sporting News*, May 20, 1978.

27. Art Spander, *Sporting News*, April 24, 1976.

28. Lon Simmons, interview with the author, March 11, 2012.

29. Bob Stevens, "Herseth Hits the Big Time," *San Francisco Chronicle*, April 3, 1976.

30. Angell, *Five Seasons*, 338.

31. *San Francisco Chronicle*, December 27, 1977.

32. *San Francisco Chronicle*, January 10, 1978.

33. *Sporting News*, February 11, 1978.

34. *San Francisco Examiner*, March 16, 1979.

35. Bob Lurie, interview with the author, October 12, 2015. In the spring of 1977, Lurie hired James Hunt as the Giants' chief counsel. Hunt represented Stoneham and the Giants in the 1976 sale.

36. *San Francisco Chronicle*, September 6, 1979; *Los Angeles Times*, September 7, 1979; *Sporting News*, September 15, 1979.

37. Robinson managed for Cleveland from 1975 through 1977. See "Frank Robinson" (Encyclopedia of Players), Baseball-Reference.com, http://www.baseball-ref erence.com/players/r/robinfr02.shtml.

38. Hank Greenwald, interview with the author, September 28, 2015.

39. Robinson's first year as manager of the Giants was in 1981, a strike-shortened season.

40. Bob Lurie, interview with the author, June 12, 2013.

9. The Humm Babies

1. The Crab was tackled by two San Diego Padres players at a game in September. The objects thrown at the crab began with resin bags from players to food items from the stands. Eventually the fans began throwing heavier objects, such as golf balls and flashlight batteries. The Crab's suit had to be reinforced midseason to protect him. For more on the history of Crazy Crab, see Art Rosenbaum, *San Francisco Chronicle*, April 11, 1984; Murphy, *San Francisco Giants: 50 Years*, 103; *ESPN: 30 on 30 Shorts: The Anti-Mascot*; and Fost, *The Giants Baseball Experience*, 162.

2. In the strike-shortened season of 1981, the Giants finished 56-55 and did not qualify for postseason play.

3. See for example Glenn Dickey, *San Francisco Chronicle*, September 19, 1985.

4. The 49ers would win four Super Bowl championships in the 1980s, prompting many to call them the team of the decade. They would also win another Super Bowl in 1995.

5. The events were numerous, including the threat of the so-called Zodiac killer, the kidnapping of Patty Hearst by the Symbionese Liberation Army, the Jonestown massacre that included the death of Congressman Leo Ryan, and the assassination of George Moscone and supervisor Harvey Milk.

6. Talbot, *Season of the Witch*, 375, 357. Talbot treats San Francisco's turbulent time between the love-ins of the late 1960s, through the social and often violent unrest of racial and gay activism of the 1970s, to the city's recovery in the 1980s—a recovery, Talbot argues, stimulated in large part by the success of the 49ers.

7. Talbot, *Season of the Witch*, 373.

8. Talbot's only mention of the Giants is to label them as a team "imported from New York in 1958," *Season of the Witch*, 358.

9. Bob Lurie, interview with the author, April 10, 2012.

10. Bob Lurie is not sure of the exact date of his call to Rosen, but Houston owner John McMullen announced on September 13, 1985, that Dick Wagner would replace Al Rosen as president and general manager of the Astros (*Sporting News*, September 23, 1985). That would place Lurie's initial call to Rosen no later than September 8 or 9.

11. Bob Lurie, interview with the author, October 12, 2015.

12. *New York Times*, September 14, 1985; *Sporting News*, September 23, 1985.

13. Al Rosen, interview with the author, March 16, 2012.

14. John McMullen replaced Al Rosen with Dick Wagner on September 13, 1985. See *Los Angeles Times*, September 14, 1985; and *San Francisco Chronicle*, September 14, 1985.

15. Perhaps Lurie's request for McMullen's permission was unnecessary given Rosen's dismissal, but Lurie wanted to avoid any appearance of "tampering"—that is, improper discussion about employment with someone connected to another club (Bob Lurie, interview with the author, July 18, 2011).

16. Bob Lurie, interview with the author, April 10, 2012.

17. Al Rosen, interview with the author, March 16, 2012.

18. *San Francisco Examiner*, September 15, 1985.

19. *San Francisco Chronicle*, September 19, 1985.

20. Bob Brenly, interview with the author, August 12, 2015.

21. Roger Craig, interview with the author, February 1, 2014.

22. "Al Rosen," SABR Biography Project, http://sabr.org/bioproj/person/40d66568.

23. Al Rosen, interview with the author, March 16, 2012.

24. Robby Thompson, interview with the author, June 15, 2012.

25. Roger Craig, interview with the author, February 1, 2014.

26. Mike Krukow, interview with the author, March 16, 2013.

27. Steve Kroner, "Brad Gulden: The Original Humm Baby," *San Francisco Chronicle*, April 9, 2006.

28. Roger Craig, interview with the author, February 1, 2014.

29. Kroner, "Brad Gulden," April 9, 2006.

30. Roger Craig, interview with the author, February 1, 2014.

31. The Giants drew 818,697, next to last in the National League, in 1985 ("San Francisco Giants Attendance, Stadiums, and Park Factors," http://www.baseball-ref erence.com/teams/SFG/attend.shtml).

32. Pat Gallagher, interview with the author, October 26, 2011.

33. Burns, "Ninth Inning."

34. "1989 San Francisco Earthquake," History Channel website, http://www.his tory.com/topics/1989-san-francisco-earthquake.

35. There were two California World Series played before the A's and Giants met in 1989. The Los Angeles Dodgers and Oakland played twice, once in 1974 and again in 1988. But these were statewide rather than from the same metropolitan region.

36. See, for example, *San Francisco Chronicle*, October 18–20, 1989; *Oakland Tribune*, October 18–21, 1989; and *Los Angeles Times*, October 18–19, 1989.

37. Peterson, *Battle of the Bay*, 174–75.

38. Peterson, *Battle of the Bay*, 181–82.

39. *San Francisco Chronicle*, October 28, 1989.

40. Roger Craig, interview with the author, February 1, 2014.

41. Dusty Baker, interview with the author, January 5, 2016.

42. The Giants' team ERA (8.21) was the second-highest in World Series history. The 92-point disparity in batting averages (.209 for the Giants; .301 for the A's) was the highest in World Series history. The winning team never trailed and the losing team never led. It was one of the lowest-rated television audiences in World Series history; see Peterson, *Battle of the Bay*, 188.

43. Peterson, *Battle of the Bay*, 188.

10. Vox Populi

1. *San Francisco Chronicle*, March 14, 1985; August 1, 1985; November 13, 1985.

2. *Sporting News*, July 13, 1968.

3. Or haunts it. See Greenwald, *This Copyrighted Broadcast*, 59–63.

4. Greenwald, *This Copyrighted Broadcast*, 61.

5. *New York Times*, January 12, 2012. See also, Gary Kamiya, "Remembering Candlestick Fondly Is a Breeze," *SFGate*, December 21, 2013, http://www.sfgate.com /giants/article/Remembering-Candlestick-fondly-is-a-breeze-5083276.php.

6. There are also general curses applied to the park. See "Believe in the Haunting Curse of Candlestick," *Santa Cruz Sentinel*, August 24, 1992; and Lawr Michaels, "The Curse of the Stick Is Lifted," *Mastersball*, November 2, 2010, http://www.mas tersball.com/index.php?option=com_content&view=article&id=772:the-curse-of -the-stick-is-lifted&catid=954:mastersdaily&Itemid=67.

7. In the 1962 World Series, torrential rains and winds forced a four-day delay before game six at Candlestick; in the 1989 World Series, the Loma Prieta earthquake caused an eleven-day delay between games two and three.

8. One writer was not so sure. See Fimrite, "Gone With the Wind?" *Sports Illustrated*, September 1, 1986.

9. Laventhol and Horwath, *The Future of Candlestick Park*, was commissioned by the San Francisco Giants and released on May 19, 1981 (quoted in Agostini, Quigley and Smolensky, "Stickball in San Francisco," 423). See also *San Francisco Examiner*, March 29, 1982.

10. Agostini, Quigley, and Smolensky, "Stickball in San Francisco," 389.

11. "Putting a Dome on Candlestick Park Would Be So . . . ," UPI, September 2, 1983; http://www.upi.com/Archives/1983/09/02Putting-a-dome-on-Candlestick -Park-would-be-so/4625431323200/.

12. *San Francisco Chronicle*, May 8, 1986.

13. *San Francisco Chronicle*, April 15, 1986.

14. *San Francisco Chronicle*, April 15, 1986.

15. *San Francisco Chronicle*, June 13, 1985.

16. *San Francisco Chronicle*, November 16, 1985.

17. *San Francisco Chronicle*, November 13, 1985.

18. *San Francisco Chronicle*, November 19, 1985.

19. Lowell Cohn, *San Francisco Chronicle*, August 2, 1985.

20. *San Francisco Chronicle*, October 14, 1985; *Oakland Tribune*, October 16, 1985.

21. Bob Lurie, interview with author, October 22, 2015.

22. *San Francisco Chronicle*, August 6, 1987.

23. Glenn Dickey, *San Francisco Chronicle*, November 19, 1985.

24. *San Francisco Chronicle*, August 7, 1985.

25. *San Francisco Chronicle*, November 2, 1987; *San Francisco Examiner*, November 1, 1987.

26. *San Francisco Chronicle*, November 4, 1987; *San Francisco Examiner*, November 1, 1987.

27. Agostini, Quigley, and Smolensky, "Stickball in San Francisco," 392.

28. *San Francisco Chronicle*, July 11, 1989.

29. *San Francisco Chronicle*, October 15, 1989.

30. Agnos, *San Francisco Chronicle*, July 10, 1989; editorial, *San Francisco Examiner*, October 15, 1989.

31. *San Francisco Chronicle*, July 10, 1989.

32. *Chicago Tribune*, October 8, 1989.

33. ABC News, "Video Vault: ABC7 News Coverage from 1989 Loma Prieta Earthquake," October 13, 2014, http://abc7news.com/news/video-vault-abc7-news -coverage-from-1989-loma-prieta-earthquake/349508/.

34. Mayor Art Agnos, "Letter to San Francisco Citizens," October 1989, quoted in Agostini, Quigley, and Smolensky, "Stickball in San Francisco," 394.

35. Agnos, "Letter to San Francisco Citizens."

36. *Los Angeles Times*, November 8, 1989.

37. *San Francisco Chronicle*, July 15, 1989.

38. *San Francisco Chronicle*, July 1, 1989.

39. *San Francisco Chronicle*, July 1, 1989.

40. Ronald E. Garratt, former assistant city manager, Santa Clara CA, email to the author, February 23, 2016.

41. *Los Angeles Times*, May 5, 1990.

42. *Seattle Times*, August 9, 1990.

43. *San Jose Mercury News*, November 8, 1990; *San Francisco Chronicle*, November 8, 1990.

44. *New York Times*, April 2, 2012; Mark Purdy, "Purdy: Bud Selig Offers Revisionist History on A's-Giants Territorial Rights Feud," *East Bay Times*, August 19, 2014, http://www.eastbaytimes.com/athletics/ci_26369112/purdy-bud -selig-offers-revisionist-history-giants-territorial.

45. Ciderbeck, "Territorial Rights—A (Not So) Brief History," Athletics Nation, April 20, 2012, http://www.athleticsnation.com/2012/4/18/2958535/territorial-rights -a-not-so-brief-history.

46. *New York Times*, October 8, 2000.

47. *Los Angeles Times*, November 8, 1990.

48. *Los Angeles Times*, May 24, 1992.

49. *San Jose Mercury News*, June 4, 1992; *Los Angeles Times*, June 4, 1992.

50. Bob Lurie, interview with the author, July 17, 2014.

11. "It's Déjà Vu All Over Again"

1. Hank Greenwald, interview with the author, September 28, 2015.

2. *San Francisco Chronicle*, July 10, 1989.

3. "The Lowdown on Lurie, Giants and a New Stadium," *San Francisco Chronicle*, June 5, 1992.

4. Rapaport, "Fast Balls and High Finance," 49.

5. The local sportswriters certainly noticed it. See *San Francisco Chronicle*, June 4, 1992; and *Sporting News*, June 15, 1992.

6. *San Francisco Chronicle*, June 4, 1992.

7. James L. Lazarus, Letter to Mayor Frank Jordan, May 7, 1992, Frank Jordan Papers.

8. *San Francisco Chronicle*, June 5, 1992; *San Francisco Examiner*, June 7, 1992.

9. Bob Lurie, Letter to Mayor Frank Jordan, June 8, 1992, Bob Lurie Private Papers and Scrapbooks.

10. Lurie, Letter to Frank Jordan, June 8, 1992.

11. *New York Times*, June 12, 1992; *Sporting News*, June 22, 1992.

12. *New York Times*, June 12, 1992.

13. *San Francisco Chronicle*, June 11, 1992; *St. Petersburg Times*, June 19, 1992.

14. *Los Angeles Times*, June 12, 1992.

15. Tuckman, "Sliding Home"; Corey Busch, interview with the author, June 17, 2014.

16. *New York Times*, June 26, 2010.

17. Grousbeck cofounded Continental Cable Television in 1964. He has served on the Stanford faculty since 1986. He is the principal owner of the Boston Celtics. See "H. Irving Grousbeck," Stanford Graduate School of Business, https://www.gsb .stanford.edu/faculty-research/faculty/h-irving-grousbeck.

18. H. Irving Grousbeck, interview with the author, February 23, 2016; Rapaport, "Fast Balls and High Finance," 53.

19. H. Irving Grousbeck, interview with the author, February 23, 2016.

20. *San Francisco Chronicle*, July 4, 1992.

21. Tuckman, "Sliding Home": 39.

22. Jenkins, "Lurie Isn't Obstructing Giants' Sale," *San Francisco Chronicle*, July 10, 1992; Stone, "The Bell Is Starting to Toll at Candlestick," *San Francisco Examiner*, July 12, 1992.

23. *San Francisco Chronicle*, July 31, 1992.

24. Mike Piazza was inducted into baseball's Hall of Fame in July 2016.

25. Tuckman, "Sliding Home," 36.

26. Rapaport, "Fast Balls and High Finance," 53.

27. *St. Petersburg Times*, August 7, 1992.

28. St. Petersburg tried to lure the Chicago White Sox in 1988 and then later the Seattle Mariners and the Texas Rangers. See *San Francisco Chronicle*, November 11, 1992.

29. Rapaport, "Fast Balls and High Finance," 52; *San Francisco Chronicle*, August 7, 1992.

30. *San Francisco Chronicle*, August 8, 1992.

31. *San Francisco Chronicle*, August 8, 1992.

32. *San Francisco Chronicle*, August 7, 1992.

33. *Los Angeles Times*, August 9, 1992.

34. I am indebted to Gabriel Schechter for pointing out the Giants' 1992 June swoon.

35. *San Francisco Chronicle*, November 11, 1992.

36. Robby Thompson, interview with the author, June 15, 2012.

37. *New York Times*, February 21, 1993.

38. *San Francisco Chronicle*, November 11, 1992.

39. *San Francisco Chronicle*, August 12, 1992.

40. *San Francisco Chronicle*, July 10, 1992.

41. Larry Baer worked for Lurie in the Giants organization from 1980 until 1983. See *San Francisco Chronicle*, September 28, 2008.

42. *San Francisco Chronicle*, November 12, 1992.

43. Peter Magowan, interview with the author, September 22, 2015.

44. *San Francisco Chronicle*, November 12, 1992.

45. *San Francisco Examiner*, August 25, 1992.

46. Herb Caen, *San Francisco Chronicle*, October 13, 1992.

47. Tuckman, "Sliding Home," 66.

48. *San Francisco Examiner*, October 11, 1992.

49. Herb Caen, *San Francisco Chronicle*, October 15, 1992.

50. *New York Times*, September 4, 1992.

51. Fay Vincent explained his decision to resign in testimony before the U.S. Senate. See Senate Hearings on Antitrust Exemption, 10–15.

52. *Los Angeles Times*, September 10, 1992.

53. *San Francisco Examiner*, September 29, 1992.

54. Peter Magowan, interview with the author, April 20, 2016.

55. Rapaport, "Fast Balls and High Finance," 55.

56. *San Francisco Examiner*, October 13, 1992.

57. Tuckman, "Sliding Home," 66.

58. Peter Magowan, interview with the author, June 25, 2013.

59. *San Francisco Chronicle*, October 13, 1992.

60. Bob Lurie's contribution was in the form of a four-year loan. See *San Francisco Examiner*, October 16, 1992.

61. Brand, "Off the Field, A Legal Donnybrook," 38.

62. St. Petersburg–Tampa was awarded an expansion MLB franchise in 1995.

63. *San Francisco Examiner*, November 6, 1992.

64. Mayor Frank Jordan to President William White, National League, October 20, 1992, Frank Jordan Papers.

65. *Los Angeles Times*, November 9, 1992; Peter O'Malley, interview with the author, September 22, 2011.

66. *San Francisco Chronicle*, November 11, 1992.

67. *San Francisco Chronicle*, November 11, 1992.

68. *San Francisco Chronicle*, November 11, 1992.

69. *San Francisco Examiner*, November 11, 1992.

70. Senate hearings on Antitrust Exemption.

71. The expansion fee was $130 million. See *Sporting News*, March 20, 1995.

72. *San Francisco Examiner*, November 16, 1992.

12. The Improbable Dream

1. Dominic J. Carboni, former Serra High School vice principal and Bonds's high school football coach, interview with the author, March 23, 2016.

2. *Los Angeles Times*, December 8, 1992.

3. *Los Angeles Times*, December 9, 1992; *San Francisco Chronicle*, December 9, 1992; *Sporting News*, December 14, 1992.

4. *Los Angeles Times*, December 9, 1992; *Sporting News*, December 14, 1992.

5. *New York Times*, December 9, 1992.

6. Peter Magowan, interview with the author, June 3, 2015.

7. Rapaport, "Fast Balls and High Finance," 58.

8. *Los Angeles Times*, December 17, 1992; *San Francisco Chronicle*, December 17, 1992; *New York Times*, December 17, 1992.

9. Dusty Baker, interview with the author, January 5, 2016.

10. Peter Magowan, interview with the author, June 3, 2015.

11. Peter Magowan, interview with the author, September 29, 2015.

12. James L. Lazarus, former staff official with Mayor Jordan, interview with the author, February 26, 2016.

13. Peter Magowan, interview with the author, September 29, 2015.

14. *San Francisco Chronicle*, April 14, 1993.

15. *2015 San Francisco Giants Media Guide*, 425.

16. Peter Magowan, interview with the author, June 3, 2015.

17. *Sports Illustrated*, October 8, 1993.

18. In 1998, Mark McGwire hit 70 HR, Sammy Sosa 66, and Ken Griffey Jr. 56. Bonds hit 37; his power numbers would increase, however, in the next nine seasons, surpassing the others.

19. Peter Magowan, email to the author, March 31, 2016.

20. Cliff Corcoran, "The Strike," http://www.si.com/mlb/2014/08/12/1994-strike-bud-selig-orel-hershiser.

21. There were some notable baseball "what-ifs" due to the 1994 season cancellation. The Montreal Expos, 74-40 on August 12, might have won their first National League pennant. The Cincinnati Reds, with the best record in the NL, might have been in the postseason. San Diego's Tony Gwynn was hitting .394 and San Francisco's Matt Williams had 43 home runs on August 12, both of them poised to break or tie records, Gwynn having a shot at a .400 batting average and Williams in sight of Roger Maris's 61 homers.

22. PBS, "Dark Days: Millionaires vs. Billionaires," from *The Tenth Inning*, directed by Ken Burns and Lynn Novick, http://www.pbs.org/baseball-the-tenth-inning/dark-days/millionaires-vs-billionaires.

23. *Sporting News*, January 30, 1995; February 13, 1995.

24. *Sporting News*, February 20, 1995.

25. *Sporting News*, April 10, 1995.

26. PBS, "Dark Days: Millionaires vs. Billionaires."

27. Peter Magowan, interview with the author, March 29, 2016.

28. Peter Magowan, interview with the author, March 29, 2016.

29. Peter Magowan and Larry Baer, "The Miracle at China Basin," *Splash Hit!*, 19.

30. Giamatti, *Take Time for Paradise*, 59–60.

31. Magowan and Baer, "The Miracle at China Basin," 19.

32. Smith, "The Construction of San Francisco's MLB Stadiums," 118.

33. Magowan and Baer, "The Miracle at China Basin," 19.

34. Magowan and Baer, "The Miracle at China Basin," 19.

35. Smith, "The Construction of San Francisco's MLB Stadiums," 119.

36. Quentin Kopp, a conservative politician, was wary of using public funds for private projects and did not support the other two ballpark initiatives in San Francisco. Roberta Achtenberg, a former member of the board of supervisors, was a prominent attorney and Democratic politician as well as the first openly lesbian government official approved by the U.S. Senate. Rev. Cecil Williams was pastor of

Glide Memorial Church and a leading advocate for African Americans, gays, and lesbians. Williams's church grew to a congregation of ten thousand and provided many social services in the city.

37. Wong, *San Francisco Voter Information Pamphlet*, 60.

38. Wong, *San Francisco Voter Information Pamphlet*, 63–65.

39. Headlines are from March 27, 1996.

40. Gabriel Schechter, former Baseball Hall of Fame librarian, email to the author, April 10, 2016.

41. Peter Magowan, interview with the author, June 25, 2013.

42. Delany and Eckstein, *Public Dollars, Private Stadiums*, 195. Tax-increment financing (TIFs), used throughout the country by local municipalities to promote development, diverts property taxes on the land into the construction costs. See deMause and Cagan, *Field of Schemes*, 175.

43. *Kajima News and Notes* 13, no. 3 (Summer 2000).

44. Peter Magowan, interview with the author, March 29, 2016.

Epilogue

1. Quoted in Murphy, *San Francisco Giants*, 179.

2. Quoted in Murphy, *San Francisco Giants*, 179.

3. In 2008 the Giants drew 2,863,843, and in 2009, 2,862,111. See 2015 *San Francisco Giants Media Guide*, 425.

4. Murphy, *San Francisco Giants*, 179.

5. Magowan and Baer," The Miracle at China Basin," 21.

BIBLIOGRAPHY

Archival Collections

Agnos, Art. Papers. San Francisco History Center, San Francisco Public Library.

Christopher, George. Papers. San Francisco History Center, San Francisco Public Library.

Jordan, Frank. Papers. San Francisco History Center, San Francisco Public Library.

Lurie, Bob. Papers and scrapbooks. Bob Lurie Private Collection.

Magowan, Peter. Papers and clippings. Peter Magowan Private Collection.

Moscone Collection. Holt-Atherton Special Collections, University of the Pacific, Stockton, California.

National League. Minutes from Special Meetings of the National League, Major League Baseball Archives.

Published Sources

Agostini, Stephen J., John M. Quigley, and Eugene Smolensky, "Stickball in San Francisco," eScholarship, University of California, Berkeley, November 1996.

Angell, Roger. *Five Seasons.* New York: Simon and Schuster, 1977.

————. *The Summer Game.* Lincoln: University of Nebraska Press, 2004.

Atlas, Ted. *Candlestick Park.* Charleston SC: Arcadia, 2010.

Avila, Eric. *Popular Culture in the Age of White Flight.* Berkeley: University of California Press, 2004.

Barra, Allen. *Mickey and Willie: Mantle and Mays, the Parallel Lives of Baseball's Golden Age.* New York: Three Rivers, 2013.

Bloom, Nicholas Dagen. *Public Housing That Worked.* Philadelphia: University of Pennsylvania Press, 2008.

Boutan, L. P. "Was Postwar Suburbanization 'White Flight'? Evidence from the Black Migration." *Quarterly Journal of Economics* 125 (2010): 117–43.

Boxerman, Burton A., and Benita W. Boxerman. *Ebbets to Veeck to Busch: Eight Owners Who Shaped Baseball.* Jefferson NC: McFarland, 2003.

Brand, Jeffrey. "Off the Field, A Legal Donnybrook," *California Lawyer*, April 1993.

Burgos, Adrian, Jr. *Cuban Star.* New York: Hill and Wang, 2011.

Burns, Ken. "Ninth Inning." *Baseball*, PBS film, 1995.

Cagan, Joanna, and Neil deMause. *Field of Schemes*. Monroe ME: Common Courage, 1998.

The City and County of San Francisco vs. The National Exhibition Company, et al. Superior Court, San Francisco, California. No. 700-534, Hearing re: Request for Preliminary Injunction. February 11, 1976.

Corcoran, Cliff. "The Strike: Who Was Right, Who Was Wrong and How It Helped Baseball," *Sports Illustrated*, August 12, 2014.

D'Antonio, Michael. *Forever Blue*. New York: Riverhead Books, 2009.

Delaney, Kevin, and Rick Eckstein. *Public Dollars, Private Stadiums: The Battle over Building Sports Stadiums*. Piscataway NJ: Rutgers University Press, 2003.

Einstein, Charles. *Willie's Time: Baseball's Golden Age*. Carbondale: Southern Illinois University Press, 2004.

Fetter, Henry D. *Taking on the Yankees*. New York: W. W. Norton, 2003.

Fitts, Robert K. *Mashi: The Unfulfilled Baseball Dreams of Masanori Murakami, the First Japanese Major Leaguer*. Lincoln: University of Nebraska Press, 2014.

Flaherty, Vincent X. "The Miracle Move of the Dodgers." In *Baseball Register*, ed. J. G. Taylor Spink. Sporting News Publishing, 1960.

Fost, Dan. *The Giants Baseball Experience*. Minneapolis: MVP Books, 2014.

Frommer, Harvey. *New York City Baseball*. Madison: University of Wisconsin Press, 2004.

Garratt, Robert F. "Horace Stoneham and the Breaking of Baseball's Second Color Barrier." *NINE*, Spring 2014, 42–53.

Giamatti, A. Bartlett. *Take Time for Paradise*. New York: Bloomsbury, 1989.

Goldblatt, Andrew. *The Giants and the Dodgers*. Jefferson NC: McFarland, 2003.

Golenbock, Peter. *Bums: An Oral History of the Brooklyn Dodgers*. Chicago: Contemporary Books, 1984.

Goodwin, Doris Kearns. *Wait Till Next Year*. New York: Simon & Schuster, 1997.

Greenwald, Hank. *This Copyrighted Broadcast*. San Francisco: Woodford Press, 1999.

Hano, Arnold. *A Day in the Bleachers*. Cambridge MA: DaCapo, 1995.

Helyar, John. *Lords of the Realm*. New York: Villard Books, 1994.

Hirsch, James S. *Willie Mays: The Life, the Legend*. New York: Scribner, 2010.

Hogan, William, and William German, eds. *The San Francisco Chronicle Reader*. New York: McGraw-Hill, 1962.

Jordan, Donald M. *The A's: A Baseball History*. Jefferson NC: McFarland, 2014.

Kahn, Roger. *The Era*. Lincoln: University of Nebraska Press, 1993.

Klima, John. *Willie's Boys: The Birmingham Black Barons, the Last Negro League World Series, and the Making of a Baseball Legend*. Hoboken NJ: John Wiley and Sons, 2009.

Konte, Joe. *The Rivalry Heard 'Round the World*. New York: Skyhorse, 2013.

Kuhn, Bowie. *Hardball: The Education of a Baseball Commissioner*. New York: Times Books, 1987.

Leavy, Jane. *Sandy Koufax*. New York: Harper Collins Perennial, 2003.

Lowenfish, Lee, and Tony Lupien. *The Imperfect Diamond*. New York: Stein and Day, 1980.

Marichal, Juan, and Lew Freedman. *Juan Marichal*. Minneapolis: MVP Books, 2011.

McCue, Andy. *Mover and Shaker: Walter O'Malley, the Dodgers, and Baseball's Western Expansion*. Lincoln: University of Nebraska Press, 2014.

Mullen, Megan. "The Pre-history of Pay Cable Television: An Overview and Analysis." *Historical Journal of Film, Radio, and Television* 19, no. 1 (1999): 39–56.

Murphy, Brian. *San Francisco Giants: 50 Years*. San Raphael CA: Insight Editions, 2008.

Murphy, Robert E. *After Many a Summer*. New York: Union Square Press, 2009.

Ostroff, David H. "A History of STV, Inc. and the 1964 Vote against Pay Television." *Journal of Broadcasting* 27, no. 4 (1983): 371–86.

Parrott, Harold. *The Lords of Baseball*. Atlanta: Longstreet, 2001.

Peters, Nick, with Stuart Shea. *Tales From the San Francisco Giants Dugout*. New York: Sports Publishing, 2013.

Peterson, Gary. *Battle of the Bay*. Chicago: Triumph Books, 2014.

Prager, Joshua. *The Echoing Green*. New York: Vintage Books, 2006.

Rapaport, Richard. "Fast Balls and High Finance." *California Business*, September 1993.

Reidenbaugh, Lowell. *Take Me Out to the Ballpark*. St. Louis: Sporting News, 1983.

Roseboro, John. *Glory Days with the Dodgers*. New York: Atheneum, 1978.

Rosengren, John. *The Fight of Their Lives*. Guilford CT: Lyons, 2014.

Schott, Tom, and Nick Peters. *The Giants Encyclopedia*. Champaign IL: Sports Publishing, 2003.

Shannon, Bill, and George Kalinsky. *The Ballparks*. New York: Hawthorn Books, 1975.

Shapiro, Michael. *Bottom of the Ninth*. New York: Henry Holt, 2009.

Simmons, Matty, and Don Simmons. *On the House*. New York: Coward-McCaen, 1955.

Smith, Maureen. "From 'The Finest Ballpark in America' to "The Jewel of the Waterfront:' The Construction of San Francisco's Major League Stadiums," The International Journal of the History of Sport 25, no. 11. Special Issue: *Cathedral of Sport: The Rise of Stadiums in the Modern United States*.

Smith, Red. *Red Smith on Baseball*. Chicago: Ivan R. Dee, 2000.

Starr, Kevin. *Golden Dreams: California in an Age of Abundance, 1950–1963*. New York: Oxford University Press, 2009.

Sullivan, Neil. *The Dodgers Move West*. New York: Oxford University Press, 1987.

Talbot, David. *Season of the Witch*. New York: Free Press, 2012.

Thorn, John, Peter Palmer, Michael Gershman, and David Pietrusza, eds. *Total Baseball*. 6th ed. New York: Total Sports, 1999.

Thornley, Stew. *Land of the Giants*. Philadelphia: Temple University Press, 2000.

Tuckman, Michael. "Sliding Home," *California Lawyer*, April 1993.

U.S. House of Representatives. Hearings before the Antitrust Committee of the Committee on the Judiciary. Eighty-fifth Congress, first session (June 17–August 8, 1957), Part 1. Washington: Government Printing Office, 1957. [Hereafter called Celler Hearings on Baseball.]

U.S. Senate. Hearings before the Subcommittee on Antitrust, Monopolies and Business Rights of the Committee on the Judiciary. One Hundred Second Congress, second session, on the Validity of Major League Baseball's Exemption from the Antitrust Laws, December 10, 1992. [Hereafter called the Senate Hearings on Antitrust Exemption.]

Veeck, Bill. *The Hustler's Handbook*. Chicago: Ivan R. Dee, 1965.

Vecsey, George. *Baseball: A History of America's Favorite Game*. New York: Modern Library, 2008.

Vrusha, Spike. *Benchclearing*. Guilford CT: Lyons Press, 2008.

Walsh, Joan and C. W. Nevius. *Splash Hit!* San Francisco: Chronicle Books, 2001.

Wolfe, Burton H. "From N.Y. to S.F." *The Californian*, June 1960, 13–14.

Wong, Germaine O. *San Francisco Voter Information Pamphlet and Sample Ballot*. San Francisco: Office of the Registrar, the City and County of San Francisco, 1996.

Zimniuch, Fran. *Baseball's New Frontiers*. Lincoln: University of Nebraska Press, 2013.

INDEX